George Bell: the greatest churchman - a portrait in letters

The Author:

Peter Raina read Modern History at St Catherine's College, Oxford, and Theology at Clare Hall, Cambridge; received his MA at Clark University (USA), and his D. Phil. from the University of Warsaw. He has been a Research Fellow at the Osteuropa-Institute of the Free University Berlin, a Visiting Fellow at the Centre of International Studies, Faculty of History, Cambridge University, and at the Centre for International Studies, London School of Economics & Political Science; Research Associate, St Catherine's College, Oxford; Senior Research Associate, Graduate Centre, Balliol College, Oxford; Honorary Member of the High Table and Senior Common Room member, Christ Church, Oxford. He is a life member, Clare Hall, Cambridge.

Peter Raina is the author of a number of books concerning European history and politics. These include a volume on George Macaulay Trevelyan (in English), Gomulka, a political biography (in German) and 13 volumes on the Polish Primate, Cardinal Wyszynski (in Polish). Peter Raina now resides in Berlin.

Peter Raina

George Bell:
The greatest churchman
- a portrait in letters

Foreword by
The Right Reverend P. K. Walker, D. D.

CHURCHES TOGETHER
IN BRITAIN AND IRELAND

Churches Together in Britain and Ireland
Bastille Court
2 Paris Garden
London
SE1 8ND

Direct Line: +44 (0)207 654 7254
Fax: +44 (0)207 654 7222
www.ctbi.org.uk

Cover design by Nial Smith Design

First published 2006 by Churches Together in Britain
and Ireland
Copyright © Churches Together in Britain and Ireland
2006

Paperback ISBN 0 85169 332 6
Hardback ISBN 0 85169 334 2

Further copies available from
CTBI Publications
4 John Wesley Road, Peterborough PE4 6ZP, UK
Tel: + 44 (0)1733 325002; Fax: +44 (0)1733 384180
orders@ctbi.org.uk; sales@mph.org.uk

THIS BOOK IS GRATEFULLY DEDICATED
TO
O. M. T. O'DONOVAN
REGIUS PROFESSOR OF
MORAL AND PASTORAL THEOLOGY
AT OXFORD
BY THE AUTHOR
IN ADMIRATION OF HIS TEACHING

Contents

Preface

On Remembrance Sunday, 2000, Bishop Peter Walker[1] delivered a moving sermon in Christ Church Cathedral, Oxford, at the dedication of an altar to the memory of the Bishop of Chichester, George Bell. It was [said the Rt Revd Bishop] "given to George Bell to be a senior leader of the Church in crucial, indeed critical, indeed catastrophic, times, as Bishop of an ancient Diocese – and as a Diocesan Bishop of the Church of England Bell saw himself always as a Bishop of England, one of the English Bishops and, as such, a bishop of the Universal Church; and the responsibilities he carried in that wider ambience(...)".[2]

Why exactly did George Bell see himself as a bishop of the Universal Church? Bell himself tells us why. It is the catholicity of the Gospel that makes the Church universal. At the heart of Christianity [Bell declares] "stands the Church. Christianity without the Church is not Christianity. The Church is the community through which God intended that the life of Christ should find continual expression. The Church needs no justification based upon utilitarian grounds. It was created by the act of God. Its existence cannot be denied or disregarded. It is here. It is a fact. It lives a life. It offers worship to God. It is a rock. It possesses the Gospel, the revelation of the love of God in Christ, who was born and was crucified and rose from the dead. This is a fact of immense significance, which the human mind is compelled to recognise. It is a fact which places the Church among the things which cannot be destroyed"..[3] Hence Christian disciples were "bound to one another, because they are disciples of Christ", who "is above the battle", and "does unite men and women". And it is in "His Church" that a "real world unity is to be found, despite the variety of confessions and communions". George Bell never tired of emphasising the maxim that he believed in "the Holy Catholic Church, the Communion of Saints!"[4]

The Church [argued Bell] "is a community of life as well as love. As such it stands over against all denials of life. It declares, because it is the Body through which Christ works, that love is the only possible basis of human unity, and that enmity and estrangement make freedom impossible and are the frustration of life's purpose. It proclaims this truth in all circumstances, and the kindred truth that God's purpose in the world is the creation of Man as a personal community of free and equal persons. Its very existence testifies to the spirit which is the opposite of war. Indeed, it bids men renounce the will to power because the will to power is the negation of the will of God for man. It bids men renounce war not only because war brings bitter suffering, but because it makes men seek power as an end in itself. As the will to power is the negation of the will of God for man, so Love is the fulfilment of His will. The Church is the divine community founded on Love. It is in God's plan the supreme means for the unification of mankind".[5]

Such were then Bishop Bell's deep convictions, and he lived up to them. The duty of the Bishop is not only to preach the Message of the Gospel, but also to act towards fulfilling this duty. To believe is to act, and to act is to transmit the Message, and indeed the Judgement. And judgement itself [maintains the learned Professor of Moral and Pastoral Theology at Oxford, Oliver O'Donovan] is "an act of moral discrimination, dividing right from wrong" – to make "the right and wrong in a given historical situation clear to our eyes".[6] That is what Bishop Bell endeavoured to do all his life. His actions bear witness to this.

Several monographs on George Bell's work and life are available to us in print. The first and only (never re-published) full "Life" remains Ronald C.D. Jasper's *George Bell Bishop of Chichester* (1967). Other studies include Kenneth Slack's brief but outstanding, *George Bell* (1971); Gordon Rupp's *'I seek my brethren'. Bishop George Bell and the German Churches* (1975); Andrew Chandler's *Brethren in adversity: Bishop Bell, the Church of England and the crisis of German Protestantism, 1933-1939* (1997); Edwin Robertson's *Unshakeable Friend, George Bell and the German Churches* (1999); Muriel Heppell's *George Bell and Nikolai Velimirovic': the story of friendship* (2001) and Giles Watson's "George Bell and the Anglican response to crisis, 1937-1949", *Humanitas* (Birmingham), No.1,Vol.1,1999.

The purpose of the present work is modest. It is merely to portray the life of the Bishop on the basis of the letters from George Bell to various people and their response to him. Bell's correspondence was copious. My selection is restricted. I have kept to such letters as will illuminate Bell's self-portrait. These letters speak for themselves, and call less for commentary than for supplementation by extracts from Bell's own most significant speeches. I have used these as generously as space has allowed.

Berlin, 2005
Peter Raina

Acknowledgements

I gratefully acknowledge my debts to all those who have helped me in my work and especially to Right Reverend Peter Knight Walker. I also tender my thanks to those who have granted me the use of copyright letters, and in particular I record my obligations to:

1. The Governing Body, Christ Church, Oxford, for having elected me to temporary Membership of the High Table of Christ Church, thus enabling me to work on the present book.

2. Dr Richard Palmer, Librarian and Archivist, Lambeth Palace Library, London (The Papers of G.K.A. Bell, Bishop of Chichester)

3. Dominik Hunger, Handschriftenabteilung, Universität Basel: Nachlaß Alphons Koechlin (Briefwechsel Bell/Koechlin).

4. Frau Marianne Leibholz, M.A.(Bishop Bell's correspondence with Professor Gerhard Leibholz).

5. The Duke of Bedford and the Trustees of the Bedford Estates for kindly permitting publication of letters from the 12th Duke of Bedford to Bishop George Bell.

6. The Earl of Halifax for kindly permitting publication of letters from the 1st Earl of Halifax to Bishop George Bell.

7. The Dean and Chapter and the Students of Christ Church, Oxford, for kindly permitting me to reproduce photos of the George Bell Altar (Christ Church Cathedral, Oxford).

Foreword

by

The Right Reverend Peter Knight Walker, D. D.
Sometime Canon of Christ Church, Oxford, and Bishop of Ely

I count it a privilege to write this "foreword" to a book which I look forward to placing alongside the three most valued books that I possess. They are G.K.A. Bell, *The Church and Humanity 1939-46* (1946); his earlier, and monumental, *Randall Davidson Archbishop of Canterbury* (1935, 3rd edition 1952), the life of the Archbishop he had served as Chaplain for ten years (1914-1924); and third, *Poems 1904-1958* by George Kennedy Allen Bell, printed privately for Mrs Henrietta Bell in 1960 "For his friends" and given to me by her as one of them.

The first of the three, never reprinted and long unobtainable, is the one I would part with last, containing in it as it does Bell's historic speech of 9 February 1944 in the House of Lords on the Obliteration Bombing of the German cities, which, it is commonly maintained, cost him the Archbishopric of Canterbury. More could perhaps be said, but what is beyond dispute is that this senior English churchman, who died a universally respected Honorary Life President of the World Council of Churches to whose foundation, on 22 August 1948, no single churchman had contributed more than he, died with no acknowledgement of his distinguished faithfulness in duty to both Church and State ever having been made to him by his own country.

It was Bell's hope that in retirement, and from the meticulous personal records he had always kept, he might write his own reflective account of the years, particularly, in which he had chaired the International Council of Life and Work, not least in holding it to the crucial business of the emergence, in defiance of Adolf Hitler's ever-increasing totalitarian ruthlessness, of the German Confessional Church. It was in those years that he found his stature as a leader, and a true prophetic calling . But that book was never written, for he died within months of standing down from Chichester.

There has been only one unitary life of Bell: R.C.D. Jasper's *George Bell Bishop of Chichester*, 1967 and never reprinted. And it has to be said that, in terms of perception of Bell's unique stature and significance from the crucial 1930s and onward, no ecclesiastical study has ever matched one single sentence of the all-too-brief monograph by the leading English Freechurchman, Kenneth Slack: "Bell saw to the heart of what was happening in our century and unremittingly called men to a very costly Christian obedience as they faced it". (Kenneth Slack, *George Bell* (1971), p. 19.) And yet one major secular historian has in recent years perceived the significance of Bell for today: Norman Davies gave two pages of his considerable *Europe, a History* (1998), to Bell's steadfast pursuit in war and peace, as a senior Christian churchman, of the principle of international European *reconciliation* (pages 922-3).

I find in that reference both a gleam of light in darkness and a pointer to the urgent need for a rediscovery of Bell's life and teaching. And it is at this point that I welcome most particularly the precise account that Dr Peter Raina offers of the method of his book. He puts this modestly in terms of seeking to allow a "self-portrait" to emerge from letters of GKAB selected for their capacity to disclose or illuminate *the man*.

When, at my request, Bishop Bell wrote his name for me in his *Randall Davidson, Archbishop of Canterbury* I remember him hurrying to the frontispiece, the grave studio portrait of the Archbishop, and letting his eye rest on it for a moment in silence. The Archbishop breathes on every page of that book, always conveying to the reader a sense of an immediate *reality*. This is the hallmark of a book compact on every page with necessary detail on the matter in hand - and I note then, the *personal* dimension of Peter Raina's title: *A Portrait in Letters*.

I had asked Bishop Bell to sign his name for me at Epiphany in Chichester in 1956. It was to prove the last time I would see him. Our friendship had begun fifteen years before when, by a remarkable fortune of war, I was in his home for a brief time, in Royal Navy uniform and just in from six months in the Battle of the Atlantic.

The phrase recalls to me at once a moment later in that last morning with him, when the Bishop and Mrs Bell stood with a group of friends below the recent portrait of him by William (later Sir William) Coldstream. Commissioned by the Diocese, to Bell's embarrassment, the picture received at its unveiling with displeasure at what was seen as its uncompromising austerity. (The whole episode is recalled in the recent major study, Bruce Laughton, *William Coldstream*, Yale University Press,

2004). The portrait was presented finally by Bell to the Tate Gallery and another painter commissioned by the Diocese.

Yet Coldstream painted always under the strict rule of *truth*. In his own words, quoted in the Tate Gallery's own Coldstream Exhibition Catalogue of 1987, "I find I lose interest unless I let myself be ruled by what I see".

I have written elsewhere of what I see in this "finest, gravest portrait, ecclesiastical or other, of the Twentieth Century"(my own words): "Bell sits lost in thought, still, silent, the man upon whom these things have come, and looking simply, steadily, forward into the middle distance. And I see there the true Christian *visionary* of the Twentieth Century".

So Coldstream saw Bell. And the Bell he saw was the Bell who would not look away from what he saw; who believed that *nothing mattered so much as the truth*; and the Bell, it should be always remembered, to whom the younger man, Dietrich Bonhoeffer, had sent his last message before Hitler's emissaries hauled him away, to be hanged next day on his explicit orders. "I was very much impressed by Bishop Bell when I painted him". So Sir William Coldstream wrote to me in a personal letter in September 1986, five months before he died.

Bell was, for me, without doubt, the greatest churchman of them all, the greatest bishop. The value of this book lies both in its concept and in its execution: the concept of allowing us to read Bell in his own spontaneous words, and in passages long and substantial enough to carry their own weight and so convey to us, in the detail which is necessary if we are to see them for what they were, the realities that faced him and demanded his response in the action he must take.

I used above the phrase "the Christian *visionary* of the Twentieth Century". I will close this foreword with a word from one to whom Bell, modest man that he was, looked often for guidance in deep and complex moral matters. "Bell", wrote Donald Mackinnon, Professor of Divinity in the University of Cambridge, "saw the problem with the clarity that only comes to the man who does not simply look on a problem from afar, but who acts in respect of it" (D.M. Mackinnon, *The Controversial Bishop Bell*, 1968).

This is a book that moves *in that dimension* of understanding and appreciation. It is an endeavour to be very grateful for, nor could it be more pertinently timed.

P.K.W.

1

"I find my belief in prayer"

George Kennedy Allen Bell[7] was born on 4th February 1883. His father, James, had gone up to Corpus Christi College, Cambridge. Ordained in 1878, his life was entirely in the pastoral ministry of the Church of England, his last appointment being as a Residentiary Canon of Norwich Cathedral. George's mother, Sarah Georgina (neé Megaw) was a dedicated housewife and mother. In addition to the first born son, George, she brought up three more sons and three daughters.

George Bell was sent to various preparatory schools, first to Malvern Lodge in Southampton, then to Stanmore Park near Harrow, and later to Temple Grove, East Sheen. In 1896 he won a Queen's scholarship at Westminster school, and in 1901 a classical scholarship to Christ Church, Oxford. He took a First in Classical Honour Moderations in 1903, but disappointingly (and perhaps by over-generosity in the two fields of undergraduate social service and poetry) fell to a Second Literae Humaniores, or 'Greats'. He won the distinguished Newdigate Prize for his poem 'Delphi' in 1904.

Finding himself called to follow his father and offer himself for the Ordained Ministry, he went from Oxford to Wells Theological College in April 1906, and on 9 June 1907 was ordained deacon in Ripon Cathedral by Bishop Boyd Carpenter,[8] to serve his title as curate of Leeds Parish Church for three years.

Early in March 1909, however, the Dean of Christ Church Oxford, Dr Thomas B. Strong[9] privately approached George Bell to ask if he would fill in an impending vacancy for a don in Holy Orders. Bell would not "have merely Chaplain's work to do" but also "take full part in the management of the whole place".

```
Christ Church
Oxford
11 March 1909
Private
Dictated

Dear Bell,
```

I want to ask you in private whether you would like your name brought forward as a Clerical Student here. It is probable that Warner will retire on a pension in June, 1910, and that then, or perhaps before, we shall want to appoint someone in Holy Orders who will be a Student. He would not have merely Chaplain's work to do, because we think it desirable that he should be on the same sort of level as all the other Students. But his work would, at any rate at first, be mainly Pass work. You know pretty well what the Clerical work here is. I think a person who came with that definite intention might make a good deal more of it than I ever succeeded in doing, or that has been done since. We should hope that the Clerical Student would be, when his time came, Censor, and take full part in the management of the whole place. Perhaps you would let me know some time what you think about this.

I was sorry to hear the other day indirectly that you have had an attack of influenza. I hope you are not over-working.

Yours very sincerely,
Thomas B. Strong

George Bell willingly accepted the offer and took "full part in the management of the whole place", combining Chaplain's duties with some undergraduate teaching of Classics and English Literature. It was in these Christ Church years that Bell developed his intense dedication, begun in Leeds, to the social teachings of the Church. He became an active member of the short lived Cavendish Association, encouraging the University members to undertake social work. He helped found Barnett House (a centre for social and economic studies) and the Oxford University Co-operative Society. As secretary of the Social and Political Studies Association and the Oxford Settlements Committee, George Bell lectured extensively for the Workers' Educational Association. He was quite happy with his work, which had the blessings of his bishop and the approval of the Canons of his College. And yet what made him less happy was the theological controversy between the Modernists and anti-Modernists, among the best Oxford theologians of the time .

The controversy began with the publication in 1911 of *Miracles in the New Testament* by Rev. J.M. Thompson, Dean of Divinity at Magdalen College, Oxford, denying the historical character of the virgin birth and resurrection of Christ. Canon Henry Scott Holland[10] of Christ Church and his colleagues (*Miracles*, 1911) vehemently challenged Thompson's arguments. Further controversy broke out when seven Oxford dons in 1912 published their *Foundations – a Statement of Christian Belief in Terms of Modern Thought*. The *Statement* was duly contested by Rev. Ronald Knox,[11] Chaplain of Trinity College, Oxford, in his *Some Loose Stones* (1913).

This theological debate excited George Bell and, even, helped consolidate his own faith. In a letter (29th December 1913) to his friend (later Canon) R.A.Rawstorne, Bell expressed his disagreement with Knox on his treatment of a priori convictions of God and the doctrinal infallibility of the Scriptures. The phrase "A deposit of faith" had an unpleasant sound for him, for it suggested ""something that's sunk to the bottom, or a kind of sediment".

> To my mind [he wrote] that is altogether foreign to the New Testament idea. Of course there must be creed and dogma, the intellectual presentation of the Word. But the Word itself is alive, quick and powerful. To me "faith" in the New Testament suggests something very living, moving, creative, rather than something settled and deposited once for all.[12]

Christianity "is a life before it is a system and to lay too much stress on the system destroys the life". He was, he wrote, "only an ordinary sort of man. But I found (and find) that my belief in prayer, in God's care for me, in the Risen Christ and therefore in Resurrection, in absolution and grace of Holy Communion were (and are) justified by practice. I found this of course by degrees. I have been led rather than taken by storm: guided by quiet thinking and doing rather than driven by tumult and violence. And so I go on, continually reassured by my own experience and the experience of those among whom I work".[13]

George Bell had been at Christ Church, Oxford, for nearly four years when in early August 1914 the Archbishop of Canterbury, Dr Randall Davidson[14] invited him to become his chaplain. Bell accepted the invitation as a call of duty, and indeed of God, despite his reluctance to leave Christ Church (as he felt, abruptly) and some personal hesitation about his own "shyness". The Archbishop gave Bell time to consider the offer. When the offer came, [Bell wrote to Rawstorne on 9th August] and "at a time when so many men all over England were obeying the King's call for service without demur or delay – how could I turn back from this call, and how hesitate a moment longer?"[15] . So he accepted; "after telling the Archbishop a little of what made me doubtful – my fondness for persons, my dislike of social entertaining, my shyness, and such detail as my views on Disestablishment: and on all these points he was extremely reassuring. Also I made a bid for having friends to see me, and also to stay, at Lambeth: and he promised to help me there, and said he had not seen enough younger people at Lambeth lately".[16].

Christ Church was not keen to lose Bell. The College was remarkably pleased with what he had been doing at Oxford. But the wishes of the Archbishop had to be respected. Yet the Dean was hesitant to relieve Bell at once, so requested the Archbishop that Bell should continue to work in his office at the College until the end of the Term. The request was granted.

Lambeth Palace, S. E.

11 August 1914

My dear Bell,
    I have heard, and probably you also have heard, from the Dean of Christ Church, who seems to be clearly of opinion that it would be a good thing that you should continue in office at Christ Church until the end of next Term. He says that this is clearly best for the College, and that there would be great difficulty in making other arrangements. This being the case, I am sure it would be your wish, as it is mine, to fall in simply with what the Dean, who has behaved with kindliest consideration throughout, thinks to be best, and we shall be quite ready to make temporary arrangements here so as to set you free for work at Oxford during next Term.
    As to the exact details of dates we can correspond later. In the great whirlpool of European affairs just now none of us dare prophesy what will be the condition of things a few months hence. We must of course act as though the arrangements we make could be fulfilled after ordinary fashion; but none of us dare say for certain that this is so.

We are all of us day by day lifting up our hearts
to our Father in Heaven for guidance and strength,
collectedness, and the true kind of peace.
    I am
    Yours very truly,
    Randall Cantuar

George Bell was to be the Archbishop's junior chaplain. His first task on taking up his appointment was to assist in the drafting of prayers for the nation at the outbreak of war. From the beginning, the personal significance of the appointment and its responsibilities were clearly put to him by the Archbishop. The Archbishop wished that "while undertaking responsibility for diocesan affairs", that Bell "keep abreast of all the bigger things going on". He "must read as much of the whole correspondence issuing from the Archbishop" as he could and "refer to old files". Bell was "also to remember the Archbishop's wish when anyone is to be interviewed that his papers and case should be prepared beforehand, not simply fetched in at the time".[17]

The work at the Palace kept Bell quite busy. He would usually retire to bed at past midnight. There was little private life. "I think it is nearly a fortnight [he wrote to Rawstorne on 7th November 1915], since I wrote any letter to anyone that was not purely a business affair. I have had so many of those letters to write lately – silly, stupid things most of them – that I am quite jaded and feel starved for lack of that nourishment which any kind of communication with my friends gives me: and friendship is my meat and drink".[18]

But then Bell was enthusiastic about his work, and, in time, became the Archbishop's most indispensable assistant. He became "an accomplished intermediary" between the Archbishop and many prominent figures, secular as well as clerical.[19] The new chaplain established good personal relations with men of importance within the Church and the State. Of course Bell's own personality played a decisive role in this state of affairs. Not only was he extraordinarily well read and informed, he owned exceedingly polite manners, was easily approachable, affectionate. He made strangers feel comfortable in his company, thus winning respect and affection whomever he met. Then again he was discreet and circumspect. No wonder that he was much in demand if ever there was a new vacancy which needed to be occupied. In 1917 the Bishop of Worcester invited him to become Vicar of St. Michael's,

Coventry. Prebendary F.N.Thicknesse desired him to come to St. Mark's, North Audley Street. Bell refused all these offers. Why he did so, we learn from his letter to Thicknesse[20]:

```
Lambeth Palace, S. E. 1
22 November  1917

Dear Prebendary Thicknesse,

     The Archbishop has shown me your letter to him
in which you make the very kind suggestion that
I might succeed Prebendary Cronshaw at St Mark's
North Audley Street.
     I am deeply grateful to you for thinking of me
for so important a post, and very sensible of the
honour you do me. Nor can I fail to realise the
responsibility involved in making an answer to the
proposal.
     Yet after the fullest consideration of all
the circumstances I believe that I ought to remain
where I am and therefore not to accept the offer
which you kindly say you are disposed to make. I am
far from understanding the importance of the work
at S. Mark's, or the richness of its opportunities;
but after careful deliberation, both in my own mind
and with Miss Livingstone to whom I am engaged,
I cannot help feeling that at present I can best
render my proper service to the Church as Chaplain
at Lambeth. I ought to add that the Archbishop
himself has been most kind in discussing the matter
with me, but he has made it quite clear not only
that the decision should be mine, that which ever
way I decided I should be sure of his goodwill.
Again thanking you very much,
     Yours very truly,
     G. K. A. Bell
```

Then again in July 1922 another serious offer came from the Bishop of Manchester, William Temple[21] to become Vicar of Bolton. The Archbishop of Canterbury did not want to stand in the way. He told Bell that he ought to go to Bolton. But really the Archbishop did not want him to go. In a moving and affectionate letter dated 2nd July 1922 the Archbishop wrote about how closely and effectively they had worked together.[22]

You and I have for all these tempestuous years
worked together, and it is our joint work, and not
my work in any narrower sense, which has had such
degree of effectiveness as belongs to it. Take away
one of the partners in the work and it is obvious
that the doing of it would either not be done at all
or done in quite a different way. And to start it
afresh with a new fellow-worker in the departments
which have been specially yours would in any case
be difficult; and the difficulty is doubled by the
fact that I am seventy four years old and can't
readily or light-heartedly open at that age a new
chapter. Next, you have by sheer effectiveness and
resourcefulness of work, got into a position in
central Church affairs which is markedly your own.
Quite apart from myself, people look to you and
don't look in vain. Bishops and others who believe
in me as Archbishop and rely upon what guidance I
can give, realise clearly your share in it all,
and, do what we will, we cannot expect them to be
other than critical and even severely critical, of
any action of yours which impairs the efficiency of
Lambeth work and words, and weakens such security as
there is for my continuous holding of the position
during the next few - they cannot be very many -
years.[23]

The Archbishop did not intend to "disregard the immense
importance, the varied interest, the educative usefulness, or the sacred
trust of such a parish as Bolton", but the Archbishop strongly felt that
"the uniqueness of your position at Lambeth, and of the qualifications
you have accumulated for holding it to the common good, outweigh
even the greatness of the call to Bolton".[24]

After this worthy assessment of Bell's position it would have been
hardly possible for him to leave Lambeth Palace. His conscience would
not have permitted it. So Bell stayed on until he was confronted with
a still more challenging a surprise at the beginning of 1924. Dean of
Canterbury, Henry Wace,[25] had been ill for some time, and in December
1923 the illness was so grave as to suggest that he would soon die. On
10th December, Bell recorded in his diary that the Archbishop had asked
him if he would like to be Dean. Bell replied that he would not "rule it

out straight", although the "public would think it an odd appointment – too great a post".[26] Wace died on 9th January 1924.

The Deanery of Canterbury is a crown appointment. The Archbishop advises the Prime Minister, who, if he approves the candidate, recommends him to the Monarch. So the Archbishop first asked Canon V.F. Storr if he would like to be Dean. Storr said no. Then on 14th January the Archbishop again turned to Bell. "I should not say NO, if you approved", Bell replied.[27] The Archbishop, relieved, said that he did not want him to go, but there was "no place in which I would rather see you than Dean of Canterbury". The Archbishop also informed Bell that he had "seen the canons and sounded them", and Bell "was the one person whom they all agreed would be welcome to them".[28] Soon afterwards the Archbishop proposed Bell's name to the recently installed Prime Minister, Ramsay Macdonald.[29] After "the most careful consideration" the Prime Minister on 14th February officially informed Bell that he was offering him the succession to the Deanery.

```
14 February 1924
Dear Sir,

        The Deanery of Canterbury has become vacant
owing to the death of the Very Rev Dr Wace.
                It is now my duty to submit to His
Majesty the name of a successor and after the most
careful consideration I have come to the conclusion
that I cannot better serve the interests of the
Church than by offering to you the succession to
the Deanery. On hearing from you that you would be
willing to accept this offer I shall be happy to
submit your name to the King.
                Until His Majesty's approval has been
obtained, I have to ask that you will treat this
offer as confidential.
        Yours very truly
        Ramsay Macdonald
```

Bell replied the same day, accepting the Prime Minister's offer.

Confidentially Bell informed his mother about the Prime Minister's offer and his acceptance of it. When the possibility was first suggested, wrote Bell, he could not feel that he was "the least big or good or worthy enough for such a post", but "I feel that as duty now". Besides it was a comfort to "know that the Archbishop and others have so much desired it".

> Lambeth Palace, S. E. 1
> S. Valentine's Day
> 1924
> Confidential
>
> My dearest Mother,
>   I have just received a letter from the Prime Minister, in the middle of a Bishop's Meeting, asking me to be Dean of Canterbury. When the possibility was first even suggested, I could not feel that I was the least big or good or worthy enough for such a post. I feel that as deeply now. I am not good or wise enough; and I can picture, from another point of view, the great surprise with which the world will receive the news. But it is a comfort to know that the Archbishop and others have so much desired it, and I know I shall have the help of those who love me in trying my best, and the help of God.
>   A Valentine for you.
>   Your loving
>   George

Bell's nomination was greeted with joy by his immediate colleagues. Senior Canon (later Archdeacon of Chichester) A.J. Mason[30] privately wrote to Bell to say that it was "great joy to feel that a friend of us all is coming to govern us, with whom we shall work happily".

> The Precincts,
> Canterbury
> 15 Feb. 1924
> Private
>
> My dear Bell,
>   The Archbishop has told me in confidence that you have, after long delay, received the momentous letter. The relief to my mind – to speak of what is personal – is unspeakable. And besides the security of knowing that we shall not have some new gospel set forth among us, it is a great joy to feel that a friend of us all is coming to govern us, with whom we shall work happily. I long to be able to tell our

two sons. How delighted they will be.

You know how rejoiced we shall be if we and our house can be of any use to you when you come to see about arrangements. Of course you have the Palace, but the Senior Canon claims the privilege of welcoming you and Mrs Bell for bed & board whenever it suits you.

Yours very sincerely,
A.J. Mason

Of course we have not breathed a word about it as yet.

Another, similar letter, expressing joy was sent to Bell from The Theological College, Salisbury, on 26t[h] February 1924.

Theological College,
Salisbury.
26 February 1924

My dear Bell,

I want to write a line to tell you how glad we all are here about your appointment to Canterbury. Two years ago we had a Principal's Conference there and I was struck then with the glory of the place and the great opportunities that the Deanery must give. It will allow you to keep in touch with much of that important work for which the Church has been owing you so much during the past few years, though I hope you will not be kept on the run too much. One does not want Deans to be too leisurely, but there is an extreme at the other end, into which some of our Deans are in danger of falling. But if our Deans have no time to be learned, where shall learning be found amongst us?

I wonder if there is any previous instance in which a Residentiary Canon of a Cathedral receives one of his old curates as Dean. No doubt Bickersteth will now be able to reap the results of having trained you in the way in which you should go at Leeds.

The right use of Cathedrals is not always easy to find in these towns of no great size. At Wells I suppose we had an extreme example of that difficulty, but even here it is not altogether absent, I don't think that we shall solve it by just making them into super parish Churches, but rather by giving a lead to the Diocese in teaching and in worship.

I had intended to write this earlier, but the delay enables me to ask about one G.H. Tubbs, who is a candidate for ordination at Canterbury. After a Course at Oxford he went to King's College, London, but now writes to apply for admission here. I gather from his letter that this is in accord with the wish of the Archbishop. If everything is in order we should be glad to have him.

Yours ever,
C.J. Dumont

On 26th February C.P. Duff[31] from the Prime Minister's office informed Bell privately as well as officially that "the King has been graciously pleased to approve Bell's appointment to the Deanery of Canterbury".

10 Downing Street
Whitehall, S. W. 1
16.2.24C.

Dear Mr Bell,
I hope you will allow me to send you my sincere congratulations upon your appointment to the Deanery of Canterbury. I have this moment had the formal notification of His Majesty's approval. The Archbishop told me last night that he hoped the announcement would be in Monday morning's papers. I shall accordingly send it out from here tomorrow: or if for any reason you would prefer any alteration in this arrangement could you ring up Colonel Waterhouse here (I am away tomorrow) who could act accordingly?

Yours Sincerely,
C.P.Duff

16 February 1924

Dear sir,
I am desired by the First Lord of the Treasury to inform you that the King has been graciously pleased to approve your appointment to the Deanery

of Canterbury, and to say that you will hear further
regarding the ordinary formalities.
     Yours faithfully,
     C.P. Duff

The news of the newly appointed Dean of Canterbury became
public on 18th February. The Bishops now formally recorded "their
heartfelt gratitude" to Bell, for "the invaluable service rendered by
him to the Bishops' Meetings by his singularly full, accurate, and lucid
minutes, and also for the ever ready and efficient help given by him to
the Bishops during his ten years' tenure of the office of Chaplain to the
Archbishop of Canterbury". The resolution was passed at the Bishops'
Meeting at Lambeth Palace on 21st May. The Archbishop conveyed the
message to Bell on 27th May.

     Lambeth Palace, S.E.1
     27 May 1924

     Dear Mr Dean,
     It is my pleasant duty to convey to you a copy
     of a Resolution passed with unanimity and, I think
     I may add, enthusiasm by the Bishops of the Three
     Provinces assembled here on Wednesday last. If you
     deem it well to send any reply it could be brought
     up at the next Meeting of Bishops.
     I am,
     Yours very truly,
     Randall Cantuar

Now that the Dean's appointment had been confirmed an
unexpected problem confronted Bell. The Statutes of Canterbury
Cathedral required that the Dean "be a Priest of unblemished life
and reputation, a man not only learned and accomplished but also
distinguished by some title of learning, that is a Doctor or Bachelor of
Divinity, or Doctor of Law". Bell therefore at once contacted the Dean of
Christ Church, Oxford, Henry Julian White[32], to explore the possibility
of his being considered for a DD at Oxford, before his installation as
Dean, which had been fixed for 31st March (1924). The Dean of Christ
Church devoted all his energies and faculties to the satisfaction of the
wishes of the Dean-Designate of Canterbury. To this effect the following
correspondence is of utmost interest:

1) Dean of Christ Church to George Bell, 22 February 1924.

```
Christ Church
Oxford
22 February 1924
Private
```

My dear Dean,

I waited a little time before answering your letter of inquiry, and consulted a discreet friend.

It is not very easy to know what to suggest; D. D. Degrees are often conferred, but the only persons contemplated in the Standing Orders of Council are Bishops, and there has been a tendency lately to restrict the conferring of these Degrees on them, as it has seemed to some members of Council that Pass men ought not to be granted such an Academic honour because they have achieved distinction in a quite different walk of life.

If your case were to come up, it would naturally have to be referred, first to the Committee which deals with such applications, and then to the whole Council; finally to convocation.

It is well to have this procedure in view; in all these matters there is sure to be a advocatus diaboli, and it is well to know what arguments he would be likely to employ; and it seems to me that two criticisms are sure to be made, 1) That you might take the ordinary course and submit your theses to the Regius Professor of Divinity and get the Degree by accumulation; or 2) That the Archbishop might give you a degree himself. I am not well acquainted with the procedure in the latter case, but the question is fairly certain to be asked and I should like to know what answer I should give.

It may well be that the Dean of Canterbury must be a Doctor of Divinity at once or as nearly at once as possible, and in that case there may not be reasonable time for you to proceed in the usual way, even by accumulation; if that is so, there is a really strong case for granting the degree by decree, and I should be very pleased to propose your name for it.

Excuse this very businesslike letter and
Believe me,
Yours very sincerely,
H. J. White

2) George Bell to the Dean of Christ Church, 23 February 1924.

My dear Mr Dean,
I most grateful for your kind letter about
the Degree and the trouble you have taken in
investigating possibilities.
I have been looking up the Statutes of the
Canterbury Cathedral (dated 1686) in order to get
the exact facts as to any requirement of a special
degree. I find the relevant Statute is as follows:
Of the Qualifications, Election and Admission of
the Dean.
We appoint and ordain that the Dean be a Priest
of unblemished life and reputation, a man not only
learned and accomplished but also distinguished by
some title of learning, that is a Doctor or Bachelor
of Divinity, or Doctor of Law.
It would therefore appear that the Dean,
before he can really be admitted Dean, must possess
the Degree of B.D., D.D., or D.C.L. In ordinary
circumstances, i.e. were the case such that it was
simply a desirable thing that the Dean of Canterbury
should be a Doctor of Divinity I should certainly
take steps to become a candidate for the Degree
of D. D. in the ordinary way by getting subjects
for a theses approved by the Regius Professor, and
then presenting the theses with a view to getting
the Degree by accumulation. This I understand in
accordance with the University Statutes I should
have been able to do according to the old regulations
if I were to complete the necessary steps by the end
of next term and no later.
But unhappily as the Statute which I have
quoted shows the Dean-Designate of Canterbury must
be a B.D., or D.D., or a D.C.L. before he can be
installed as Dean. The late Dean died on January
9th and had been in failing health ever since his
accident in the Summer. As, among other reasons it
is not desirable that the office of Dean should remain
vacant for too long, the date of my installation

has been fixed for Friday, March 31st. Therefore the question of time is a very important factor; and I think you will agree that I am practically prevented from proceeding as a candidate by theses or examination in the ordinary way.

As to the second possible criticism that it is open for me to ask the Archbishop of Canterbury to give me a Degree himself. I could undoubtedly apply to the Archbishop, and I should do so with the hope that he would be kindly willing to confer a Degree if it became absolutely necessary. But from the general point of view the Archbishop himself would I know always encourage those who desire or are required to be honoured with the title of learning to seek such title from their own University, if there were reasonable hope that the University might grant it. And on grounds of a more personal character which you will appreciate it would I am sure be better that I should (if it were possible) obtain the Degree from some degree conferring authority other than himself. And certainly, but in no way reflecting on the Lambeth Degree on which I should be the last person to reflect, I should particularly, on this occasion, prefer to seek, and if so it might be, gratefully to receive a Degree from the University where I worked in different ways for nearly ten years as scholar and student of Christ Church.

Perhaps these considerations do not altogether meet the criticism of the advocatus diaboli, and in that case and if you think the advocatus diaboli likely to prevail I am sure you would tell me so, and I should then (though reluctantly) apply to the Archbishop of Canterbury. If, however, you are of opinion, after thinking over what I have said, that there is a good case for the granting by decree (or by whatever process is proper) a Degree which would meet the Statutory requirement relating to the Office of Dean of Canterbury, and if you are willing to propose my name, I should be very grateful indeed.

Yours very sincerely,
GB

3) Dean of Christ Church to George Bell, 25 February 1924.

```
Christ Church
Oxford
25 February 1924
```

My dear Dean,

Thank you for your letter, which gave me just the information I required. I gave notice in Council this afternoon that I would "state qualifications" for a D.D. degree next Monday, and I think the Committee which recommends will probably give their verdict in favour; and if that is so, we may hope to carry it in Council at once, and then in Convocation in due course; and should the advocatus diaboli object I will know how to answer him.

    (Private. Does His Grace know what an admirable Secretary S.C.E. Legg would make, if he could get him? He is the only man I can think of who would be worthy to succeed you.)

    Yours very truly,
    H. J. White

4) Dean of Christ Church to George Bell, 28 February 1924.

```
Christ Church
Oxford
28 February 1924
```

My dear Dean,

I am glad to inform you that the Committee of Council is unanimous in recommending you for the D. D. degree by decree. This will come before the actual Council on Monday next, when I will state qualifications and do my best to have the matter voted on there and then. If that is done, the decree could be sent to Convocation for March 11.

    Meanwhile, will you kindly inform me what is your exact description? Are you already actually Dean, or Dean-designate? I shall be very obliged if you will let me have an answer to this question by return, as your name must be properly described in the agenda-paper for Monday.

    Yours very sincerely,
    H. J. White

A Postcard will do.

Bell held the Deanery for five years. He brought with him fresh life and significant changes at the Cathedral. The new Dean instructed that the Cathedral be opened to public free of charge from Whitsunday every Sunday between services and in Summer until 7 p.m.; and ladies could enter the Cathedral without hats. Short leaflets describing briefly various historical aspects of the Cathedral, written by Bell himself, were available to visitors at a modest price. Visitors were pleased to make voluntary gifts. Bell set aside a special altar in the nave to be used for private prayer. And at the daily Eucharist and at Evensong, the Dean "instituted a scheme of prayer for all parishes in the diocese and their incumbents, so that each parish was remembered once a year by name", thereby strengthening the link between the Cathedral and the diocese.[33]

Bell established a society called "Friends of Canterbury Cathedral". Any churchman could join it by paying a membership fee of 5s. Gifts of larger sums were welcomed. Among the first to be entered on the roll was the Prince of Wales. The income thus earned covered the costs of repairing and restoration in the Cathedral.

It was on Bell's initiative that the BBC began broadcasting the Cathedral services at regular intervals, at least four times a year. Then came the precious thought of performing religious plays in the Cathedral. Nothing of the sort had happened since the Middle Ages. Bell invited John Masefield[34] to write a special play, *The Coming of Christ*. Gustav Holst[35] composed the music. In Whitsun week 1928 the play was performed in the Cathedral five times before six thousand people.[36] Bell hailed the event as "an incident of great significance in the history of the Cathedral", and looked upon it "as a religious event, an act of religious dedication and inspiration, very proper to the Whitsuntide Festival".[37] The entry to the performances was free, but those who attended offered voluntary contributions. The money thus collected was used for commissioning new plays. One of the first distinguished authors commissioned was T.S. Eliot[38] to write *Murder in the Cathedral*. Christopher Fry[39] and Dorothy Sayers[40] followed.

A Canterbury Festival of Music and Drama was next on the agenda. It took place in August 1929. At Canterbury, wrote *The Times*, the Church was "resuming her old and proud connection with the Arts". Bell himself in a letter to *The Times* on 17th August 1929 emphasised the fact that "the special and intimate association of the festival with

Canterbury Cathedral recalls the old inspiration which religion gave to art of all kinds and not least to drama and music".[41]

The organisational work alone did not keep Bell busy at the Deanery. He took time off to publish (together with Rev. W.L. Robertson)[42] *Documents on Christian Unity* in 1924, *The Church of England and the Free Churches* in 1925; *The Stockholm Conference on Life and Work* in 1926; *The Modern Parson* in 1928 and *A Brief Sketch of the Church of England* in 1929.

In 1929 Bell left the Deanery. On 11th March he was nominated Bishop, by the then Prime Minister, Stanley Baldwin,[43] to the See of Chichester, made vacant by the death of Bishop Winfrid Burrows[44] (on 13th February 1929). After some hesitation Bell accepted the offer and was consecrated in Canterbury Cathedral on 11th June 1929. As a diocesan bishop Bell's voice now carried weight, and no one could have been more conscious of that than the new Bishop of Chichester himself.

Annex 1

G. K. A. Bell: Divinity Degrees at Oxford

<u>Private.</u>

CHRIST CHURCH,
OXFORD.

March 11, 1909.

Dear Bell,

   I want to ask you in private whether you would like your name brought forward as a Clerical Student here. It is probable that Warner will retire on a pension in June, 1910, and that then, or perhaps before, we shall want to appoint someone in Holy Orders who will be a Student. He would not have merely Chaplain's work to do, because we think it desirable that he should be on the same sort of level as all the other Students. But his work would, at any rate at first, be mainly Pass work. You know pretty well what the Clerical work here is. I think a person who came with that definite intention might make a good deal more of it than I ever succeeded in doing, or that has been done since. We should hope that the Clerical Student would be when his time came, Censor, and take full part in the management of the whole place. Perhaps you would let me know some time what you think about this.

   I was sorry to hear the other day indirectly that you have had an attack of influenza. I hope you are not over-working.

         Yours very sincerely,

         Thomas Bishop

Rev. G. K. Bell.

36

Christ Church,
Oxford.

Sir,

Many people are likely to agree with Professor Margoliouth that a degree in Divinity is a degree in something which implies religion as well as learning, and ought not therefore be awarded, save with the greatest reluctance, to candidates writing from a definitely non-Christian point of view. But many will also feel with Professor Oman that it is only right to admit the "the orthodox Nonconformist etc degree" — and, we may add, Roman Catholic.

The Divinity Professors have been

driven to admit all candidates alike,
whether Christian or non-Christian,
simply by their being that the University
as such can no longer be called upon to
decide what is orthodox and what is not.
On the other hand, Professor Holland
for instance has emphatically declared
that Theology cannot be adequately
studied or taught out of relation to a
society, i.e. it must have a
denominational basis. It is with the
greatest timidity that I venture to
make the following suggestion. Let the

3

Christ Church,
Oxford.

Divinity degrees be definitely limited to Christians — I say nothing about a possible degree in comparative Religion later on — but let the candidates for these degrees present themselves with their theses, no longer as individuals or, so to speak, in *vacuo*, but as members of a particular society, — the denomination to which they belong. Each of these societies has one or more theological colleges of its own for the training of its ministers, and it would,

Christ Church,
Oxford.

Undergraduate must become a member of some Society before taking the University Examination and eventually the B A degree, and if, as punctually happens, the Society which he enters satisfies itself as to his character, is it quite unreasonable that graduates seeking for a degree in Divinity should enter for that degree through a Theological College belonging to the particular denomination of which they are members? It may, of course, be objected that the University will still have to decide what constitutes an "orthodox

Society"; but I believe that even that question could be settled and settled amicably, & especially when we remember that the Theological Colleges of several denominations have already been made welcome in Oxford.

Your obedient servant

G. K. A. Bell.

2

"War is incompatible with the mind and method of Christ"

After the end of World War I several Western European Church leaders felt that the Church had not done enough to carry Christ's message and that it was time now for the Church to play an ever increasing a role in the maintenance of world peace. The leading figure behind this thought was the Archbishop of Upsala, Nathan Söderblom.[45] He initiated and brought into effect his idea of holding an international conference of Church representatives from various countries. Over sixty delegates gathered at Oud Wassenaar near the Hague. This "International Committee of the World Alliance for promoting International Friendship through the Churches" discussed, from 30th September till 4th October 1919, a variety of topics on the problems of peace and war, and especially the proposal by Söderblom for a world conference of the Churches to tackle moral and social questions facing society. The Anglican delegation at this conference included George Bell, who was fascinated by Söderblom's views, and devoted his life-time to their achievement.

The first opportunity offered to Bell in this direction came when he acted as an assistant secretary to the 1920 Lambeth Conference. The "Appeal to all Christian People" owed "something" to Bell's initiative.[46]

Archbishop Söderblom, with the help of his Swiss and American colleagues, convened further international gatherings first in November 1919 in Paris, and then again in August 1920 in Geneva. These were mostly Protestant gatherings, thus not ecumenical in the sense Söderblom wished them to be. He wanted a conference of all Churches, including Roman Catholic and Orthodox Churches. The Archbishop of Canterbury, Randall Davidson, fully supported the Swede, who with unique enthusiasm and devotion succeeded in assembling five hundred churchmen from thirty-seven countries in Stockholm from 19th to 30th August 1925. Only the Roman Catholic Church did not send its delegates, though invited to do so. Thus the Conference of Life and Work became the first ecumenical Christian conference of its kind. Its chief aim was not to enter into questions of Creed or ecclesiastical organisation, but to "unite the different Churches in common practical work, to furnish the Christian conscience with an organ of expression in the midst of the great spiritual movements of our time, and to insist that the principles of the Gospel be applied to the solution of contemporary social and international problems".[47]

Bell of course was intensively involved in the proceedings of the Stockholm Conference, putting at the disposal of the Conference his volume of Documents on Christian Unity, produced in 1924, as a result and direct consequence of the 1920 Lambeth Conference Appeal. At Stockholm now Bell was invited to join a six-member international team to draft the Conference Message. The Message expressed penitence for the past failures of the Churches and "affirmed the duty of all Churches to apply the Gospel to all realms of human life – industrial, social, political, and international".[48] The mission of the Church was "above all to state principles, and to assert the ideal, while leaving to individual consciences and to communities the duty of applying them with charity, wisdom and courage".[49] Christians all over the world were appealed to, to realise God's will in order to achieve His Kingdom: "The nearer we draw to the Crucified, the nearer we came to one another, in however varied colours the Light of the World may be reflected in our faith".

An international Continuation Committee of sixty-seven members (Bell among them) was appointed to carry on the work of the Stockholm Conference. The duties of the Committee included the publication of the Conference proceedings; to co-ordinate information on methods of co-operation among the Churches and to prepare further conferences on Life and Work. Individual Churches were encouraged to set up committees to promote mutual co-operation. To this effect George Bell introduced a motion in the Church of England Assembly in November 1925. However it was not until 1932 that a Council on Foreign Relations was appointed.

At Bell's instigation the Continuation Committee appointed a sub-committee under the chairmanship of the German theologian, Adolf Deissmann, to attempt at "closer co-operation between the Churches and teachers and theological professors".[50] And it was in this spirit that an Anglo-German theological conference to discuss "The Kingdom of God" took place at Canterbury in April 1927. Bell was very satisfied with the results. It "was a great conference", he wrote to Deissmann. "The week was very fruitful, very vital, and the source of friendship which all hope will be lasting".[51] Another Anglo-German conference followed a year later in August 1928, this time at the Wartburg, Eisenach in Germany. The subject matter of both conferences was published in English and German, under the title *Mysterium Christi*, edited jointly by Bell and Deissmann. The third Anglo-German conference took place in March 1931 at Chichester.

The Stockholm Continuation Committee held its next meeting in September 1929 in Eisenach. Bell, now as Bishop of Chichester, made his presence strongly felt. He presented a resolution, which endorsed:

> - the clauses of the Treaty of Paris of August 1928 (the Kellog-Briand Pact), undertaking to "condemn recourse to war for the solution of international controversies and renounce it as an instrument of national policy";
> - the Stockholm statement that war, considered "as an institution for the settlement of international disputes, is incompatible with the mind and method of Christ, and therefore incompatible with the mind and method of His Church";
> - the need of revising existing treaties and the necessity for arbitration;
> - "an appeal to the respective authorities of all Christian Communions to declare in unmistakable terms that they will not countenance any war or encourage their countrymen to serve in any war, with regard to which the government of their country has refused an offer to submit the dispute to arbitration".

Bell also advocated the creation of a permanent executive body to be called the Universal Christian Council for Life and Work. The Council was to include women and youth organisations as well as greater representation from Asia and Africa. The Council was to have a small Executive Committee, which would meet annually, but the entire Council would gather biennially to discuss "some special subject of vital moral importance". The Council's constitution was adopted by the Continuation Committee at Chexbres in September 1930.[52]

In England Bell worked effectively towards realising the Eisenach resolutions. An interdenominational body "Christ and Peace Campaign" was established under the chairmanship of Bell. He prepared his second volume of *Documents on Christian Unity*, 1924-30 for the 1930 Lambeth Conference, to which he now acted as episcopal secretary. At this conference Bell also sat on two committees: Life and Witness of the Christian Unity and the Unity of the Church.[53] We owe it to Bell that the 1930 Lambeth Conference fully supported the spirit of the "Christ and Peace Campaign". The following letters throw some light on how Bell worked together with various peace organisations to put into practice the principles of the Gospel.

   1) Letter from the Fellowship of Reconciliation to the Bishop of Chichester, 25 October 1929.

```
The Fellowship of Reconciliation
17, Red Lion Square,
London, W. C. 1
25 October 1929

My dear Bishop of Chichester,
     I should not be happy not to send you a brief
note of very sincere thanks for the kind way in
which you presided and spoke at the Central Hall on
Tuesday. Everybody seems to be thoroughly pleased
with the meeting and the prospects for further work
are most promising. Such success would of course
have been quite impossible without your help.
Please accept very warm thanks.
     It has just occurred to me that it might be
useful to let the Prime Minister know about the
meeting. If a letter embodying the resolution were
awaiting him on his return from America it would
suggest that the Churches were ready to support
a forward peace policy. Would you feel able to
write to him? I shall prepare a draft for your
consideration.
     If you will kindly let me know when you are
likely to be in London again and able to spare half
an hour I should be very glad to consult you as to
next steps.
     Again, very many thanks,
     Yours sincerely,
     Percy W. Bartlett
     [General Secretary]
```

2) Draft letter to the Prime Minister (no date).

My dear Prime Minister,
You will be in no doubt about the cordial welcome awaiting you here on your return from your peace mission to America. Everybody would like to thank you personally for what you have been able to do and to assure you that you have the good will of the country behind you in pressing farther along the path of disarmament and pacification.

As one token of the attitude of thoughtful people I think the resolution adopted unanimously by an overcrowded meeting in the large Central Hall on the 22nd of this month, over which meeting I had the privilege of presiding, will be of special interest. The meeting was called under the title, "Christ and Peace: a Call to the Church to end War", and followed a well attended service of intercession conducted by the Bishop of Kensington in the Church of St Martin-in-the-Fields. With other meetings on the same lines likely to be held in provincial centres, it will show that the Churches are anxious to add to political efforts for peace a moral and spiritual contribution which I believe you will consider indispensable.

The resolution was as follows:

I am, my dear Prime Minister, etc.

3) The Churches and Arbitration – Resolution proposed by the Bishop of Chichester (no date)

The Churches and Arbitration.
Resolution
proposed by the Bishop of Chichester (Dr Bell)
seconded by Dr Simons
supported by Wilfred Monod.

The members of the Continuation Committee of the Universal Christian Conference on Life and Work, belonging to many Christian Communions in Europe and America, and assembled at Eisenach for their first meeting after the signing of the Pact of Paris desire to issue the following statement:

1.   We whole-heartedly welcome the solemn declaration made by the leading statesmen of the world in the names of their respective peoples that they condemn recourse to war for the solution of international controversies, renounce it as an instrument of national policy in their relations with one another, and agree that the settlement or solution of all disputes or conflicts, of whatever nature or of whatever origin they may be, which may arise among them shall never be sought except by pacific means.

2.   We believe that war considered as an institution for the settlement of international disputes is incompatible with the mind and method of Christ, and therefore incompatible with the mind and method of His Church

3.   While convinced that the time must come for the revision of existing Treaties in the interests of peace, we maintain that all disputes and conflicts between nations, for which no solution can be found through diplomacy or conciliation, ought to be settled or solved through arbitration, whether by the World Court or by some other tribunal mutually agreed.

4.   We therefore earnestly appeal to the respective authorities of all Christian communions to declare in unmistakable terms that they will not countenance any way, or encourage their countrymen to serve in any way, with regard to which the Government of their country has refused an offer to submit the dispute to arbitration.

4) Secretary, Christian Organisations Committee, League of Nations Union, to the Bishop of Chichester, 25 November 1929:

League of Nations Union
15, Grosvenor Crescent,
London, S.W.1
Honorary Presidents:
Rt Hon. Stanley Baldwin, M.P.
Rt Hon. The Earl of Balfour, K.G.O.M
Rt Hon J. R. Clynes, M.P.
Rt Hon. D. Lloyd George, O. M., M.P..

Joint Presidents:

Rt Hon. The Viscount Grey of Fallodon, K.G.
Rt Hon. The Viscount Cecil of Chelwood, K.G.
Chairman of Executive Committee:
Professor Gilbert Murray, LL.D., D. Litt.
Secretary:
J. C. Maxwell Garnet, C.B.E., Sc.D.

25 November 1929

My dear Lord Bishop,
Thank you for letting me show to my Committee
the findings of the group of Anglican clergy, set up
in connection with the Christ and Peace Campaign.
From what you said at the last meeting of the group,
I understood that the formation of such a group was
a prelude to the setting up of a Council to run the
Campaign, and until such a Council had been set up
and a programme agreed upon, the Campaign would not
go forward. That, I gather, was the purpose of our
considering upon what basis it might be possible
for us to co-operate in the Campaign.

I now hear, however, that meetings are already
being arranged by a central Committee under your
chairmanship, and that money is being appealed for,
and that the arrangements are being made from Red
Lion Square. You will remember that the point was
raised at the group as to what address should be
given to the Campaign, and we all agreed it would
be inadvisable to run it from Red Lion Square, as
this would identify it in the minds of many people
with the Fellowship of Reconciliation. I should be
most grateful if you would let me know what truth
there is in the above report, as I was quite under
the impression that the Campaign was going to be
unconnected with the Fellowship of Reconciliation
as such. I think there is great danger that if it is
associated in the minds of Church people with the
Fellowship of Reconciliation the cause of peace in
this country, so far from being strengthened, would
be considerably weakened.

We of the League of Nations Union feel that the
call to the Churches has already been given by the
Archbishop of Canterbury in his sermon in St Paul's
Cathedral on Armistice Day, when he said, "With
whatever authority belongs to the office which I
hold I would on its tenth anniversary call upon all

my fellow-churchmen to be foremost in their support of the League of Nations, and of the Union which in this country exists to strengthen its cause". We think there is very much more chance of arousing the Church of England, at any rate, in this cause of peace upon such a basis than of confusing the issue between support of international co-operation through the League of Nations and the renunciation of war in the Kellogg Pact with the purely individualist pacifist position of the Fellowship of Reconciliation.

I should be very glad if I might hear from you on the subject.

Yours sincerely,
Secretary,
Christian Organisations Committee.

5) Secretary, League of Nations Union, to the Bishop of Chichester, 18 December 1929.

League of Nations Union
18 December 1929

My dear Lord Bishop,
I am looking forward with pleasure to seeing you on Tuesday.

In view of your answer to my note, and of the further facts stated in your letter to Fox, I think you may rely on a friendly and sympathetic attitude on the part of the League of Nations Union towards your "Christ and Peace" Campaign.

But may I make three suggestions?
They should be:
1.   That clergymen and ministers invited to interest themselves in the Campaign will include those clergymen and ministers who have done most to promote the cause of peace through the League of Nations, and especially those whose Churches or Parochial Church Councils are Corporate Members of the League of Nations Union.
2.   That when letters are written in connection with the Campaign, they be neither written on F.O.R. notepaper nor signed by officers of the F.O.R.
3.   That support of the "Christ and Peace"

Campaign should never be prepared as an alternative to support of the League of Nations Union or the World Alliance.

```
    Yours sincerely,
    Maxwell Garnett
```

6) Archbishop of Canterbury to George Bell, 20th February 1930.

```
    Lambeth Palace, S. E.
    20 February 1930
    Private
```

```
    My dear George,
    I have received your letter of the 19th. I have
heard all about the Services and Intercessions
proposed for Saturday, March 1st, from a very devoted
lady from the United States a Mrs. Leland, and while
showing I hope every sort of sympathy with her
efforts I also gave her some reasons why I did not
feel able to identify myself officially with these
particular demonstrations of zeal for the cause of
peace. I have, as you know, long ago asked for the
continued prayers of all members of the Church for
the Disarmament Conference, and to be continually
repeating these Calls to Prayer  deprives them of
their full significance. I have before me at this
present moment no less than four earnest pleas for
formal and official requests for Prayer. I note that
you yourself describe the campaign as unofficial,
and great as my sympathy with it is I fear that any
such letters as you ask for would be regarded as
giving it an official character; and to speak the
truth I am not so sure about all the language used
by the more ardent protagonists of Peace as to feel
justified in taking the responsibility of writing a
special letter for publication in regard to these
Services on March 1st. You, who have been here so
long, know well the difficulties of anyone holding
my office in these matters! But you also know that I
wish Godspeed to every endeavour ...
```

7) Bishop of Chichester to General Secretary, The Fellowship of Reconciliation, Percy W. Bartlett, 4th April 1930.

The Palace,
Chichester
4.IV.30

My dear Bartlett,
Many thanks for your letter. It is very difficult for me to know quite what I can manage during the Autumn in the way of big meetings.

I would do my best with two of them, supposing you could get two meetings on two days running e. g. 10th & 11th November at Manchester & Leeds.

Canon Raven has made me promise to recover my expenses of last week from the Liverpool collection & I propose to do that. As I have so far not been a contributor to the Campaign Funds I do not want to draw upon them, for my expenses.

I wonder about C. J. Wigan. I have corresponded with him but own to being a little doubtful whether he has had the necessary experience. He is a good man but I have an impression that he is not very strong in health. (...)

8) Bishop of Chichester to the Archbishop of Upsala, 6th December 1930.

My dear Lord Archbishop,
I am delighted indeed at the award to you of the Nobel Peace Prize. It is a matter for the very highest congratulations – a splendid tribute to you and fine for the Christian Church. It is a fine recognition of your leadership and inspiration in setting on foot the Stockholm Conference and all that has followed. But it goes back far behind that, for many years behind the Conference at the Hague in 1919 to the early days of the War when you issued your appeal to the Archbishop of Canterbury and others, and no doubt behind that too.

I wonder whether it is at all possible for you as yourself and also as Nobel Prize man, to take part, either for the whole three days or for one of them, in a Convention on peace at Oxford under my presidency – April 15 -18? The Secretary, Percy

Bartlett, is most anxious to get you, and you will see from the enclosed preliminary circular what is proposed generally. The person who has put his best into it is A. Herbert Gray – I am not sure whether you know him – a Presbyterian and a fine man. I also enclose a circular about the Christ and Peace Campaign generally. If you can come you will indeed be conferring a very great favour and rendering a big service.

Yours ever,

9) Open letter from the Bishop of Chichester, 15 December 1930.

The Palace,
Chichester
15 December 1930

My dear Bishop,
A small interdenominational Council, in the leadership of which the Dean of Canterbury and I were asked to share, has during the past twelve months or so been able to arrange a quite useful series of large public meetings up and down the country under the heading "Christ and Peace: a call to the Church to end War". The position adopted at these meetings has been precisely that laid down in resolution 25 of the recent Lambeth Conference: War as a method of settling international disputes is incompatible with the teaching and example of Our Lord Jesus Christ.

It has been throughout the hope of the Christ and Peace Council that the campaign of meetings might culminate in an interdenominational convention to declare that the Church as an institution was ranged against war and committed by the Gospel to the construction of peace.

Our Free Church friends unite with us in feeling that the Lambeth resolutions render part of this plan unnecessary, and suggest a revision in our plans. It therefore is proposed to hold a rather smaller conference in Oxford, from the 15th to the 18th of April next year for the purpose of working out some of the implications of what may be called the Lambeth position. Without being alarmist it is very true to say that the world is full of danger spots and that there is very little time in which to stave off another world war. The question of what the Church in this country ought to do probably in concert with the Churches in other countries in face of this situation is one that demands very careful thought.

I write to ask whether you would be good enough to put me into touch with say half a dozen fairly representative men and women in your diocese already deeply interested in the problem of peace from a Christian point of view, who would be likely to accept an invitation to a private conference of the kind I have indicated, and who would be able to help. I should be glad to send them personal invitations.

Yours sincerely,

10) Bishop of Chichester to the Master[54] of Balliol College, Oxford., 16th March 1931.

Private.

My dear Master,

A Convention on Peace organised by the Christ and Peace Campaign is being held at Oxford, April 15-18. Somerville College is going to put up the members of the Convention up. There should be something between 78 and 100 people. I do not know Somerville myself from the inside and I wonder whether I could ask you in confidence whether they have a conference Hall, that is to say apart from a Lecture Room, in which 100 people could sit as a Conference ordinarily would sit.

The Secretary of the Convention – Mr Percy Bartlett – has been talking to me about the arrangements and is going up to Oxford shortly to look round, but it would help very much if you could tell me whether in fact in addition to their Dining Hall and their general accommodation (or as part of their general accommodation) they have a large room capable of seating 100. What Bartlett is a little afraid of, I think, is that the room may be more lecture-room shape than conference chamber.

If by any chance (and I think it very unlikely that the fear is justified) Somerville has not such a

Conference Hall, would there be any chance of Balliol supplying one, as being fairly near? Or could you suggest a place sufficiently near Somerville for the same purpose?

Yours sincerely,

Annex 2

1. Bishop of Chichester to Rt. Hon. Stanley Baldwin, MP, 14th March 1933.
2. Stanley Baldwin to the Bishop of Chichester, 16th March 1933.
3. Editor of *The Times* to the Bishop of Chichester, 4th June 1933.

14th March, 1933.

Dear Mr. Baldwin,

I venture to ask you to spare half an hour to see a most interesting and able man who has something **very** definite and, as it seems to me, very practical to suggest with regard to the Air Forces and Disarmament. He wishes to **follow** up what you said in the House of Commons on November 10, about War by Air, with a concrete and reasonable plan for giving what you said international practical expression.

His name and address are:-

J. R. Bellerby Esq.,
Bourn,
Cambridgeshire.

His Age is 36. He served four years in the War where he lost his right arm, and ended up as a Major in the Machine Gun section. At the end of the War he went to Leeds University for three years and took his Degree in Economics. From 1921 to 1927 he was on the staff of the International Labour Office at Geneva in the Diplomatic Division, and was, while at Geneva, a member of the Joint Committee of the International Labour Office and the League of Nations which dealt with the economic crisis. In 1924 he was Secretary of the International Unemployment Commission. In 1927 he went to Cambridge as Fellow of Caius till 1930 when he was appointed Professor of Economics at Liverpool University. He gave up that position at the end of last year in order to be free for work in connection with Disarmament and the Economic Depression. He is an extraordinarily self-less man so far as I know. He is married but has nothing to live on except his disablement pension; but he has studied the art of living on a very little. He is a man of very high ideals as you will judge. He is also a man who has very definite practical ability and experience of an international kind. He tells me that through his work at Geneva, he knows exactly how to make a scheme with regard to Air Disarmament go through in a practical way. He is an easy person to talk to. I asked him to come and see me because he has interests of a Christian social international kind which appeal to me. It is not he who has been at me in any way for anything.

I know how very busy you are, and I know also that I am doing something very unusual. But I believe that it really

- 2 -

would be worth while for you to have direct personal conversation with him, because I think he might really be useful
in following up what you have already declared last November.

Yours sincerely,

The Right Honorable
Stanley Baldwin, M.P.

F N

PRIVY COUNCIL OFFICE,
WHITEHALL, S.W.1.

16th March 1933.

My dear Bishop,

Thank you for your letter of the 14th March about Mr. Bellerby.

I am afraid that in present circumstances, sorry though I am to refuse any request that comes from you, it is really quite impossible for me to see him, at any rate in the near future. While Parliament is sitting I am always extremely busy, but in the absence of the Prime Minister and the Foreign Secretary I haven't a free moment.

I am, however, suggesting that Mr. Bellerby should come and see my Parliamentary Secretary, Geoffrey Lloyd, who is rather knowledgeable about air matters; and Geoffrey Fry is writing to him in this sense. Lloyd will of course pass on to me any points that Mr. Bellerby makes.

Yours sincerely,

Stanley Baldwin

The Right Reverend
The Lord Bishop of Chichester.

60

THE TIMES

1785

THE TIMES PUBLISHING COMPANY, LTD.,
PRINTING HOUSE SQUARE,
LONDON, E.C.4.

PERSONAL.

4th June, 1933.

My dear Bishop,

I am glad you wrote to me. In this difficult question of "police bombing" we are all anxious to get our facts right and your letter enables me to justify Lord Winterton and his co-signatories in their inclusion of Sir Henry Dobbs ✱ among the great political officers who have borne witness to the efficiency and humanity of the Air arm.

With experience of punitive work by the Air Force and by ground troops on the Indian Frontier and in Iraq, he vouched in his letter to us last autumn "for the immense superiority of air operations in efficiency and humanity."

"In the first place, a mere demonstration by aeroplanes over disturbed areas, if promptly made before the spark had become a blaze, brings insurgents to heel in nine cases out of 10 without the dropping of a single bomb. Contrast this with the difficulty, delay, and provocativeness of a reconnaissance in force by 'ground troops.' In the second place, villages are not bombed until the inhabitants have had time and opportunity to clear out, and the destruction of property wrought by air-bombs is much less than that wrought on the-

-2-

Indian frontier under the old 'scuttle and
burn' policy by ground troops, when not only were
all buildings razed to the ground and grain stores
burnt, but even the village fruit-groves, the result
of the labour of generations, were by order destroyed.
This was a much more embittering experience for the
villagers. Lastly, on several occasions since the
Afridi operations the Air Force has proved its
capacity for dispersing tribal concentrations on
the Indian frontier."

Dobbs's doubt about the use of the Air Force in
Iraq arose from another cause. Under the new treaty of
alliance he feared that with less responsibility and less
knowledge we might be drawn into lending the services of
the Air Force to cope with domestic trouble caused by a
tyrannical or mistaken policy on the part of the Iraq
Government over the inception of which our Government had
been unable to exercise influence. And he wanted it laid
down that except to provide for the safety of British
communications the Air Force should abstain from air
demonstrations as much as from actual operations in aid
of the Iraq Government in internal affairs. Otherwise,
while keeping to the letter of our understanding, we might
incur the odium of supporting maladministration for which
we were not responsible.

-3-

      I was talking last week with a senior officer
not long back from the Indian frontier who took the same
line as Dobbs in asserting the efficiency and humanity of
air operations. It was not the bombs but the fleas, he
said, which subdued the turbulent tribesmen. This may
sound a flippant saying, but his point was that our bombs
merely drove the tribesmen into their caves and that the
fleas drove them out again to make their submission to
the authorities. I think, indeed, it is impossible to
deny efficiency and humanity to our police operations in the
air against primitive peoples. But to impede or prevent a
general renunciation for the sake of a cheaper and more
humane policing of our frontiers is a price which many
will be disinclined to pay.

                    Yours sincerely,

The Right Reverend
    The Lord Bishop of Chichester.

3

"An hour of great danger for the German Church"

Because of Bell's involvement in the ecumenical movement one could imagine that he might have disregarded his diocesan obligations. Far from it. Bell was committed heart and soul to his diocese. Right after his enthronement as Bishop of Chichester on 27th June 1929, he set out to undertake the needed organisational reforms. To begin with he proposed to establish personal and close relations with the clergy. He invited rural deans to meet him, thus winning their confidence. He believed the restoration of synodical government was "one of the great needs of the English Church". He therefore determined to constitute "a Bishops' Council of Clergy to meet quarterly for the confidential discussion of issues relating to the welfare of the diocese. Twenty-four members of this council were to be elected by the parochial clergy themselves, and to these would be added one representative of the unbeneficed clergy elected by themselves, three co-opted members, and five ex officio members – the bishop suffragan, the dean and the three archdeacons – a total of thirty two. This would be in addition to the full Diocesan Council, which included representatives of the laity; and it was through these bodies that Bell sought the co-operation of both clergy and laity in his various projects for the diocese".[55]

One of these projects was to raise the standard of religious education in schools. A Bishop's Chaplain for Schools was appointed to co-operate with the local Education Authorities. The diocesan Religious Education Committee subsidised public lectures by distinguished academicians in the major towns, and under the Home Study scheme courses in bible study, history and current problems were arranged.[56]

Bell decided to edit the Diocesan Gazette himself. He gave it a new format, life and style. Under the title "The Bishop's Window" Bell wrote not only about matters of Church interest, but also on current social and economic problems. Men of letters (among them T.S. Eliot) wrote for the Gazette. A special section "Book of the Month" included book reviews.

Bell was an exceptional host. Once a month he entertained at his week-end parties noted politicians, actors, authors and artists. In October

1931 Bell hosted Mahatma Gandhi,[57] at a time when the guest from India was being jeered at by Churchill.

Much grief was caused by the economic crisis of the thirties. Bell collected all sorts of sources to provide material help for the unemployed and to maintain various social centers. Later (in 1937) he joined a committee of competent public figures (including the Master of Balliol, A.D. Lindsay), who were to study the roots of unemployment. The investigations of this committee, headed by Archbishop Temple, appeared in a report: *Men without Work* in 1938.

There were other things to be done. The Archbishop of Canterbury, Randall Davidson, died in May 1930. Before his death he had desired, and even so arranged, that Bell would write his biography. Bell began writing soon after the Archbishop's death. A two volume work appeared in the autumn of 1935. This was an astonishing achievement.

With Hitler's rise to power in January 1933 the German Evangelical Church came increasingly under pressure to adopt Nazi doctrine. In fact a group , who called themselves "German Christians" had already founded an organisation "Evangelical National Socialists" in 1932. Now from 3rd - 5th April 1933 they held a national conference, at which they proclaimed loyalty to the Nazi leadership. This action of the "German Christians" was strictly opposed by the members of the "Gospel and Church" movement, who, determined to maintain religious independence of the Evangelical Church, denounced the Nazi ideology as un-Christian, and thus totally unacceptable. The situation saddened Bell. But it also worried him much. Before he would act, Bell asked his colleague, Dr. Alfons Koechlin[58], well acquainted with the German Church, to assess the recent situation.[59] Koechlin came to Chichester at the beginning of June 1933. What he told Bell must have strongly agitated the Bishop's feelings. Bell later (14 June) wrote to Koechlin that it "was a great pain and pleasure to have that good talk with you". He had then "thought much about it afterwards", and been "moved to write by my confidence in yourself and your own strong feeling that a letter to *The Times* over my name at the particular juncture would do real good". Here is what Bell wrote to *The Times*[60]:

Sir,

With your permission I should like to call attention to a crisis in the Evangelical Church of Germany which may have serious implications in both the political and religious fields.

In your issue of June 6 your Berlin correspondent stated that "the political conflict in the German Protestant Church became more marked than ever at Whitsuntide". In ordinary circumstances it would be improper for an English Churchman to make any comment in a public way on such a situation. But the circumstances are not ordinary, and by the result of the present – please note the word – "political conflict" in the German Church we, as well as members of many Churches in Europe and America, may be profoundly affected.

The situation at present is this. A strong national religious movement is now astir in Germany. It is partly expressed in the plan of uniting the different Evangelical Churches in a single Protestant Communion in the German State. This unification, with the full assent of Herr Hitler himself, was entrusted by the representatives of the German Churches to a committee of three – Dr. Kapler, the president of the Evangelical Church Federation, the Lutheran Bishop Marahrens, and the Reformed Church leader, Pastor Hesse, of Elbefeld.

The three plenipotentiaries had many talks, but their most urgent was the nomination of a Reich bishop or Primate. They were in very close touch with the different trends of Christian opinion throughout Germany. At the end of their deliberations they unanimously recommended the appointment of Dr. F. von Bodelschwingh.[61] This nomination was significant. Dr. von Bodelschwingh is very well known as a spiritual leader without any political attachment. He is the superintendent of the great Christian Social Institute, or mission, at Bethel, near Bielefeld, which his father founded at the end of the last century. His work at this mission has brought him into touch with men of all political opinions. Here thousands of sick and epileptic people are cared for, and through it there travel tramps and unemployed men and lads from the ends of Germany. Dr. von Bodelschwingh is not only a spiritual force and in touch with German scholarship, but a man of uncommon administrative ability. His nomination was announced in the week before Whit Sunday. It was widely welcomed and when put before the delegates of all the German Evangelical Churches who had been specially summoned to Berlin was endorsed by the overwhelming majority of 83 votes to three. So far all was well. Dr. von Bodelschwing was undeniably the choice of the Church and he immediately took up the duties of his office.

It is against this appointment by the votes of the Church that a political agitation has now begun. The promoters of the agitation are the body known as the "German Christians". This body consists entirely of members of the National Socialist Party, pledged to promote that party's political principles. Its leader is Pastor Müller.[62] The object of the agitation is the overthrow of the Primate chosen by the Church and the putting in his place of Pastor Müller as a Nazi Primate. It is an hour of great danger for the German Church, and it is significant that the "German Christians" are being given the full use of the Nazi machinery, the radio, and the Press.

Conflict between churchmen competing as rivals for election to the post of German Primate would in any event be a grave misfortune. But still graver, and much more damaging to the religious influence of the church, would be the suppression, through political means, of the Primate whom the Church has chosen by the nominee of an all-powerful political party. Herr Hitler, in his official declaration of policy on becoming Chancellor, solemnly guaranteed the independence and constitutional rights of the German Evangelical Church. It is the adhesion to this solemn guarantee which is of such vital importance today.

Yours faithfully,
George Cicestr
The Palace, Chichester, June 12.

Koechlin had not yet read Bell's letter to The Times of 14 June. And yet it was on June 14th that the two exchanged letters. Koechlin in his letter thanks Bell for his hospitality and supplies further information:

14 June 1933
The Lord Bishop of Chichester,
Chichester

Sir,
I am anxious to express to you once more my
sincere gratitude for the very kind reception you
have given me Friday last. I am holding the two
hours I was privileged to spend with you in grateful
memory.

The purpose of my visit was an extraordinary
one. It was, as I quite feel, somewhat unusual to
bring to you on my own initiative information and
suggestions concerning the German church situation.
I was and still am quite aware of the responsibility
it meant to ask a leading personality of the church
in England to take an action in so delicate a
matter.

I would not have done anything if it had not
been my firm conviction that the developments were of
the utmost importance for the churches of Germany,
for their ecumenical relations in the great church
movements as well as in the mission field, and if
I had not known that leading German personalities
were anxious to hear some voices expressing the
thought and anxiety of other churches.

Since I came home the situation has again
developed. Dr. Kapler,[63] as you will have read,
has resigned, apparently under the pressure of the
difficulties created by his opponents. The thought
of a popular election of the Bishop, which had
been announced at the beginning of last week, has
apparently been given up, as every one seems to see
that it would lead to quite an impossible situation.
The efforts are tending towards some compromise
between the national-socialist current and those
holding for Dr. von Bodelschwingh.

Though they on all parts declare to stay for
a complete independence of the church, it remains
thoroughly true that the political influences are
prevailing far more than their adherents see or
believe it. The situation is in principle as acute
and critical today as I told you Friday last.

May I in closing tell you that one of my
information was not quite accurate. I told that the
vote for Bodelschwingh had been taken by 83 to 3

voices. In fact it was taken by 83 to 11, the three churches of Mecklenburg, Hamburg and Württemburg possessing together 11 voices, having voted against him. Please excuse that I have misled you in this question. When I got the information by a quite trustworthy man, I had expressively asked him if I could rely on the correctness of his saying. Returning home yesterday, I found the correct indication.

You will receive under separate cover as an expression of my gratitude the little report I had written some years ago on the Stockholm Conference. May be that you find time to have a short look in it.

Will you kindly remember me to Mrs. Bell and believe me, Sir,
        faithfully yours,
                [A. Koechlin]

Here is what George Bell had written to Dr Koechlin on 14th June.

        The Palace,
        Chichester
        14 June 1933

        Dear Dr Koechlin,
        It was a great gain and pleasure to have that good talk with you on Friday about the German Church. I thought much about it afterwards. Though I hesitated lest I should be causing embarrassment rather than helping, I decided to write to *The Times*. The letter ultimately sent, a copy of which from *The Times* of today I send herewith, was very much what I drafted when you were here, but better in composition. I most earnestly hope that I have not caused trouble - but the contrary. I shall be thankful for anything you can tell me of any reactions. I was moved to write by my confidence in yourself and your own strong feeling that a letter to *The Times* over my name at this particular juncture would do real good.

        The Bishops of Gloucester and Lichfield wrote off as I suggested to Dr von Bodelschwingh to wish him well. I have asked the Archbishop of Canterbury to approach the Foreign Office with a view to a report on the situation from the British Ambassador in Berlin. His Grace has promised to consider my suggestion very carefully, but not unnaturally feels a considerable hesitation at taking any step, however slight, which even suggests Intervention.

I shall be thankful for any news you can tell me as the days go by. Once more with kindest regards,
    Yours very sincerely,
    George Cicestr

Bell answered Koechlin's letter of 14th June on 20th June.

    The Palace,
    Chichester
    20 June, 1933

    My dear Dr Koechlin,
    Many thanks for your letter of June 14th which crossed one from me to yourself. I am grateful for what you say and also for the report about Stockholm which you send me. I am delighted to have this.

    The difference between 5 and 11, in the note especially in the circumstances you describe of there being three Churches, is very slight, and I do not think material.

    Perhaps, if it is not troubling you too much you could give me a list of the Churches actually concerned in the Unification, including the Reformed Churches. I am very anxious to get any information from time to time.

    I am rather afraid from what I hear that the Archbishop of Canterbury feels that it would be rather too much interference for him to take the step which you and I talked over. Any further news that you can tell me will interest me greatly. The Times is now giving reports as to what is happening from time to time.
    Yours sincerely,
    George Cicestr

Koechlin replied on 27 June.

    27 June 1933
    The Right Rev. The Lord Bishop of Chichester,

The Palace,
Chichester

Dear Sir,

I am very thankful for your kind letter of June 20th. To answer your question concerning the different German churches, I am sending herewith the list I found in the handbook of the churches, edited 1930 by the International Christian Press Commission, Berlin-Steglitz, Beymestrasse 8.

As you will have seen, the events have developed in a very dangerous way. Bodelschwingh stood as long as he was able to stand, though different church leaders and churches, having originally voted for him, had submitted themselves to the Nazi pressure and refused to give him their further support. The "German Christians" dictated to all their members to stay against Bodelschwingh. They managed to refuse him the possibility of seeing Hitler and even Hindenburg and were able under the pretext that the church could not put order into the existing divisions, to get in Prussia a Kommissar for the church business. This Kommissar has put aside Kapler and the former church governing body. He has put aside Generalsuperintendent Schian in Breslau, who dared to stay for Bodelschwingh and to speak openly against the German-Christians´ convictions.

To illustrate the situation, I can tell you that all the social work of Professor Siegmund-Schultze[64] has at once been closed and that all his papers were searched through in the hope that he might be compromised by any foreign letter. He himself was a prisoner for some days, could get his liberty again, but on the advice of his doctor and his nearest friends has decided to leave the country as a refugee. He passed Basle on Sunday last and will hardly be able to go back to Germany in the time to come. We are trying to help him to get out of Germany his wife and his children, hoping that they might get a permit to come over to Switzerland.

I know confidentially that Professor Karl Barth[65] in Bonn is facing the great possibility to be seized by the Nazis and that he has already taken all his measures necessary in such a case of urgency.

However he is decided to stay on his post as long as he ever can for the sake of the church, especially of the reformed church of Western Prussia, of which he is the leading theological adviser. It will be relatively easy to help him if anything is happening, as he is still a Swiss citizen. Please do not make any official use of these facts. I mention them only to illustrate the situation.

If one asks how it is possible that so many most respectable and even leading church men of Germany are following the trend of thought of the German Christians, one is facing the following facts:

1)   They see in the Hitler-movement the only possible solution, even the way of God having saved Germany from the danger of Bolshevism and having given back to the Germans the national feeling they had lost. They see in the awakening of the nation even a religious awakening after the time of Marxism and feel as church men obliged to throw their influence, the built up forces and deep educational possibilities of the church into this great national rising movement. They think it necessary to go new ways, to risk a part of the Church's existing formal life, to be trusted by the movement and to get the possibility of decisive influence on the leaders and on the people. They are afraid of reactionary political and economic forces staying behind the former church leaders and even behind Bodelschwing. For these main reasons they are inclined to accept Wehrkreispfarrer Müller as bishop because he is fully trusted by Hitler and his movement, even though they know that as a religious and theological personality there can be no comparison between him and Bodelschwingh.

2)   A second very peculiar reason is that some of the theologians and church leaders feel the danger of racism swallowing the Christian principles and think the only way to overcome it is to stay in the midst of the nationalistic movement unfolding in that battlefield the flag of Christ. They do not seem to see how much the cause of Christ might be and is compromised by such an alliance and how impossible it is, to overcome the nationalistic Satan by a nationalistic Beelzebub who remains Beelzebub even if he becomes German-Christian nationalist.

Nevertheless there are signs of hope giving

in the dark picture the possibility of confidence. I am meeting these very days at the convention of the Basle Mission men whose thoughts concerning all these questions might be very different from mine, but who very earnestly, even fervently stay for the cause of mission, the cause of only propagation of the gospel of Christ. There you feel quite united in spite of all differences of view and judgement. You experience the reality of the fellowship in Christ, the living Christ, realising in himself the unity of his Church.

I am glad to know that in your prayers and thoughts and with your sympathy you are following the situation and am thankful that you are giving me the possibility of sharing with you the concerns I feel we have in common.

With the expression of this deep gratitude, I am,

faithfully yours,
[A. Koechlin]

Bell wrote to Koechlin on 1st July.

The Palace,
Chichester
1 July 1933
Private

My dear Dr Koechlin,

Very many thanks for your letter of June 27th and for the information which you give me concerning the different German Churches. I am very glad to have this.

I am deeply interested in what you say about the present situation. I saw Fraulein Lucas, the Private Secretary of Siegmund Schultze, in London on Wednesday, twice. At that time she thought that he was a prisoner and not likely to be released from Germany. I am thankful that he is free at any rate.

This is a letter sent to you rather urgently to let you know that the Dean of Chichester, the Very Rev. A. S. Duncan-Jones, as Vice-President of the Church of England Council on Relations with Foreign Churches, left by air for Berlin this morning, and will reach Berlin this afternoon. He has gone as an observer to report to the Archbishop of Canterbury and the Council on the situation. It was represented to the Archbishop that it was specially important that a responsible English Churchman should be in Berlin for tomorrow.

What you say about the trend of thought of the German Christians is very interesting, though it shows how serious and sad the situation is. To-day's news of Hindenburg's intervention is a sign of great hope.

The Dean's address is: Grand Hotel am Knie, Berlin-Charlottenburg.

I shall be thankful for any further information.

During Thursday and Friday the question was being closely considered by the Archbishop of Canterbury, amongst others, as to the possibility and advisability of a declaration on the part of the British Churches, headed by the Archbishop, and of Life and Work and the World Alliance jointly, viz. two separate declarations following one another protesting against the attacks on the spiritual independence of the Church. I have written to Dr Cadman in the U.S.A., and other enquiries about signatories are being made. But we are also – and this is the most important point – trying to find out, especially through Fraulein Lucas who has returned to Holland and is in touch with German Church leaders, whether such a declaration or protest would embarrass our friends in Germany, or whether it would help them. Much, no doubt, depends on what is said in such a declaration. I enclose a draft. The Dean of Chichester will return on Tuesday or Wednesday and we shall hear more from him. I should however be very thankful to know your own opinion in the matter, quite privately.

Yours sincerely,
George Cicestr

The proposed drafts of the two declarations ran as follows:

Draft 1
In the name of the Christian communions which we represent, we desire to make an earnest protest

against attacks on the liberties and constitutional rights of the Churches in the German State which were guaranteed by Chancellor Hitler in Reichstag speech of March 23. German church members and leaders as loyal and patriotic German citizens do not dispute authority of State in all purely state concerns. But in spiritual matters they have a spiritual allegiance. Such high-handed actions as those recently reported to have been taken by German government against spiritual independence and properly elected authorities of Church cause widespread distress in whole Christian world.

Draft 2

In the name of the Christian communions which we represent, we desire to make an earnest protest against the present attacks on the religious liberty and the constitutional rights of the Churches in the German Empire, especially in Prussia. These liberties and rights are based on fundamental principles inherent in the Gospel of Jesus Christ and the character of the Church. They were guaranteed by the Chancellor Hitler in his programmatic speech before the representatives of the nation in the Reichstag, March 23rd 1933.

We are certain the German church members and leaders, to whatever fraction they might belong, as loyal and patriotic German citizens do not dispute authority of state in all purely state concerns. But in a spiritual matter they are bound by an allegiance to our Lord Jesus Christ, to deny it, even under extreme pressure of political and state forces, would mean to deny the only Lord of the church. To refuse the duly instituted church leaders the possibilities of governing the organised Church in the realm of their indispensable constitutional rights and to monopolise by high-handed actions as those recently reported all church government in the hands of state officials, is creating a situation of great concern and distress for all Churches connected to the German Evangelical Church in the fellowship of the spirit and in co-operation for God's kingdom all over the world.

Bell air-mailed a copy of draft 2 to Koechlin. In a letter to Bell on

3rd July Koechlin expressed his thanks to the Archbishop of Canterbury for having sent an observer (Dean of Chichester, the Very Rev. A.S. Duncan-Jones) to Berlin, "who will, I am certain, be able to bring to you the news I am getting relatively late". Koechlin hoped that "a word of protest" from outside Germany might act as "serious warning in view of the nearly incredible developments taking place presently". The letter also confirmed "that Siegmund-Schultze, Mrs. Siegmund-Schultze and four children, that is the whole family, anxious to leave Germany, are safe in Switzerland".

Since the Dean of Chichester was to meet Hitler, it was thought inappropriate to manifest a protest from outside Germany. The Dean, after having met Hitler, reported in his letter to *The Times* (6th July) that he was satisfied that Hitler had no desire to interfere with internal working of the German Church. Bell was sceptical. In his letter of 10th July to Koechlin Bell noted that he thought that the Dean "was a little too easily impressed by Hitler's assurance".

Bell to Koechlin, 10th July 1933.

```
    The Palace,
    Chichester
    10 July 1933

    My dear Dr Koechlin,
    Very many thanks for your letter of July 7th.
I quite understand. I am grateful for the trouble
you have taken. The Dean of Chichester was in Berlin
from July 1st to July 5th and saw Hitler*. He also
saw many Church leaders including Müller. It was
clear that anything in the nature of a protest
from outside Germany would, be embarrassing to our
friends, so I am sure that we must do nothing for
the moment.
    I am much, interested in what you tell me
about Karl Barth and his theological students.
What an extraordinary situation! Do please keep me
informed. I wonder very much what happened at the
Friday conference with Frick.
    Yours sincerely,
    George Cicestr
    *He was a little too easily impressed by
Hitler's assurances, I think!
```

Bell had evaluated the situation correctly. Hitler did not mean to keep his promises. This became quite clear at the National Church Synod election held on 23rd July. The Synod was entirely dominated by the pro-Nazi German Christian delegates, who overwhelmingly elected Dr. Ludwig Müller as State Bishop. Müller was Hitler's choice.

The "nearly incredible developments taking place" to which Koechlin had referred became evident with the adoption of the Aryan Paragraph, whereby Christians of Jewish origin could no longer be welcomed in the German Church. Further, serious restrictions were placed upon those who supported or belonged to the Confessional Church. These "incredible developments" were unacceptable to Bell, who was now (since August 1932) also the chairman of the Council of Life and Work. The situation of the German Church was one of the chief topics of discussion at the Council's annual meeting on 9th-12th September 1933 at Novi Sad in Yugoslavia. Among those attending the meeting were delegates from the Churches of Denmark, Sweden, England, Germany, France, Switzerland, Greece, Yugoslavia, Hungary, and the USA. The delegates desired to have full information on the existing position in Germany. The German delegates attempted to "give full information as to what was taking place in their country". The debate, Bell wrote to the Editor of *The Times*, was "frank and friendly, and there were various differences of opinion. But grave anxieties were expressed in particular with regard to the severe action taken against persons of Jewish origin, and the serious restrictions placed upon freedom of thought and expression in Germany".[66] It was felt that a Universal Christian Council could not "keep silent at such a moment". The Executive Committee of the Council therefore resolved to "ask the Bishop of Chichester, as their Chairman and President of the Oecumenical Council, to write a letter to the temporary governing body in order to bring before the German Protestant Church the distress and anxiety which these disabilities caused to the members of the Committee and the Churches which they represented".[67]

Bell sent the desired letter to State Bishop Ludwig Müller on 23rd October. He called the State Bishop's attention to the adoption of the Aryan Paragraph and the suspension of the spiritual ministry: "all opposition and criticism (wrote Bell) has been prohibited; and still sterner methods of coercion are apparently projected". How, Bell asked, can such a state of things be harmonised with the principles of the Christian Gospel?

Forgive me, Herr Reich bishop , if I express myself too strongly, but my feelings are strong, and I should be deceiving you and failing in my duty as President of the Universal Christian Council for Life and Work if I did not declare to you that such action, and such policy, must cause universal dismay, and must, if persisted in, evoke the strongest protests from the Christian Churches abroad ...[68]

Bell sent a copy of this letter to Koechlin, and kept him informed over his other activities. Bell wrote to Koechlin on 25th October.

The Palace,
Chichester
25 October 1933

My dear Dr Koechlin,

I enclose for your private information a copy of a letter to Bishop Müller. It was written in accordance with the Resolution of Novi Sad. I shall be interested to hear what reply it evokes. I am reserving the right to publish. Have you any views on this?

Bishop Hossenfelder was In England last week and I think he was rather busy with propaganda. The Bishop of Gloucester, whose letter to *The Times* yesterday was not very helpful on the general situation (though intended to be kind to Germany, missing the point) was persuaded by him.

The Archbishop writes to me, after seeing the Bishop of Gloucester, to say that Bishop Hossenfelder definitely informed the Bishop of Gloucester the other day that the Aryan Paragraph was to be withdrawn. Do you know whether this is the case or not? I should be glad of an answer from you on this point. My own impression, for what it is worth, is that the Prussian Synod, applies the Paragraph and that it is the Synod which matters, while the National Synod did not in fact raise the question. That non-raising of the question was no doubt all to the good, but it does not alter facts by mere omission to legislate one way or another, does it?

I shall be deeply interested to hear how your own journey to Germany is faring.

Yours very sincerely,
p.p. George Cicestr
Secretary.
S. Rowe
(Dictated by the Bishop but signed for him in his absence.)

And then again on 30ᵗʰ October.

The Palace,
Chichester
30 October 1933

My dear Dr Koechlin,
Very many thanks for your most kind letter and for the very interesting information which it contains. A young theological student from England has just published an article on the new regime in the monthly periodical "Theology". I have only just set eyes on it myself and have not read it when dictating this letter, but I will send the copy to you in case you have comments or criticisms.

I shall look forward with the greatest interest to receiving your confidential report. I will certainly maintain fully the position taken in my letter to Bishop Müller. I am under the impression that while the withdrawal of the Aryan Paragraph is very important, it is the application of the principle underlying these restrictions that has to be so carefully watched, and that the fair treatment of the minority, or rather of the people disagreeing with the official Church government, is the vital thing.

I agree with what you say about "Wait and See". I am very much interested in what you tell me about the German Missionary Conference.

Yours sincerely,
George Cicestr

Next to Koechlin the man who updated Bell on the position in Germany was pastor Dietrich Bonhoeffer,[69] who in 1933 took charge of the German Church in London. Bonhoeffer was a staunch supporter of the Confessional Church, and strongly opposed the Nazi programme. The two churchmen cultivated a close personal relationship, and worked together for the independence of the Church in Germany. The following letters bear witness to this relationship.

London, 16. November 1933
23, Manor Mount, S.E.23

My Lord Bishop,
I thank you very much for your kind invitation to come to Chichester on November 21st. It is indeed a great pleasure for me to come. May I ask you what time would be convenient for you for my arrival.
You certainly know of the recent events within the German church, and I think that there is a great likelihood for a separation of the minority from the Reichskirche, and in this case an action of ecumenical support would certainly be of immense value in this tense situation. There is no doubt that any sort of separation would become at once a strong political issue, and for this reason would probably be dealt with by the government in an exclusively political way. It seems to me that the responsibility of the ecumenical work has perhaps never been so far-reaching as in the present moment. If the ecumenical churches would keep silent during those days, I am afraid that all trust put into it by the minority would be destroyed. Undoubtedly Müller is now in a very precarious situation, and a strong demand from the side of the ecumenical churches could be the last hope for the Christian Churches in Germany. We must not leave alone those men who fight — humanly spoken — an almost hopeless struggle. I get news with every mail and also by telephone. If I may, I will forward to you the recent information.
In the enclosed paper you will find some very typical formulations of the Teutonic Christians.
I think one ought to try to drive a wedge between Müller and the radicals. On the other hand one cannot rely by any means on Müller's personal

theological insight and it is dangerous to put too much trust into such a break.

With many thanks, I remain, My Lord,
Yours very sincerely,
Dietrich Bonhoeffer[70]

Bell to Bonhoeffer

17 November 1933

Dear Dr Bonhoeffer,
I am delighted that you can come to Chichester on Tuesday, November 21st.

I appreciate what you say about the ecumenical movement and its task just now. Have you seen my letter to Müller? I enclose the English original text and a German translation. It was printed in full in *The Manchester Guardian* on Monday, and the main portions appeared in *The Times* and other papers. Bishop Müller knew it was to be published and I received no objection. Dr Schönfeld[71] tells me that he has seen Bishop Müller and Bishop Schöffel, and that my letter had made an impression. I understood from Schönfeld that Bishop Müller was going to send me a preliminary reply and that he might possibly ask for a delegation from the ecumenical movement to visit Berlin and see Church leaders. But I have heard nothing more.

Yours sincerely,
George Cicestr

Bonhoeffer to Bell

London, 25 November 1933

My Lord Bishop,
The two days which I spent in your home meant so much to me that I beg to thank you once more for this opportunity which you so kindly gave to me. I have received your letter, and I shall certainly keep all you told me to myself. Things in Germany are getting on – as it seems – more slowly than one could expect, and I am almost afraid that the influence of the radical German Christians becomes once more very strong, and that Müller will yield

under this heavy pressure. I shall give you new
information as soon as something important will
occur.

I remain, My Lord, yours very sincerely,
Dietrich Bonhoeffer

Bonhoeffer wrote again a couple of days later.

London, 27 November 1933

My Lord Bishop,
May I draw your attention to the enclosed
leaflets. Three pastors have been dismissed only
because of their sincere confession to Christ as
the only Lord of the Church. One of them Pastor
Wilde is father of seven children. The case is not
decided yet definitely, but perhaps the moment has
come when the ecumenical movement ought to provide
for subsidies and financial support for those who
will lose their positions for the only reason of
their being confessors of their faith. Things are
becoming very acute. Schöffel has resigned. Prof.
Fezer[72] has left the German Christian Movement.

Yours, My Lord, very sincerely,
Dietrich Bonhoeffer

A month later Bonhoeffer sent another letter, telling the Bishop in detail the latest information he had received from Germany.

London, 27 December 1933

My Lord Bishop,
Thank you very much for your most kind Christmas
greetings. It means very much for me indeed to know
that you are sharing all the time the sorrows and
the troubles which the last year has brought to
our church in Germany. So we do not stand alone
and whatever may occur to one member of the Church
universal, we know that all the members suffer with
it. This is a great comfort for all of us, and if
God will turn back to our church sometime now or
later, then we may be certain, that, if one member
be honoured, all the members shall rejoice with
it.

Things in Germany are going on more slowly than

we expected. Müller's position is, of course very much endangered. But he seems to try to find closer contact with the state to be sure of its protection in case of danger. Only from this point of view I can understand his last agreement with the Hitler Youth. But it seems as if the State is nevertheless very much reserved and does not want to interfere once more. I do not think personally that Müller can keep his position and it will certainly be a great success if he falls. But we must not think that the fight is settled then. On the contrary, it will without any doubt start anew and probably sharper than before with the only advantage that the fronts have been cleared. The trend towards Nordic heathenism is growing tremendously, particularly among very influential circles; and, I am afraid, the opposition is not united in their aims. In Berlin they are going to form an Emergency Synod under the leadership of Jacobi[73] next Friday. This is meant to be a legal representation of the oppositional congregations against the illegal synods of last August and September. Jacobi is probably the wisest of the oppositional leaders in the moment and I put much trust into what he is doing. There is a great danger that people who have had a very indefinite attitude toward the German Christians last summer, jeopardise now the success of the opposition by mingling in and seeking their own personal advantage.

The letter of Müller is as expected very weak and anxious, it really does not mean anything at all. It does not come out of a sound theological but much more of political argumentation — though one always has to realise that his position now is so difficult as never before.

If you allow me 1 shall be only too glad to come once more to Chichester. I am still having continuous information by telephone and airmail from Berlin.

Please, give my most respectful regards to Mrs. Bell.

I remain, in sincere gratitude, My Lord,
Yours truly,
Dietrich Bonhoeffer

Before the end of the year (1933) the editor of *The Round Table* wrote to Bell proposing that he secure an article on the crisis in the German Protestant Church, for the March (1934) issue. Bell wrote back on 2nd January 1934 suggesting Bonhoeffer - "a man who would do the article with great ability and first-hand knowledge". With this in mind, Bell wrote to Bonhoeffer on 4th January:

> My dear Bonhoeffer,
> Very many thanks for your letter. I am very anxious to see you at an early date, for I have an important proposal with regard to a long article in a very important periodical to put before you. As it turns out, I shall be away myself tonight and probably tomorrow night, for personal reasons. Could you send me your telephone address on a postcard, so that I may talk to you? When are you most likely to be in?
> I want you to reserve yourself for a luncheon engagement which has been suggested, if you will, on Tuesday, January 23rd, at 1.15 p.m. Let me know about this.
>
> Yours sincerely,
> George Cicestr

Bonhoeffer refused to write the article. At this very moment an important event occurred. Hitler commanded State Bishop Müller to meet him on 17th January. However, the meeting took place on 25th January. Unaware of the postponement Bell wrote to the Editor of *The Times* on 16 January, and the letter appeared the following day.[74]

> Sir,
> The eyes of Christendom at this moment are on the German Church. To-morrow the Reich Primate, Bishop Müller, is to meet the Chancellor. And the question to which the answer is so anxiously awaited is this. Is force to be invoked, against the constitution of the German Church, to determine issues in which the spiritual nature of the Church and the Gospel are at stake? Is the State to intervene, against the solemn promises of Herr Hitler himself, in a fundamentally religious dispute?
> There is no doubt of the loyalty of the

dissenting Bishops, or of the 6,000 pastors and their lay supporters, to the German Reich. There is no taking sides for or against a political party. Indeed, practically the whole body of churchmen opposed to Bishop Müller are supporters of the Nazi régime. Their stand is for the Gospel and the Church - spiritual principles and spiritual facts - and they declare that these cannot be dragooned into a "German Christian" system.

The German Church crisis may not be dismissed as a purely German concern, for anything which weakens the spiritual nature of the Church loosens the ties with the Christian Churches abroad which, as Bishop Müller said, it is his task to preserve. Bishop Müller has himself appealed to the Churches abroad in his Open Letter of September 1:

"The German Protestant Church, founded upon the Gospel, feels itself a limb of the 'One Holy Catholic Christian Church'. It is our earnest hope that the mutual esteem and spiritual unity with the Christian Churches abroad will ever be strengthened and lead to a constantly increasing mutual service".

And again:

"The German Protestant Church consciously takes its stand with the Christian Churches abroad under the banner of the Gospel".

There is no doubt that the Churches abroad, Orthodox, Anglican, Lutheran, Reformed, represented on the Universal Christian Council for Life and Work, desire the closest co-operation with the German Church. But they have already expressed their grave anxieties to the Reich bishop about the suppression and silencing of opponents. It had been hoped, as a result of Bishop Müller's reply to the letter expressing these anxieties, that the coercion would cease. The restoration of coercive methods, or the use of superior force now, would be a wrong to the Christian conscience and a wrong to the Gospel and to the whole Christian Church.

Yours faithfully,
George Cicestr
The Palace, Chichester, Jan. 16.

Bonhoeffer was exceedingly gratified to read Bell's letter in *The Times*. And he conveyed his thanks to Bell the very same day.

London, 17 January 1934

My dear Lord Bishop,
It is my strong desire to thank you most heartily for your letter which I have just read in *The Times*. I am sure, it will be of great importance for the decisive meeting of today. We German pastors in London have sent a telegram to Hindenburg, Hitler, Neurath,[75] Frick,[76] Müller, saying that only the removal of Müller could pacify the highly excited German congregations here in England. You have certainly seen the new order of Rust forbidding all professors of theology to take part in the opposition against Müller and to be members of the Pastors' Emergency League. If this order is the beginning of a state action against the opposition, then, I think, your letter should be enforced by a most drastic disapproval of Müller's policy and approval and support for the opposition, directed to President von Hindenburg as a "membrum praecipuum of the protestant Church". Any delay of time would then probably be of great danger. A definite disqualification of Müller by the ecumenical movement would perhaps be the last hope – humanly spoken – for a recovery of the German Church. It may be, of course, that Rust's order is one of the many attempts from the side of the Prussian government to anticipate the decision of the Reich and to overrule the Reich government. The first prints of your book in German have just arrived.[77]
I thank you once more for your help.
Yours very respectfully,
Dietrich Bonhoeffer

Bell thanked Bonhoeffer for his "most kind letter", and informed him of the further steps that he, Bell, had undertaken.

18 January 1934

My dear Bonhoeffer,
Ever so many thanks for your most kind letter. I have today written a letter to the Reich bishop,

a copy of which I enclose. It has gone by air mail – two copies, one to Jebenstrasse 3, the other to Marchstrasse 2, under direction to Wahl.

I am considering the question whether it would be a wise and legitimate action on my part to send a copy of this letter to President Hindenburg. If so, I wonder whether it would be embarrassing you if I asked you to translate the letter into German – both the covering letter to the President and the letter to Bishop Müller. I particularly do not want you to do anything injudicious. I shall probably in any case send copies of my letter to Bishop Müller in English to Deissmann and Dibelius, but one is anxious not to embarrass one's friends, and even that may be unwise. Will you, if you think there is anything in it, translate both the covering letter and the letter to Bishop Müller into German, and let me have the copies by return of post? But use your own judgement, and if you would rather have nothing to do with it, I shall understand.

Yours ever,
George Cicestr

Bonhoeffer's response was immediate and positive. He replied the very next day (19th January).

My Lord Bishop,
Thank you very much for your wonderful letter to Reich bishop Müller. One feels that it comes out of such a warm and strong desire to stand for the Christian cause and to "open the mouth for the dumb in the cause of all such as are appointed to destruction" (Proverbs 31.8), that it must undoubtedly be convincing for everybody.

I am sending you the translations of the letters and I am absolutely convinced that it would be of immense value, if Hindenburg would learn to know this point of view. It has always been the great difficulty to have a free discussion with him about that matter, because there were many people who wanted to prevent it. So it is all the more important, that he gets your letter.

Once more many thanks.
I am always yours very respectfully,
Dietrich Bonhoeffer

Among those who attended the meeting with Hitler on 25 January were State Bishop Müller, Pastor Niemöller[78] (Berlin-Dahlem), bishops Meiser (Bavaria), Wurm (Württemberg) and Marahrens (Hannover). Hitler rebuked the bishops for creating disunity within the German Church and commanded that they should all support Müller. That was that.

Hitler's stance strengthened Müller's position. Anyone who challenged Müller now was duly suspended or simply dismissed. Niemöller was the first victim. This indeed worried Bell. He desired to know more about Müller's actions from the German Ecumenical Bishop, Heckel, who had led the German delegation at Novi Sad Life and Work Conference. Heckel,[79] together with two of his colleagues (Krummacher and Wahl) came to London to speak to Bell. They met at the Athenaeum on 9th February. Bell raised various questions at the meeting and then handed to Heckel "Informal Notes", which contained the following points:

    1.   The prohibition of opposition to actions
or decrees objectionable on spiritual grounds.
    2.   The power taken by the Reich bishop to
abolish posts, enact or suspend decrees, at his
simple unfettered discretion.
    3.   The use of the police to help the
suppression of opponents.
    4.   The dismissal of pastors because of
their opposition to a German Christian policy.
    5.   The putting of State considerations above
religious considerations, and especially above the
principle of the freedom of the Gospel.
    6.   The grave danger of the Church being used
as the instrument of the National Socialist Party;
and being absorbed by the State.

A public statement on the outcome of the meeting was made by Bell on 10th February.

    The Bishop of Chichester on Friday received
representatives of the German Evangelical Church in
London. In connection with the correspondence which
has passed during the past month between the Reich

bishop and the Bishop of Chichester as President
of the Universal Christian Council for Life and
Work, it was agreed to promote a common study in a
frank and brotherly spirit of various problems now
before the Churches, including the investigation of
the religious and theological principles involved,
under the auspices of the Universal Christian
Council.

The language of the statement sounded accommodating. However, the discussion at the meeting had been quite controversial. Heckel had wanted Bell not to interfere in the German affairs, and even to seek his assurance that he should keep silent. This Bell "firmly declined to give".[80] Bell would not remain indifferent to what was happening in Germany. In fact he had already requested Dr Koechlin to write a detailed article on the German situation for *The Round Table*.

In the meantime Bell had also received a letter from Dr Hans Schönfeld, the Director of the Research Department, Committee of Life and Work, Geneva, communicating a suggestion by certain German and Swedish Church leaders that Bell and the Archbishop of Upsala, Eidem,[81] might visit Berlin and personally meet Hitler. "The aim of the discussion with Hitler", wrote Schönfeld, "would be to give him a very clear and concrete impression of how much harm the methods and procedure of the present Church government are creating for Germany in all the countries, how the Churches abroad are continually trying to create a fair understanding of the developments in Germany, but how all this work for mutual understanding is constantly being seriously endangered and even destroyed by such methods and action on the part of the present Church government".[82] Bell was sceptical about visiting Hitler. He conveyed his doubts in his letter dated 23rd March 1934 to Dr Nils Karlström, a Swedish member of Life and Work. By going to the Chancellor, wrote Bell, he would "in fact be asking for state intervention". "I am most anxious to avoid putting Hitler into the position of the final authority in spiritual questions of this order. Supposing, as the result of our interview, he did remove Müller, could he not, with some justice, claim that Churches outside Germany had requested him to determine the form of Church government in Germany? And would not this tie our hands in advance if later Hitler wished to take other action which might not please us so well, with regard to the Church?"[83] Bell's arguments were convincing, and the whole idea was dropped.

Earlier Bell had again written to Bonhoeffer, to ask if he could come to Chichester to help him with regard to an article on Germany.

```
10 February 1934

My dear Bonhoeffer,
    I enclose a copy of a letter to Schönfeld for
your information. I should very much like to see
you, for I want your help with regard to the Round
Table article which is now in manuscript. Would
it be at all possible for you to spend Wednesday,
February 14ᵗʰ, here, arriving at 11 a.m.? The article
has to be in the printer's hands by Thursday, and
if you could stay Wednesday night as well, we could
get on I think. I rang you up last night but you
were out.
    Yours ever,
    George Cicestr
```

Bonhoeffer wrote back on 12ᵗʰ February that he was unable to come to Chichester.

```
My Lord Bishop,
    Thank you very much for your very interesting
letter. I should like to come to Chichester on
Wednesday very much, but last night, I received a
telephone call from Germany and I was asked most
urgently to come to Germany for a meeting which
shall take place tomorrow afternoon at Hannover.
The Emergency League will take this decision about
its future, separation, etc. So I will leave to-
night and shall unfortunately not be able to come
to see you on Wednesday. I shall be back probably on
Saturday. If you want some information from a German
I should propose to telephone to Pastor Rieger, my
colleague, Greenwich 2613. I will try to read the
paper still before I leave and to make some notes.
I am very sorry not to be able to help you as much
as I should like to.
    Yours very respectfully,
    Dietrich Bonhoeffer
```

On 13ᵗʰ February Bell wrote a long letter to Dr Koechlin on his meeting with Dr Heckel in London, and at the same time thanking Koechlin for the article for *The Round Table*.

Bell to Koechlin, 13th February 1934.

```
The Palace,
Chichester
13 February 1934.
```

My dear Dr Koechlin,

Very many thanks for your letter and for the article for *The Round Table*. Before it came I had seen the original with the Editor of *The Round Table*. He has gone over the article, shortening it in certain ways and bringing out some points more clearly in the English. He has asked me to look through the article from the point of view of seeing whether a little more could not be added so as to inform a forgetful public as to some more of the main facts, and I am going through the article carefully with this in view. I think that a little more history (not more philosophy but more facts) might be included, and I hope you will not mind if a few points of this factual kind are inserted. The article is most useful, and will be a great help to the public.

You may have seen in *The Times* that Dr Heckel and other representatives of the German Evangelical Church came to see me in London on Friday. What they wanted was to persuade me that the situation was much more complicated than I thought, and could not be understood except from within; and to extract a promise from me that I would not write more letters or make more statements, say for another six months, while the "pacification" went forward! They brought me a special confidential message from the Reich bishop to the effect that the Aryan Paragraph was not to be enforced and that all the Bishops had agreed to this. Dr Heckel said he would put this in writing in a letter to me for me to use. I said however I could not use it unless it was a very positive and substantial statement – not a mere general pious hope. They were very anxious to have the note of their interview communicated to the Press, and suggested a form of words to the effect that it was the task of the oecumenical movement to have brotherly theological discussions

– the implication, I suppose, being that it must not deal with burning issues in a practical or public way. I could not agree to this, but I thought that no harm would be done in the announcement that they had seen me and that we agreed to promote steps for frank and brotherly discussion of various problems before the Churches. At the same time (and we had a discussion in two parts, lasting two hours each) I went over the points with regard to the use of force, which I said disturbed members, of other Churches so greatly. I wrote the points out and gave the paper to Dr Heckel. I enclose for you a copy of the paper. You will see that they are put with a certain bluntness. Obviously Dr Heckel and Co. are most anxious to keep in touch with the oecumenical movement, and do not want to lose their contact. But I am afraid that a breaking point may come unless there is a change in policy. I wish your letter with the article had come before I saw them, and that I had known of the visits of the police to pastors' houses reported in Saturday's *Times*. I am however now writing to Dr Heckel calling his very serious attention to these incidents, and reminding him of the danger to relations with other Churches which such a policy creates. They told me that a Reich Minister for dealing with the relations with the Evangelical Church was in all probability to be appointed. I said that I viewed this prospect with a good deal of alarm, and pressed the dangerous character of such an appointment upon them: for in the present circumstances of the Evangelical Church, such an appointment would seem to carry far more in the way of control with it than happens in the case of other Churches, even though those Churches, like our own, are Established.

I hear today, privately, that there is a very important Meeting taking place in Hannover, of leaders of the Pastors' Emergency League, to consider future policy and whether they are to work for separation and so forth. It is a very anxious moment indeed. Any news that you hear will be most gratefully received.

Yours ever,
George Cicestr

Bell was now anxious to see Bonhoeffer, most probably concerning the suggestions made by Dr Schönfeld:

24 February 1934

My dear Bonhoeffer,
I am very anxious to see you. I wonder whether you have returned from your wanderings? I hope very much you are better, for I was very sorry to learn from Pastor Rieger that you had fallen a victim to a chill or influenza. I am in London on Wednesday evening and Thursday morning. What would suit me best of all would be if you could come and have breakfast with me at the Athenaeum at 9 O'clock on Thursday morning. Is that too outrageous?
    Yours ever,
    George Cicestr

Bonhoeffer replied after he had returned from Berlin. He informed Bell, how desperate the situation was in Germany and how the Confessional Church was earnestly expecting help from Bell.

London, 14 March 1934

My Lord Bishop,
May I just let you know, that I was called last week again to Berlin - this time by the Church Government. The subject was the ecumenical situation. I also saw Niemöller, Jacobi, and some friends from the Rhineland. The free Synod in Berlin was a real progress and success. We hope to get ready for a Free National Synod until 18th of April in Barmen. One of the most important things is that the Christian Churches of the other countries do not lose their interest in the conflict by the length of time. I know that my friends are looking to you and your further actions with great hope. There is really a moment now as perhaps never before in Germany in which our faith into the ecumenical task of the Churches can be shaken and destroyed completely or strengthened and renewed in a surprisingly new way. And it is you, my Lord Bishop, on whom it depends whether this moment shall be used. The question at stake in the German Church is no longer an internal issue but is the question

of existence of Christianity in Europe; therefore a definite attitude of the ecumenical Movement has nothing to do with "intervention" – but it is just a demonstration to the whole world that Church and Christianity as such are at stake. Even if the information of the newspaper is becoming of less interest, the real situation is as tense, as acute, as responsible as ever before. I shall only wish you would see one of the meetings of the Emergency League now – it is always in spite of all gravity of the present moments a real uplift to one's own faith and courage. Please, do not be silent now! I beg to ask you once more to consider the possibility of an ecumenical delegation and ultimatum. It is not on behalf of any national or denominational interest that this ultimatum should be brought forward but it is in the name of Christianity in Europe. Time passes by very quickly, and it might soon be too late. The 1ˢᵗ of May the "Peace in the Church" shall be declared by Müller. Six weeks only.

I remain, my Lord Bishop,
Yours very gratefully and respectfully,
Dietrich Bonhoeffer

Bonhoeffer also wrote to the Secretary, Life and Work, Henry Henriod, stationed at Geneva, urging the Oecumenical movement to take strong action in support of the Confessional Church. This is how Henriod responded.

Genf, le 16 mars 1934
Dr D. Bonhoeffer
Forest Hill, London

My dear Bonhoeffer,
Thank you for your letter of March 14ᵗʰ. As you say, the situation is becoming more critical and some action should be taken up without any delay by the ecumenical movement. I have discussed your letter fully with Dr Schönfeld and we have consulted also one or two other leaders and Christian workers here.

I have written a few days ago already to the Bishop of Chichester, urging him to follow up his correspondence with Bishop Heckel by a strong letter. I am writing him today asking for a small conference of leading theologians, most of whom would be in Paris at the beginning of April for our Study conference on Church and State – a conference which would be separate from that Study week, and to which the Reich bishop would be asked to send delegates, so that straight forward questions can be put to them and strong statements made, which will make it possible for an outspoken disapproval of the attitude adopted by the Church and probable action by the Churches belonging to the ecumenical movement. This would follow up naturally steps taken before and might lead to a delegation to Berlin. If the Bishop of Chichester prefers to have a delegation go to Berlin – which I doubt very much, as most of the members of our Administrative Committee were not in sympathy with this method – I would fall in with him of course.

At the same time we are preparing as fast as we can documentation on the attitude of other Churches toward the present German situation, which can be used in the press and thus become known in Germany.

It is not in my competence to prepare for a delegation or to send an ultimatum without the consent of my committee and as you know, the Bishop of Chichester was asked to take up responsibility in the direction of relationships with Germany and I am keeping in close touch with him.

Those who stand for the Gospel in Germany should not get desperate. There are declarations and messages which are coming out from various countries by pastors and others, which will indicate how much deep feeling there is outside Germany with regard to the situation of the government of the German Church. I can only repeat that stronger action might have been taken earlier if our best trusted friends in Germany had not urged us again and again even these last few days, not to break relationships with the German Church, as it is our only means of influencing the situation by getting at the present government again and again with strong criticisms.

If you have to return to Germany, please let me know before you leave London your address, and whether one can write to you and comparatively freely.

Through our press service and through every

means we have at our disposal, we are doing our utmost to pass on the truth as we receive it with regard to the German situation.

I shall be away from Geneva in Austria, Hungary and Czechoslovakia up till Easter time. I trust you keep in close touch with the Bishop of Chichester. As you say the issue is plainly Christian and it touches the future of Christendom in Europe. You can count on my full sympathy and we know how terrific the situation must be for those who suffer bodily, mentally as well as in their soul. May God give us His clear lead so that we act at every point according to His will and for His cause.

Yours ever,

H.L. Henriod

Bonhoeffer was indeed keeping in close touch with Bell. He sent another letter to the Bishop on 15ᵗʰ April.

London, 15 April 1934

My Lord Bishop,

It is on the urgent request of one of my German friends, whose name I would rather mention to you personally, that I am writing to you again. I have received yesterday this letter which has upset me very much indeed and I think it is necessary that you know how our friends in Germany are feeling about the present situation and about the task of the ecumenical movement now. The letter is really an outcry about the last events in the German Church and a last appeal for an "unambiguous" word of the ecumenical movement. This man who speaks for a few thousand others states frankly: "in the present moment there depends everything, absolutely everything, on the attitude of the Bishop of Chichester". If such feeling arises in Germany, it means that the movement has definitely come for the ecumenical movement either to take a definite attitude – perhaps in the way of an ultimatum or in expressing publicly the sympathy with the oppositional pastors – or to lose all confidence among the best elements of the German pastors – an outlook which terrifies me more than anything else. It is for this very reason that I am repeating to you this statement of my friend. Of course, Pastors in Germany do not realise all the implications which are connected with such a step taken by the ecumenical movement, but they certainly have a very fine feeling for the right spiritual moment for the Churches abroad to speak their word. Please, do not think our friends in Germany are losing all hope, it is only humanly spoken when they look to the ecumenical movement as their "last hope" and it is on the other hand for the ecumenical movement the moment to give test of its reality and vitality. As to the facts there is firstly the appointment of Dr Jäger,[84] which is considered to be an ostentatious affront to the opposition and which means in fact that all power of the Church government has been handed over to political and party authorities. It was much surprising to me that *The Times* gave a rather positive report about this appointment. Jäger is in fact the man with the famous statement about Jesus being only the exponent of Nordic race etc ... He was the man who caused the retirement of Bodelschwingh and who was considered to be the most ruthless man in the whole Church government. Furthermore he is - and remains – the head of the Church Department in the Prussian Ministry of Education and a leading member of the Party. So this appointment must be taken as a significant step towards the complete assimilation of the Church to the state and party. Even if Jäger should try to make himself sympathetic to the Churches abroad by using mild words now, one must not be deceived by this tactic.

The situation in Westphalia seems even to be much more tense than we know. I could tell you some details personally.

On the other hand it is still the great danger that the attempt of the Church Government to win the sympathy of the leading men of the Churches abroad will succeed as we know of one such case - because many of them do not have enough knowledge to see what is going on behind the scenes. It is therefore that the mentioned letter proposes very strongly if you could not send a letter to all other churches connected with the ecumenical movement warning them not to take any personal step towards a recognition of the German Church Government and giving them the real Christian outlook of the situation which they want. The Reich bishop himself is reported to have said, if we get the Churches abroad on our side, we have won. Excuse this long letter, but everything looks so frightfully dark. It is always a great comfort to me that I may tell you frankly and personally our feelings. I hope to have the chance to hear from you soon.

    With deep gratitude, I remain,
    Yours very respectfully,
    Dietrich Bonhoeffer

Another letter followed the very next day.

    16 April 1934

    My Lord Bishop,
    May I just add a few words to my letter of yesterday – with regard to the recent decree of Müller. The only reason by which it can be explained is this: the Church government has become aware of the fact, that the secession of the Westphalian Church could no longer be detained, and it was a clever move to delay once more this decision by issuing this new decree. That this offer of peace can not be taken seriously at all, can be proved by a comparison with the Good Friday message. There Müller refuses an "amnesty", today he has changed once more his mind. The new amnesty is not even complete, Niemöller and other important pastors do not come under the decree. It is undoubtedly the only intention of this decree to split up the opposition and then to go on freely. The Aryan clause is still in force, since the law of Nov. 16th is expressly once more cancelled. So we can watch this move only with the greatest mistrust.

    I remain,
    My Lord Bishop,
    Yours very respectfully,
    Dietrich Bohhoeffer

It had become obvious now that the two churchmen should get to see each other personally. Bell invited Bonhoeffer to come to Chichester. Bonhoeffer could not make it on the date suggested and so proposed an alternative meeting.

25 April, 1934

My Lord Bishop,
Thank you very much for your kind letter and
invitation to Chichester. Unfortunately I could not
change another arrangement made for Tuesday and so I
could not come. In the meantime things are going on
rapidly in Germany and the information I get is more
optimistic than ever before, at least with regard
to the stand of the opposition. The last number of
our Church paper "Junge Kirche" brings your letter
to *The Times* and in addition to that a few voices
from Sweden and Switzerland. Today I have received
the answer of the Emergency League in Berlin to the
Peace-offer of the Reich bishop and I have dared
to translate it for you as well as I could, because
I thought it very important. I think the moment has
come, that you should and could speak a final word on
this conflict. There are thousands who are anxious
to hear that word soon. May I come to the Athenaeum
on Friday at 6 o'clock. If I do not hear anything
else, I shall be there.
    I remain,
    My Lord Bishop,
    Yours very respectfully,
    Dietrich Bonhoeffer

The two met at the appointed hour. After the meeting Bell received
more information from Bonhoeffer:

1 May 1934

My Lord Bishop,
Referring to our conversation last Friday, I
thought it might be of interest to you and even for
the circular letter that you see the new seal of our
German Church. It needs no comment.
    Secondly, I have just received the message from
my Berlin student friends that they have to prove
their Aryan ancestry and descent in order to be
admitted to the theological examinations.
    Thirdly, two letters of leading oppositionals
foretelling a very dark near future. The government
seems to be willing to maintain Müller at any cost,

even with force. In Saxony the situation seems to be most critical.

There is an idea going about in Berlin concerning the organisation of a Council of all parties and to bring about the split on such an occasion.

I hope very much that your letter will contain a word of sympathy for the suppressed opposition over there. It would help them much. Sometimes they seem to be rather exhausted.

I remain, My Lord Bishop,
Yours very respectfully,
Dietrich Bonhoeffer

Bell, immensely moved by the plight of the opposition in Germany, was now preparing to respond to its wishes. On this he communicated with Bonhoeffer:

The Palace, Chichester
2 May, 1934

My dear Bonhoeffer,
I send you a draft letter to members of the Oecumenical Council. I should be most grateful if you would tell me how it strikes you. I think myself it is too long. I hope it is properly balanced. Any points which you think might be better expressed, or omitted or added, will be most thankfully received. I should naturally be grateful for the earliest possible reply.

You will note a guarded reference to the Ulm Declaration at the end of the second paragraph.

Yours ever,
George Cicestr

Bell wrote again the following day.

3 May,1934

My dear Bonhoeffer,
I got your letter with the seal of the German Church this morning. It was posted to Winchester, Chichester having been misread for Winchester, so it reached me after I had sent my draft letter to you. Comment is indeed unnecessary on the character of

that seal. Thank you too for the other information you give me in your letter of May 1st.

My trouble with my draft letter is that it is too long - amongst other things. But I am waiting for your comments.

Yours ever,
George Cicestr

Bonhoeffer sent his comments immediately:

London, 3 May 1934

My Lord Bishop,
Thank you very much for your most interesting letter. I think it will be a very helpful and important document in the present situation. May I just add a few words with regard to details: You speak "of the loyalty (of the pastors) to what they believe to be Christian truth". Could you not say perhaps: "to what is the Christian truth" - or "to what we believe with them to be the Christian truth"? It sounds as if you want to take distance from their belief. I think even the Reich bishop would be right in taking disciplinary measures against ministers, if they stand for something else but the truth of the gospel (even if they believe it to be the truth) - the real issue is that they are under coercion on account of their loyalty to what is the true gospel - namely their opposition against the racial and political element as constituent for the Church of Christ.

Is not perhaps the word "one sided" (page 2) misleading? It could seem as if one possibly could sympathise with both sides at the same time and as if the difference between both sides were not ultimate, so that one just has to decide for either side. I am afraid, Heckel will make use of this "one-sided" in a way you do not want it to be used.

P.3 "the introduction of racial distinction" and political principles - could that be added? It is always the same error - the Swastica in the Church seal! Many sources of revelation besides and except Christ. Other constitutive norms for the Church than Christ himself.

Finally, I think the stimulating effect of your letter would be still a bit stronger if you would hint at the absolute necessity of unanimity with regard to some crucial principles, and that any further co-operation would be useless and unchristian, if such unity would prove unreal.

If there would be no word of that sort, Müller and his men will not be afraid of any definite action from your side in the near future anymore. The policy of the more intelligent people in the Church Government has always been: "discuss the problems as much as you want, but let us act" – the thing they are afraid of is not discussion but action. If they could gather from this letter that the ecumenical movement would leave them alone for a certain while, they would consider it a success for themselves. So I think it necessary not to give them the possibility of such an illusion (of which they would make any political use they can!)

Excuse my frank comments to your letter. You know that I am most thankful to you for giving me the chance of expressing my opinion to you so frankly.

I remain with great gratitude,
Yours very respectfully,
Dietrich Bonhoeffer

Bell welcomed the suggestions made by Bonhoeffer and changed his text accordingly. On 10th May Bell issued an Ascension Day Message, which read as follows:

A Message
Regarding the German Evangelical Church
To the Representatives of the Churches
On the Universal Christian Council
for Life and Work
From the Bishop of Chichester

I have been urged from many quarters to issue some statement to my fellow members of the Universal Christian Council for Life and Work upon the present position in the German Evangelical Church, especially as it affects other Churches represented on the Universal Christian Council for Life and Work.

The situation is, beyond doubt, full of anxiety. To estimate it aright we have to remember the fact that a revolution has taken place in the German State, and that as a necessary result the German Evangelical Church was bound to be faced with new tasks and many new problems requiring time for their full solution. It is none the less true that the present position is being watched by members of the Christian Churches abroad not only with great interest, but with a deepening concern. The chief cause of anxiety is the assumption by the Reich Bishop in the name of the principle of leadership of autocratic powers unqualified by constitutional or traditional restraints which are without precedent in the history of the Church. The exercise of these autocratic powers by the Church Government appears incompatible with the Christian principle of seeking in brotherly fellowship to receive the guidance of the Holy Spirit. It has had disastrous results on the internal unity of the Church; and the disciplinary measures which have been taken by the Church Government against Ministers of the Gospel on account of their loyalty to the fundamental principle of Christian truth, have made a painful impression on Christian opinion abroad, already disturbed by the introduction of racial distinction in the universal fellowship of the Christian Church. No wonder that voices should be raised in Germany itself making a solemn pronouncement before the whole Christian world on the dangers to which the spiritual life of the Evangelical Church is exposed.

There are indeed other problems which the German Evangelical Church is facing, which are the common concern of the whole of Christendom. These are such fundamental questions as those respecting the nature of the Church, its witness, its freedom and its relation to the secular power. At the end of August the Universal Council will be meeting in Denmark. The Agenda of the Council will inevitably include a consideration of the religious issues raised by the present situation in the German Evangelical Church. It will also have to consider the wider questions which affect the life of all the Churches in Christendom. A Committee met last month in Paris to prepare for its work, and its report will shortly be published entitled, "The Church, the State, and the World Order". I hope that this meeting will assist the Churches in their friendship with each other, and in their task of reaching a common mind on the implications of their faith in relation to the dominant tendencies in modern thought and society, and in particular to the growing demands of the modern State.

The times are critical. Something beyond conferences and consultations is required. We need as never before to turn our thoughts and spirits to God. More earnest efforts must be made in our theological study. Above all more humble and fervent prayer must be offered to our Father in Heaven. May He, Who knows our weakness and our blindness, through a new outpouring of the Spirit enable the whole Church to bear its witness to its Lord with courage and faith!

George Cicestr
Ascensiontide 1934

Bonhoeffer was exceedingly satisfied with Bell's message:

London, 15th May 1934

My dear Lord Bishop,
Your letter has made a very great impression on me and on all my friends here who have read it. In its conciseness it strikes at the chief points and leaves no escape for misinterpretation. I am absolutely sure that this letter of yours will have the greatest effect in Germany and the opposition will be very much indebted to you. And what I think is most important, this letter will help the opposition to see that this whole conflict is not only within the Church, but strikes at the very roots of National Socialism. The issue is the freedom of the Church rather than any particular confessional problem.

I am very anxious to learn what the effect on the Church Government will be. Once more I wish to thank you for your letter which is a living document of ecumenical and mutual responsibility. I hope, it will help others to speak out as clearly as you did.

```
I remain, my Lord Bishop,
Yours very respectfully,
Dietrich Bonhoeffer
```

Bell wrote back on 16th May 1934:

```
My dear Bonhoeffer,
I am very glad indeed to get your letter and to
know that Message appeals to you so strongly, and I
hope it may help to do the good you say.(...)
```

Bell's message served as great encouragement to representatives of the Confessional Church who held their first Synod at Wuppertal-Barmen from 29th - 31st May. The Synod voiced unanimous protest against the policies of the German Christians. The Synod declared in what came to be known as Barmen Declaration, that the Church could not act against the truths of the Gospel and that the State could not assume the responsibilities of the Church. *The Times* published the Barmen Declaration on 4th June and Bell explained the sense of this declaration to the English bishops on 7th June in the Upper House of the Convocation of Canterbury. The Convocation resolved to support the spirit of the declaration.

Bell kept Dr Koechlin informed of his actions:

```
The Palace,
Chichester,
10 June 1934

Dear Dr Koechlin,
The Bishop of Chichester desires me to send
you the enclosed cuttings from The Times of Friday,
June 8th. One is a report of a resolution which
the Bishop moved in the Upper House of Canterbury
Convocation on Thursday, and which was adopted
unanimously by the Bishops of the Province of
Canterbury. The other is a leading article on this
discussion in Convocation.
The Bishop hopes that you will not think that
he was not too strong in what he said!
Yours sincerely,
Lancelot Mason
Chaplain
```

At the same time Bell continued his correspondence with Bonhoeffer:

> 29 June 1934
> Private
>
> My dear Bonhoeffer,
> I enclose a letter from Professor Fabricius
> to the Archbishop of Canterbury which speaks for
> itself. The Archbishop has sent it to me, asking
> me to make any comments which occur to me for his
> consideration. I send this by express in the hope
> that it will reach you while Dr Winterhager[85] is
> staying with you. I should be glad if you could tell
> me something about Professor Fabricius, but more
> important if you would indicate what sort of comments
> you would think would be most likely to pierce
> Professor Fabricius' armour. The Aryan Paragraph,
> unreserved homage demanded for the State, the use
> of force and prohibition of free elections, and
> the introduction of the leadership principle with
> the autocratic powers given to Bishop Müller, seem
> clear points to be made. But is Professor Fabricius
> likely to be influenced thereby? I also enclose, so
> that if he likes Dr. Winterhager could take it with
> him to Berlin, a copy of a pamphlet just issued,
> with a report of the two speeches in Convocation.
> Beyond giving my consent to the reproduction of the
> debate in Convocation I have had nothing to do with
> the preparation of the pamphlet, which is just out
> today.
> Yours sincerely,
> George Cicestr

Bonhoeffer replied the same day.

> 29 June 1934
> Private
>
> My Lord Bishop,
> I am very grateful indeed for your letter and
> the excellent booklet which have both reached me
> before Dr Winterhager's departure. We find that this

publication of the "Friends of Europe" will be very helpful to all Protestants in our country. We have sent it to our friends of the Emergency League at once and have ordered several more copies.

I have then dealt with the enclosed letter thoroughly. Dr Fabricius is an Assistant Professor in the University of Berlin. He is considered to be ill and much embittered. His influence among the younger generation and his theological significance have always been limited. There may be certainly some connection between his recent activities and Bishop Heckel's foreign church office, but there does actually not exist any ecumenical basis of his new "Zentralstelle". If there were not a tendency of the present Church Government possibly acting as an influence behind it, the letter itself had not to be taken very seriously. It is doubtful, at least, that Dr Fabricius himself will be much influenced either by theological arguments or even facts.

I heartily disapprove of the whole tone and tenor of Dr Fabricius's letter. Yet I have dealt with all the strange arguments contained therein, and after a long talk with Dr Winterhager, I should like to submit to you the following points as possibly forming an outline to the answer, however shortly any answer should be stated in replying to Dr Fabricius's letter. Dr Fabricius maintains that there is a large difference between the official German Christians and the "German Faith Movement". In fact, this difference is extremely small! We may prove this by three statements.

1.   Dr. Krause's party, affiliated to the German Faith Movement ("sport palace") is still officially within the Church "communion" and is entitled to send its representatives to both parish councils and governing bodies.

2.   An "ecclesiastic" member of the German Faith Movement (a curate) has recently (at an open meeting attended by Dr Coch,[86] the Bishop of Sachsen) read the following "passage" from the Gospel according to St. John: "In the beginning was the Nation, and the Nation was with God, and the Nation was God, and the same was in the beginning with God, etc." – Bishop Coch has not expressed one word of disagreement with this new version of the New Testament. But several ministers of the

opposition who witnessed this event have written
to Bishop Müller and have asked him to correct
the reading curate afterwards. But no such measure
has been taken by Bishop Müller. In this way has
a "version" of Scripture reading been authorised
which could not be surpassed by anything else in
heresy.

3.   The High President of Brandenburg, Herr
Kube, Member of the General Synod of the Church in
Prussia and at the same time one of the responsible
leaders of the German Christians, has concluded
his latest Midsummer-Night speech in saying: "Adolf
Hitler yesterday, today and for evermore!"

We believe these three points to be sufficient
proofs against Dr Fabricius's ignorant statement.

We would also point out that his description
of Karl Barth's theology is very superficial and
inadequate and does not require much consideration.
Moreover, Dr Fabricius's reproach of the Barmen
synod is drastic in extravagance as he wishes
the Protestant Opposition to be responsible
for introducing the leadership principle and
for imitating the political methods of National
Socialism. One should rather keep in one's mind that
the initiative to the election of a Reich bishop
was never taken on our side and that it was not
the opposition which elected Dr v. Bodelschwingh.
It was the old (conservative) Church Government
which did that when still in power (early in 1933).
Neither Dr v. Bodelschwingh himself nor the Free
Synods have ever dreamt of securing leadership of
any political bearing in the Church.

Dr Fabricius himself expresses a desire for
information "in what behalf (which probably means
'to what extent') the German Evangelical Church is
in danger to cease to be fully Christian". Now we
should like to make Dr Fabricius concede that the
points which you, My Lord Bishop, stated in your
letter today, are all based upon facts which make it
doubtful whether the German Church has not already
ceased to be a Christian Church at all – the Aryan
Paragraph, unreserved homage demanded for the State,
the use of force and prohibition of free elections,
and the introduction of the leadership principle
with the autocratic powers given to Bishop Müller.

Dr Fabricius finally accuses the Protestant

opposition of the same thing on account of which
Bishop Müller has felt entitled officially to issue
the High Treason Threat! We openly declare and
emphasise that the Opposition Movement has never
caused the foreign press to interfere in any
question of political bearing. On the other hand
the Protestant opposition particularly enjoys and
highly appreciates the intercession and the active
assistance given by the world-wide fellowship of
Christ.

The Protestants who wish to be loyal to Jesus
Christ believe in a universal Church, and they will
always remain grateful to the Church of England and
other Churches because they have helped to keep
that ecumenical faith strong.

When I was in Germany last week, I saw Praeses
Koch.[87] He asked me to offer you his kindest regards
and the expression of his sincere gratitude and
appreciation of all the help you have already given
to our Protestant Movement, again and again.

With thanks and with kindest regards also from
Dr. Winterhager,

Respectfully yours,
Dietrich Bonhoeffer

The Council of Life and Work was to meet at Fanö, Denmark from
23rd to 30th August 1934, and Bell very much hoped that representatives
of the Confessional Church would be able to attend the meeting. This
in mind Bell wrote to the Danish Bishop Dr Ammundsen.[88]

The Palace, Chichester
7 July 1934
Private

My dear Bishop,
It has been suggested to me that I should invite
representatives of the Confessional Synod of the
German Evangelical Church which met at Barmen to
send representatives to the Denmark Meeting of Life
and Work. The point made is that the Confessional
Synod is in fact a Church, whether or not one admits
its claim to be the legal Evangelical Church of
Germany – a claim that is very strongly supported on
legal and constitutional grounds by learned German

lawyers. I am given to understand (by Bonhoeffer, with whom I have discussed the matter) that if an invitation were to be presented to Praeses Koch it would be welcome, and that representatives would undoubtedly be sent. I admit that I should like to send an invitation. In ordinary circumstances it rests with the Churches in the countries concerned to agree amongst themselves as to their respective quotes in their national delegation. But clearly one cannot expect Bishop Heckel to negotiate with Praeses Koch as to the proportion in this case. I do not at all know whether Bishop Heckel is in fact coming, or how far the German Evangelical Church will be represented. I think one wants to do anything within reason to give encouragement to the Confessional Synod.

I am writing to Schönfeld in the same way as I am writing to you. I should be most grateful if you would give me the help of your very wise advice, and if you could let me have an answer during this coming week it would be particularly welcome.

The present situation in Germany generally adds an urgency to the whole question.

Yours ever,

George Cicestr

Bishop Ammundsen positively responded to Bell's suggestion, and so Bell, as President of the Universal Christian Council for Life and Work, invited a recognised leader of the Confessional Church, the Rt. Revd Praeses Koch, to attend the Fanö meeting.

The Palace, Chichester
18 July, 1934

Right Reverend and Dear Sir,

The Universal Christian Council for Life and Work is holding its Meeting at Fanö, in Denmark, from August 23 to August 30. It is expected that the Meeting will be one of grave importance. On the Saturday the Council will engage in a discussion on the recent Message which I sent as President to the representatives of the Churches on the Universal Council at Ascensiontide. On the Monday and the Tuesday the theme for discussion will be "The

Church and the modern conception of the State" and also "The Church and the World Order".

I write as President, after consultation with Bishop Ammundsen and some others, to invite you to attend the Meeting of the Council and to bring a colleague with you: or if you are for any reason unable to attend yourself, to send two representatives. If it happened to be convenient for Dr von Bodelschwingh to be one of such representatives his presence would be very valuable. I invite you and your colleague or representatives as guests and as authoritative spokesmen in a very difficult situation, from whose information and advice the Universal Christian Council would be certain to derive much benefit.

I am well aware that you may yourself perceive difficulties which you will no doubt carefully consider as this invitation reaches you. The Universal Council will be obliged to hold a discussion, and in all probability to express an opinion, on the German Church situation. It will be very difficult for the Council to deal with the questions raised without the assistance of spokesmen representing different positions and points of view. I also appreciate the fact however that attendance may have its embarrassment for those who take a different view from that of the Church Government. I would only say that if you are able to come – or send representatives – you and your colleagues would be most welcome.

With much respect and sympathy,
I am,
Yours very faithfully,
George Cicestr
President

Praeses Koch declined the invitation fearing that his presence at Fanö might provoke the Nazis to repress further the Confessional Church. Instead Koch invited Bell to visit him on his return journey from Denmark. The German Church delegated Bishop Heckel to attend the Fanö meeting, where he had to do a lot of explaining. His position, Bell owned, "was very difficult. He was watched from all sides, and a warm tribute must be paid to him for the increasingly favourable impression which he made by his firm presentation of the

German Church case, coupled with frankness and friendliness".[89] But, contended Bell, "it simply was not possible to keep silent. To say nothing would be grievously misunderstood. In fact it would be a grave wrong to the Christian religion in Germany and a betrayal of the truth by the Universal Council ... The duty of the Council was therefore to speak and speak strongly so that there would be no disguise of the gravity of the position, but at the same time to speak in a spirit of friendship and good-will".[90]

The Fanö meeting expressed anxiety at "the present time in the life of the German Evangelical Church", and declared "its conviction that autocratic Church rule, especially when imposed upon the conscience in solemn oath; the use of methods of force; and the suppression of free discussion are incompatible with the true nature of the Christian Church". The Council asked "in the name of the Gospel for its fellow-Christians in the German Evangelical Church – freedom to preach the Gospel of our Lord Jesus Christ and live according to His teaching, freedom of the printed word and of Assembly in the Service of the Christian Community, freedom for the Church to instruct its youth in the principle of Christianity and immunity from the compulsory imposition of a philosophy of life antagonistic to the Christian religion".[91]

Bell, together with Koechlin, Ammundsen and two other Council members, had been chiefly instrumental in drafting the Council's resolution. The Council also co-opted Koch and Bonhoeffer as its members. The Confessional Church was greatly satisfied. On the way back from Fanö Bell visited Koch in Germany, thus gaining first-hand knowledge of the situation there. Bell then took a short holiday, and on reaching England reported to Koechlin on his "most illuminating talk" with Koch and other members of the Confessional Church.

```
The Palace,
Chichester
1 October, 1934

My dear Dr. Koechlin,
     I returned home from my holiday on Friday. As
you can imagine, after Fanö I was really tired,
and am thankful that my holiday had already been
```

arranged to follow the Council Meetings instead of preceding them. I spent most of a day in the difficult task of preparing my article for *The Times* for they wanted it as soon as possible. I wrote this at Lund, before going on to Dalecarlia. But I had a most refreshing holiday in Sweden then, and had the opportunity of very full talks with the Archbishop of Upsala ten days ago. He, you may like to know, was not in favour of a delegation at the present moment as he thought it would certainly achieve nothing, though it might be used by the Church Government as an indication of friendliness. He thought that it would be much wiser and much more profitable if from time to time leading members of the Council happened to pay visits to Berlin and to drop in on the Church Government officials and express their anxieties and difficulties. If a more or less steady stream of anxieties, at intervals of a month or six weeks, expressed by personal visits, friendly but critical, could be kept up, the total effect might be very valuable. I agree.

I am really writing however to tell you that last Wednesday, at the request of Praeses Koch, I passed through Germany on my way home and had six hours' conference with Praeses Koch and other members of the Confessional Synod. Incidentally I explained why I had not read his letter to the Council. I think that they understood the reason, and they certainly never intended to claim that their Praesidium was the governing body of the true German Evangelical Church but simply a committee of management to carry on in between Meetings of the Confessional Synod, which of course is the authoritative body from their point of view. We had a most illuminating talk and I was much impressed by the earnestness, statesmanship and courage of Praeses Koch and his friends. It is a great thing to have got into personal contact and to know the kind of men who are leading the Confessional Synod.

One particular request they made. The nomination of Praeses Koch to the Council has caused much objection in the German Church Government. But the Church Government is consoling itself with the thought that it is a paper action as the Council will not meet for two years and much may happen before then. Hence the importance, says Praeses

Koch, of making the connection between himself and the Council real, and to give evidence of it from time to time. I assured him that the Council wanted to make the fellowship a very real thing. When he asked me therefore whether I thought a member of the Council could come officially as a representative of the Council to the next Meeting of the Confessional Synod, which they might have to call in the fairly near future should a crisis arise, I said that I should certainly hope that this could be arranged. I did not make a promise and he understood this. But I said that I was sure that it would be the wish of the Council that steps should be taken to bring this about, and he was very much cheered by this and said "Schön" . They all seemed pleased.

I think that I ought not myself to go, at any rate just yet, as I am President. It would be too strong a step unless some quite new calamity takes place, apart from the question of my not speaking German. I am writing therefore to ask whether you, than whom none could be better, could hold yourself free to attend the next Meeting of the Confessional Synod. It would be an enormous encouragement to me personally to feel that I could count on you as the person representing the Council, for I have the greatest confidence in your wisdom and your ability to say the right thing. May I ask you to do this? Of course your expenses will be paid.

Yours very sincerely,
George Cicestr

At their second annual conference of 22nd-23rd September the German Christians had confirmed Müller as State Bishop. This was understood as a further step towards the establishment of the State Church in Germany. The Confessional Church stood in principle against it, and determined to state its disapproval publicly at the second Synod meeting at Dahlem, Berlin, from 19th-20th October. Koch had asked Bell privately if he could not be present at the October meeting. Bell delegated Koechlin to go to Dahlem, and wrote to Koch in prison to explain why he could not be there in person.

The Palace,
Chichester

15 October, 1934
Private and Confidential.
My dear Praeses Koch,

At the very first moment, nearly three weeks ago, when you asked whether it would be possible for a member of the Oecumenical Council to be present at the next Meeting of the Confessional Synod, I raised the question in my own mind whether it would be right for me, as President, to attend myself; and I have already discussed the possibility with others. I have the feeling, and I find that this is definitely shared by other wise counsellors whose sympathy with the Confessional Synod is beyond all doubt, that, as I am at present advised, it would not be the most helpful thing that I could do for me to come to Berlin to attend the Meeting.

My reason is that while other members of the Oecumenical Council may most usefully attend, if the President of the Council comes now, there is nobody left in reserve for further action at what may even be a more crucial stage; and also that other action of a private kind is being taken by myself, and a public step of the nature which your messenger invites me to take, at this juncture, would I fear destroy the chance of useful results from this private course.

You will I am sure agree that if the Oecumenical Council is to be of greatest service in a crisis which concerns the whole Christian Church, we must conserve our strength and see that it is used to the greatest possible effect at the really vital moment for affecting decision.

I have summoned the Administrative Committee of the Oecumenical Council to an emergency Meeting at Chichester next week (October 25 – 27) so as to precede the Meeting of the Confessional Synod. The situation may be clearer then and more light may have come as to the wisest and most effective way of helping in these tragic days. I hope that it may be possible for one of the members of the Administrative Committee to see you, or another prominent leader, so as to have your latest wishes and news before we confer at Chichester.

May God guard you and guide you!
Precibus oecumenicis conjuncti sumus.

Yours very sincerely,
George Cicestr
P.S. Pastor Koechlin of Basel has promised to
attend the Confessional Synod, at my request, and
I have also asked, and am hoping to secure the
presence of, a prominent Lutheran from Sweden.

Bell separately and confidentially communicated to Koechlin the
action he was taking:

The Palace,
Chichester.
15 October 1934
Private and Confidential.

My dear Dr Koechlin,
          I enclose a copy of my reply to a
question brought to me today personally by Pastor
Hildebrandt from Praeses Koch. I think that you
will agree with it. I have sent a copy to Henriod
and asked him to keep in touch with you. Please note
the final paragraph of the letter. I think it very
important that you should come to Chichester if you
possibly can for the Administrative Committee, as
a guest. And I very much want you if this is also
possible to see Koch on your way to Chichester. If
you cannot see Koch, then I am asking Henriod to do
so. I feel that we ought to have the latest from him
before we meet.
     Yours sincerely,
     George Cicestr
     P.S. Koch also sent a message asking us to
investigate the Church situation in Bavaria &
Württemberg. Can you do anything about it?

Koechlin reported to Bell on the Confessional Synod. For
this "valuable" information, Bell was personally "deeply grateful" to
Koechlin.

The Palace,
Chichester
1 November 1934

My dear Koechlin,

Ever so many thanks for your most valuable letter of the 30th October, and for your great kindness in translating the Message of the Confessional Synod, which is most admirably clear. It is a very great help to have the text so accurately put into English. May I thank you too for all the very great help that you have given during these many months, and especially in these last weeks. I think the Universal Council and the German Evangelical Church owe you a great debt, and I personally am deeply grateful. It is a very real satisfaction to me that we should be in such close contact and friendship on such a matter at such a time.

The situation develops with somewhat startling rapidity. *The Times* today suggests that the State will not only declare itself but prove strictly neutral. At the same time it looks as though this neutrality does not remove the National Church idea by any means from the sphere of practical polities, and the steadfastness and vitality as well as courage of the Confessional Synod and their friends, will be tested in new ways. However that eventuality is rather in the future, and we must be profoundly thankful for the present measure of independence which has been secured for the Evangelical Church, and the freedom won by the Confessional Synod. I shall naturally be very anxious to hear from you any further light you get on the developments. I entirely agree that it would be very difficult and even dangerous for an outsider to go to Berlin at the present juncture. The situation is too complicated, and a word or a deed might prove most embarrassing.

Thank you too very much for the photograph of the Confessional Synod.

Yours very sincerely,
George Cicestr

If it had not been possible for Bell to manifest his support by being present at the Confessional Synod, he would not hesitate to do so privately and firmly. He arranged a meeting with a man very close to Hitler. Bell and Joachim von Ribbentrop,[92] met at the Athenaeum on 6th November. It was a lengthy talk, lasting over three hours. Bell made detailed notes of their conversation:

CONFIDENTIAL
Interview with Herr Joachim von Ribbentrop
November 6, 1934.

I met von Ribbentrop as Weigall's guest at the Athenaeum, and we had three hours' talk. He is an able business man of, I should think, 45, who knows England well and has had dealings with England for some 25 years. He likes sport and is having a holiday in this country. At the same time he is seeing Arthur Henderson, Lord Cecil and others about Disarmament, and making other opportunities for private conversation on questions of German policy. He is a close personal friend of Hitler. It was in his house that Hitler met von Papen,[93] and the decision was formed to make Hitler Chancellor. He said that Hindenburg[94] refused to make Hitler Chancellor, and there were some very difficult moments. One such occasion Hitler brought his fist down with a bang and said "Fools! Don't they realise that I am a Conservative of the Conservatives !"

Von Ribbentrop spoke as a layman and did not profess to be au fait with theological questions. His main point was that Hitler had saved Christianity. "Why", Hitler asked, "did not the Churches outside Germany, in the midst of our struggle against Communism in the last fifteen years, lift up their voices, when their help would have been far more potent?". I explained what had been said and done by the Archbishop and others, including the Universal Council in its smaller way, with regard to Bolshevism in Russia. I made it plain that I realised that the German Church was, in large parts of it, in a state of semi-death, but I pointed out that it was very strong just where the Confessional Synod was strong, in Bavaria, Württemberg, Westphalia, parts of Berlin and Hannover. Was it not common sense, I asked, for Hitler, to use the help of the Church where it was strongest, rather than to bring in new creatures altogether? Von Ribbentrop and Hitler with him, I think were sceptical about the ability of the Church to get at the masses. He said more than once that it was a question of technique, how to get Christianity across to the masses. He said that millions of Germans were in a state of desperate poverty and depression, confined in their miserable tenements. They could not understand the language of the ordinary Church, so new methods must be devised, getting hold of them out of doors in the open air, and so on. He even suggested that the Churches might well be filled as a result of the new movement, but that there were not enough Churches to accommodate all the multitude that ought to be brought in. Did the German Church realise the urgency of the matter and the need of new measures being taken? We talked about the so-called National Church. I agreed that there were eccentric people in Germany whose ideas about uniting the Faith Movement, the Protestants and the Catholics in one great organisation called a National Church, might not perhaps be very seriously regarded. But the influence of much present education on the young, without the help of the Church, was dangerous. And more important, I said that the National Socialist system was such as not really to brook any other point of view in the State, and that the real fear of a National Church was of a Church which put a religious complexion on the National Socialist system and said "Ditto", in religious language, to National Socialism; that such a Church was not really what we meant by a Church, and that some measure of independence was necessary in a proper Church. He appreciated the point of this, but he kept saying that this great battle was with Communism, and that nothing must be allowed to interfere with this battle; that you did not know what people like bishops and Church leaders would say if you tolerated a measure of independence. I pointed out what the Archbishop of Canterbury had done in the way of criticising the Government with regard to Disarmament, with regard to the Irish Troubles and on many public occasions - how the present and the late Archbishop had claimed the right of speaking freely on public and political questions. This puzzled von Ribbentrop a great deal, and he did not think such an attitude would be possible in Germany. I asked whether, to take an instance of independent criticism, it would be possible for a Church leader to speak - though not necessarily in Church - about public affairs, in the same sort of way as von Papen had spoken at

Marburg? He thought that that was an unfortunate speech, and was not very encouraging about the analogy.

I pressed that perhaps one of the reasons why the Church had been so out of touch with the people in Germany was the great chasm between Lutheran theology and religion, and ordinary social and political interests. He thought there might be something in this. He said that it was most important that some arrangement should be come to with regard to the future of the German Church. If only the right head of the Church could be found, it was a question of personality. Of course such a head of the Church must be a hundred per-cent pro-Hitler. From what he said, clearly Bishop Müller is not to be quite easily thrown over. Why should not Müller remain, and have a strong man doing the work with him in a general vague way behind, as Reichbischof? He stressed the fact that Müller was Hitler's personal friend, and trusted by him; and where was another such man to be found? He was obviously afraid of the particularism of some of the Church leaders in Bavaria and Württemberg. He said that the unification of the Church was vital. I said that I was certain that the Church leaders like Koch were thoroughly convinced of the necessity of unification, and that there was no going back on their part to separate Churches. They claimed (and he took this point as an important point) that the Constitution of the National Synod which had been agreed in July last year, had been entirely thrown overboard by the Reich bishop , but that there was no reason why it should not be the basis of a proper unification today. I said that the Opposition leaders had no confidence in Müller and did not trust him, and. I did not see the possibility of reconciliation under him as Reich bishop. Further, that there was a great deal of tidying up to be done, so much confusion had been brought about that it would be good to have an interval of straightening things out, with the help perhaps of a lawyer or two on the Church side; that, given time, a man fit to be Reich bishop could emerge. I asked about von Bodelschwingh and he did not rule him out by any means, though I do not know that he knew very much about him. I said that I thought it would be quite reasonable that

Hitler should claim the right of veto. He was very much interested in the English method of appointing Bishops which gave the Crown so much power.

He obviously distrusted some of the leaders of the Opposition, and told me a curious story about Pastor Niemöller. He himself is in Niemöller's parish at Dahlem. He has not himself been much of a churchman, though he is now a German Christian, but his children have been christened by Niemöller. In July 1933 he wanted his youngest girl christened, and asked Niemöller to tea with himself and his wife. They discussed matters in a friendly way in which Ribbentrop said that "in that chair" (pointing to a chair) Hitler sat when it was decided that he should be Chancellor. Niemöller braced himself up and assumed an attitude of reserve. Then Frau von Ribbentrop said something about the German Christians, asking whether there was not something in what they stood for, in a way asking for information. They were not German Christians then themselves. And they both noticed that Niemöller's reserve became all the stronger, and that there was a sort of atmosphere of hostility. They did not understand it. They made proposals for the baptism of the child. It was arranged that the arrangements should go forward subject to a convenient date. Niemöller left, and they tried, a day or two later, to fix a day on the telephone, but though they tried several times, they could never get hold of Niemöller personally; Niemöller did not make any appointment for the baptism so the baptism lapsed and the child is not yet christened. This has obviously affected von Ribbentrop's feelings towards Niemöller. I said that I could not understand such action on Niemöller's part. I thought that possibly at the moment when they were discussing the christening, feeling was very acute owing to the election and the influence Hitler had exerted to secure the return of German Christians. But he obviously looked upon Niemöller as an opponent of National Socialists and Hitler.

We talked also about Concentration Camps a little. I asked whether he had come across Wyndham Deedes[95] who came to Berlin last spring with a letter from the Archbishop of York. At first he said. "Was that the letter about Oberammergau, protesting against the use of the swastika, at the Oberammergau Festival?". He thought that such a protest was unfortunate as the swastika, was the national flag of Germany. I said no, it was about the Concentration Camps, and roughly explained the contents of the letter. He said, no, he had not heard of this, though he seemed to recollect in a vague sort of way the fact that some messenger had come. He said that in England the whole Communist question was entirely misunderstood; that there were only 2000 or 3000 persons in the Concentration Camps; that the vast majority of these were Communists guilty of definite crimes, of really bad character - though there were a few intellectual leaders. He said that there were undoubtedly things which one might not wish to happen, but Hitler was fighting a great battle with Communism and that in such a battle, certain things might be done which would not be done in peaceable times or in a peaceable country. He said that Hitler was a great statesman and that in later years, with a proper perspective, people would look on these things in an entirely different way, and would see that Hitler really had saved Europe. He said that Hitler claimed to have added to the numbers of the Church since National Socialism had come in, by several hundred thousands of Church members. He also said that Hitler's method of action was rather by intuition than by systematic consideration of every possible detail. Von Ribbentrop would say something to him of which he might not take any notice at the time. Then some weeks later he would say "You remember saying so-and-so? I have done so-and-so". When our talk ended I said that I hoped von Ribbentrop might some day come to Chichester. He was very friendly and said that he thought it would be very useful for us to keep in touch with one another. I had the impression that he would very likely write again, or want to see me if some difficulty arose, and that he really did want to see a way through the German Church question, though not really sensitive enough to the inner nature of the conflict, or alive to the spiritual independence of a Christian Church. But he was a friendly man and the talk was useful.

One point I should have made much plainer at the beginning of my memorandum. Von Ribbentrop said

repeatedly that the fundamental thing was to save
the nation. Hitler had saved and was saving the
nation. If there were no nation there would be no
Church. This he regarded as fundamental. He also
pointed out the great financial difficulty which
would be involved if Church people were compelled
to raise their own funds supposing the State denied
them financial assistance, though. I pointed out
that presumably the State financial assistance was
in lieu of ancient Church endowments which the
State had long since taken over.
    G. C.

Bell now sent a copy of his notes to Koechlin. Ribbentrop's
assertions did not enthuse Koechlin. The actual position was far from
perfect. On this Koechlin reported to Bell in detail.

15 November 1934
The Right Rev. The Lord Bishop of Chichester
The Palace,
Chichester

My dear Lord Bishop,
    I have been very interested indeed in reading
your notes on the conversation you had with Herr von
Ribbentrop, though one has not the impression that
the man has a deeper understanding of what Church
and Church life mean. He is certainly in a position
to throw some light on different aspects of the
situation, not easy to understand for those staying
far away from national-socialist leadership. From
what Mr. Ribbentrop said, it seems quite evident
that the position of the Reich bishop might last
some weeks or even months longer.
    This morning I saw Pastor Riethmüller, the
leader of the German Young Women's Christian
Association, who told me that Praeses Koch and his
colleagues had their headquarters in their house,
Berlin-Dahlem and that he had been asked to organise
the whole evangelical Youth Work, YMCA, YWCA, etc.
in the new frame-work of the Confessional Church.
The latter is hoping that some time might be given
to it to build up, starting with each individual
congregation and parish, a strong Church life, able
to resist new attacks and sufferings coming may be

not only from the official Reichs Church Government, but even from State Government. Riethmüller, certainly one of the strong men in the Confessional Church, with a very clear vision of spiritual as well as other realities, who had just some weeks of rest in Lugano, is most perplexed in realising the nearly desperate international situation of Germany. Being inside Germany, he had not been in a position of seeing things as they are. He told me of the depths of demonic forces revealed June 30th and certainly not cleared up. He stressed the fact that it was hardly possible to influence Hitler himself, who has no idea whatever about the spiritual reality of a Church. He counted even with the possibility that the Church and in first line the Confessional Church, driven more and more in opposition to official ideology and official policy, would be in some vague or direct way declared to be the cause of unsuccess and be the object some day of a new 30th of June, no one having in circumstances of such critical days real control over the forces of evil. At any rate the Confessional Synod is convinced of the growing seriousness of the situation in to which it might be led.

On the other side it seems evident that the Reichswehr is developing its forces so as to be able to control the situation inside Germany at any critical moment and that some day, may be not very far away, it will take in hand, if not directly so indirectly, the destiny of the country. The Reichswehr is not interfering for the moment with other plans of Hitler, because Hitler is giving to it what it likes. It is however waiting for its hour.

Military Government is certainly not ideal, looked at from the point of view of the Church. New dangers might be expected then, but certainly the army, as has been proved through different incidents, will not allow Church oppression and Church persecution to go on. It would probably give the way free to new men, waiting to undo some of the biggest mistakes of the present Government resulting from the national-socialist philosophy of life.

These indications do not pretend to throw light on the future. Nevertheless they gave me some help to visualise some possibilities on which one feels unable to express any judgement.

Riethmüller said that it would be an invaluable service to help them inside Germany to see things as they are and to express to them our anxieties in view of their own attitude, behaviour and policy. He is seeing very closely, how difficult it is for them to judge and to avoid mistakes bringing irreparable harm on the Church of Christ in Germany. I promised him that all of us in the ecumenical Movements do our very best to stay united with them and to share with them with full sincerity our thoughts, our hopes and our anxieties and that you especially were fully aware of the great responsibility of the Churches outside Germany towards our Brethren in a situation full of perplexities.

I received a letter of my daughter Elizabeth this morning. She is looking forward with greatest pleasure to be allowed to stay for the week-end at Chichester. May I express in the name of Mrs. Koechlin and myself to Mrs. Bell and to yourself our deep gratitude for the kindness you are showing to Elizabeth. Will you give her our best greetings if she is already in your house when this letter is coming in.

Very cordially yours,
[A. Koechlin]

Koechlin wrote again to Bell on 21st December, this time on Karl Barth's dismissal from his University Professorship.

My dear Lord Bishop,
Receiving this letter, you will have heard that Karl Barth has been dismissed. He telephoned yesterday night with his friend Thurneysen and told him briefly that the proceedings of the disciplinary court (Disziplinargericht) had taken place yesterday in Cologne. The accusation was built up on the fact that Karl Barth refused to swear the oath to the Leader Adolf Hitler as prescribed for every State official. The sentence Karl Barth wished to put in and which I have quoted to you in a former letter, was declared to be unacceptable. The oath could only be a total oath to the Leader, who better than anyone else in Germany knew if what he asked the

State officials to do, was in agreement with God's command or not. The State official, putting his case, mentioned especially that as well the utterances of the Reformed Church as of the Marahrens Church Council, stating that every evangelical Christian would swear the oath under the mental reservation put expressively forward by Karl Barth, was inacceptable interpretation and could not stand.

Following the official act of accusation, the Court dismissed Karl Barth as University Professor and granted him for 6 months half of the amount he would have been entitled to receive as retirement pension. As Karl Barth has only been official State Professor for 9 years, this amount comes to a very small sum.

Evidently Karl Barth is still allowed to stay in Germany. If it will be possible for him to remain there in connection with some institution of the Confessional Church, has to be seen. I hope that he and his family won't be the object of ill-doings. Being not any more State official, he has lost his German citizenship and is only Swiss citizen. I know that the Swiss Government is doing every thing possible to give him protection. But one has to count with irresponsible acts of Nazi students or other people.

The other day, when a picture of Karl Barth was exhibited in the window of a bookshop, the owner was asked to take it off at once if he did not wish to have his window broken and the picture taken away from outside.

What seems to be the most important feature is the officially accepted statement of the totalitarian character of the Hitler oath, excluding explicitly the interpretation of all theological professors and Christian State officials and thought to be entitled to accept when swearing the oath. Their situation does not become easier by the decision of the disciplinary court of Cologne! In fact the judgement is proving that Karl Barth had seen clear in the whole matter.

I trust this letter will reach you before Xmas. May I send Mrs. Bell and yourself once more my heartiest wishes for the coming days. Mrs. Koechlin is joining me with Elizabeth who came home safely this morning with very happy memories and full of gratitude for all those who had contributed to make her England stay a real event in her life.

With kindest regards, yours very sincerely,

[A. Koechlin]

Bell replied on 29th December:

The Palace,
Chichester
29 December 1934

My dear Koechlin,

Very many thanks for your letter of December 21st telling me the facts about the dismissal of Karl Barth. I have seen a statement in one of the papers that Karl Barth has since been offered a Professorship in Basel and has accepted it. Is this so? Of course I appreciate the seriousness of the dismissal and the circumstances in which it is made.

The whole position inside the German Church at the moment seems more obscure than ever. *The Times* today leads one to anticipate rather more difficult conditions when negotiations are resumed next week, and also the intensification of the conflict between Christianity and paganism. I have not heard anything from Germany for a little while. I wrote to Koch about a fortnight ago sending my letter through Cragg who wrote acknowledging it from Berlin on December 19. But my letter was simply to tell Koch of the proposal which had been made for a visit from this country of English Church leaders, and to ask him what he thought about it and explain that of course there would be no following up of the proposal unless it was welcome to him. Bonhoeffer was in Berlin for a fortnight at the end of November and beginning of December. 1 saw him on his return, but he had not any very special news, except signs of a good deal of unsettlement generally. Incidentally he gave me the most curious information that quite recently - that is I think last month - the order had gone out that no member of Hitler's bodyguard must be attached to any Church, while simultaneously another order had gone out that every member of the Reichswehr must be a member of a Christian Church.

I need not say that I shall be thankful for any news that comes your way.

I hope you have had a very happy Christmas and will have a very happy New Year.

Yours sincerely,

George Cicestr

It seemed that Bell's interventions were helping the Confessional Church. So further requests for help became a common feature. Bonhoeffer again wrote to Bell at the beginning of January 1935:

7 January 1935

My Lord Bishop,

I must apologise for answering so late. The foggy weather last week kept me in bed and made me absolutely unable to work. Thank you very much for your kind letter. You had given me the address of the young German girl before and I had forwarded it to my friend Pastor Jacobi. I have not had any important news from home. I think they do not want to go on with their fight before the Saar plebiscite. The thing which occupies me most at the present moment is the question what could be done for the refugees from the Saar who will number about 3—5 thousand. I am thinking of taking a few children and giving them into the homes of my people in the congregation. But how is the whole problem going to be solved, not individually but fundamentally? I enclose a copy of a "memorandum" by one of the refugees who is here with his family and is trying to find some sort of work in the office of a lawyer, he himself having been a well known and very serious lawyer in Nürnberg. With regard to the idea of sending some British clergymen over to Germany for the time after the Saar plebiscite, I believe, it could be very helpful indeed. I do not think Rev. Cragg[96] could be offended. Pastor Forell from Sweden, who is devoting most of his time to the cause of the Confessional Church, himself asked for such a delegation from Sweden. But it might be, of course, that this Swedish delegation would be sufficient for the time being. Do you still think of the plan of an official British delegation to the Confessional Church on behalf of world-peace? The more I think of this idea, the more it strikes me as most important and helpful. At the beginning of a new year I wish to thank you most sincerely and heartily for all you have done for us in the last year. May God bless all your work and all the fellowship He is establishing through your work between our churches. Your work will never be forgotten in the history of the German Church.

I remain yours gratefully,
Dietrich Bonhoeffer

Bell replied the very next day:

8 January, 1935

My dear Bonhoeffer,
Very many thanks for your letter and the enclosure, I am very sorry you have been poorly, and do hope you are better now. I wrote to Praeses Koch and asked him if the sending of a group of five or six English churchmen to talk with German churchmen about peace and friendship between our two countries would be embarrassing or welcome. I sent the letter through Mr. Cragg. I also said that I did not think it would do for the Universal Council to be mixed up in it, as that had concerned itself with the Church question. After some delay I had a short letter back. He says that he would like five or six English churchmen to come out to Germany but he wants them to be connected with the Universal Council, and he wants them to discuss the grave German Church questions. He does not say a word about peace and Anglo-German friendship. I am rather perplexed, for that was not at all what my lay friend was proposing to finance. I have written to Mr. Cragg to that effect. In the meantime I am in touch with Dr Cross on the bare possibility of my being able to send him out to Berlin for a few days after seeing me, and to come back with a report; but I do not really know whether this be feasible.

I heard from Archbishop Eidem yesterday and I gather that Ehrenström is going to Berlin almost at once. I have not heard from Henriod about the proposed office of the Youth Committee at Berlin, but I do not know why he is so long in answering, except that the Christmas holidays were rather long at Geneva. Praeses Koch suggested that the party should go out to Berlin, if it went, about January 20th. I am going away to the Isle of Wight for a week on Saturday, and shall be in London on January 21st for most of that week. Thank you for what you have done about the young German girl. I do understand your principal occupation at the present moment with the question of what can be done for refugees from the Saar. Do you really think that they will number 3,000 to 5,000? I wish one could think of some method of dealing with the problem fundamentally. Thank you so very much for all your kind words about my poor efforts. I appreciate them greatly

    Yours ever,
    George Cicestr

And as usual the diligent observant of the German situation was Dr Koechlin.

1 April 1935
The Right Rev. The Lord Bishop of Chichester,
The Palace,
Chichester

My dear Lord Bishop,
    I thank you most heartily for your air mail letter received yesterday morning. Reverend Cragg might of course have in Berlin an insight into the situation inducing him to "deprecate your attendance" to the Confessional Synod. I could also imagine that the far-reaching general responsibilities in regard to world peace, entrusted at this highly critical moment to the English Nation and its Government, might lead the responsible leaders of England to look unfavourably to your personal mingling with the internal German political situation. From the point of view of the Confessional Church of Germany however I would regret if the invaluable help of your personal presence at the Confessional Synod could not be given to it, provided of course that the Reichs-Church Government urgently feels the desirability of your attendance.
    You might be interested in the following news I

received yesterday through Dr Hartenstein, Director of the Basle Mission, from Dr Lilje,[97] still the right hand of Bishop Marahrens, decided to stay there, refusing finally the general-secretaryship of the World's Student Christian Federation:

1. The German Christians are becoming more and more weak. Their theological leader, Pastor Christiansen is in prison because involved in a bad money business of the League for "Mother and Child".

2. The Reich bishop has been badly received by Hitler on February 28th. The Chancellor did not hide his discontent that Müller had not succeeded in reaching any result in the affairs entrusted to him. Müller in response pledged that he had no executive power, asked Hitler to be summus episcopus of the Evangelical Church and to nominate a Minister in evangelicis with full power for all questions of legislation, jurisdiction and finance, leaving to the Reich bishop only the spiritual leadership. Hitler refused the first offer, being catholic. The question of the Minister in evangelicis is not answered yet.

3. The Government of Bishop Marahrens is in daily close contact with State officials. The Reichsminister of Justice, Gürtner (catholic) is helping to reach a favourable settlement. A memorandum of Bishop Marahrens is asking for opportunity of a year's time to build up an independent Church organisation with power to put aside personalities like the Reichsbischopf and his followers.

4. The document against new paganism has been issued by Praeses Koch without the knowledge of Bishop Marahrens, but Bishop Marahrens was afterwards backing the document and Praeses Koch, especially in protesting most energetically against the State interference by which 800 (eight hundred!) Pastors had been for a day or two put into prison.

This State interference is due as it seems to Dr Frick being at that moment under the influence of Dr Jäger's friend Stuckert. The agitation in the population, the congregations assembling hundreds and thousands of faithful Christians at the doors of the prisons, singing hymns, was such, that even

Goebbels,[98] furious the Bekenntnis [Confessional] Church had got the possibility of such reaction and strengthening of its life, insisted to give free all these pastors at once.

Of the six Pastors of Hessen, who had lately been put to prison, three are in the concentration camp of Dachau, all too famous for ill-treatment of its prisoners. Grave anxiety is felt in regard to these faithful servants of the Church.

5. Praeses Koch had after these events such a breakdown, that he had to go for complete rest to a sanatorium.

6. Actually the State is considering the fight of the Confessional Church as a political one, because the national-socialist ideology is attacked in its foundation. That makes at present the situation particularly dangerous, the whole extreme wing of the Party most anxious to destroy a Church being a stronghold of anti-national-socialist philosophy.

The Confessional Synod is expected to be held at the latest next week 1) to take most energetic position against the new paganism of German faith and 2) to claim for the freedom of the Church and the Gospel.

With kindest regards,

Yours very sincerely,

[A. Koechlin]

P.S. In case you should wish me to attend the Confessional Synod, I am at your disposal except from April 26th to May 5th.

Worried about the recent developments in Germany, Bell this time wrote directly to Ribbentrop on 11th April. "If it is desired [wrote Bell] to preserve Evangelical Christianity in Germany and therefore the Evangelical Church, it is only through the stabilisation of the Confessional Synod and its government and organisation that this can be achieved. I am quite certain that the persecution of the Confessional Synod or the shattering of its organisation will be regarded in the Church of England and amongst the Free Churches in this country, and Scandinavia, and America, to say nothing of other countries of Europe, as a blow aimed at Evangelical Christianity itself".[99] Bell informed Koechlin on 17th April about his protests to Ribbentrop and also about how prepared he was "to help in case of need".

The Palace,
Chichester
17 April 1935

My dear Koechlin,
Very many thanks for your two letters. The first
letter about the article in the Berliner Tageblatt
was most useful and I have acted upon it. The
article is a religious article and if I get a spare
copy sent me I will send it along to you.
I saw Bonhoeffer on Monday in London. He was on
his way to Berlin. He is now, I think, giving up his
Pastorate in London and will certainly be away for
six months at least, possibly for good. He told me
that the situation in the German Evangelical Church
was critical but at the same time he did not think
that very drastic measures were going to be taken
immediately. He thought rather that the Government
policy was to let things drift a little, and
especially to see how far the lay people supported
the Pastors when such oppression and persecution
as you described in your letter of April 12 was
attempted. In other words they wanted, without
committing themselves too far, to see how much the
people would stand. He is to keep me in touch with
what is happening, and Pastor Rieger in Blackheath
will be a very useful link. I sent a line to Praeses
Koch through Bonhoeffer assuring him of my sympathy
and my desire to help in case of need.
I think that Bonhoeffer believes that a need
may arise in the not distant future when an appeal
might have to be made to the Oecumenical Church. I
have talked the matter over, and keep talking the
matter over, with the Archbishop of Upsala who is
spending Holy Week, with his wife and daughter, in
my house. I have showed him your letter. Before I
got your letter, having seen similar news in *The
Times*, I wrote a personal strong protest to Herr
von Ribbentrop, telling him that if it really was
desired to maintain Evangelical Christianity it
must be recognised that a Confessional Synod, from
the point of view of the Churches outside, was the
only instrument, and that an attack on that, or
the suppression of that, would be interpreted as
an attack upon Evangelical Christianity. I took as

my starting point the attacks on the Pastors and
their imprisonment, and sent him a cutting from
the "Christian World", to show how strongly Church
people from different Churches in this country felt
on the matter.

Yours ever,
George Cicestr

Bell wrote to Koechlin again about his proposed intentions:

22 May, 1935

My dear Dr. Koechlin,
We had a Meeting of the Administrative Committee
of Life and Work in Paris last week at which Dr
Oldham[100] gave a full report on his visits only a few
days before to Berlin and Hannover. I had been ready
before the Meeting, as I had let some friends know,
to go with Bishop Ammundsen to Düsseldorf in order
to see some of the leaders of the Confessional Synod
privately if that were considered useful. Oldham
however, after talking it over with Praeses Koch and
others, reported at Paris that it was not desirable
in the interests of the Confessional Synod leaders
who might be exposed to danger. Nevertheless on
Saturday night, just after my return from Paris,
Bonhoeffer rang up, having flown over from Berlin
to see me, at the special request of Koch. Praeses
Koch said that he was sorry that I had not come to
Düsseldorf and he had advised against my coming,
for it would have been useful, but he realised what
had happened. He wanted me to write a letter for
the Meeting of the Confessional Synod today and
tomorrow. He also wanted me to be ready to come at
the shortest possible notice if there were a very
grave necessity. I am of course ready to go if such
a grave necessity arose. The reason I am writing
to you is this. I should be of little use by myself
owing to my ignorance of German. Supposing — which
Heaven forbid — that such a necessity arose, would
it be possible for you to meet me in Berlin? I
could telephone to you from here to ask whether you
could come if the day were to arrive. This letter
however can state the situation more easily than a
telephone call. I expect what it would mean would be

that 1 should, if the necessity arose, fly to Berlin
and ask you to meet me at some convenient place in
Berlin, say at the Grand Hotel am Knie.
　　With all best wishes,
　　Yours ever,
　　George Cicestr

Ribbentrop replied to Bell's letter on 25th May, justifying the course of events because "quite a number of members of the Confessional Synod are evidently misused by certain irresponsible forces who are opposed to our National Socialist State: a great deal of the trouble comes from this source".[101] Ribbentrop's excuses hardly impressed Bell.

A further step to bring the Church under State control was undertaken on 16th July by the creation of a new Ministry of Church Affairs, headed by Dr Hans Kerrl.[102] It turned out to be a bad omen. Bell desired to know what Kerrl was up to. He thought Koch and Bonhoeffer would up date him on this event at a meeting (from 18th to 25th August) of the Executive Committee of Life and Work at Chamby – sur - Montreux, Switzerland, to which both the pastors had been invited. The Germans did not come. So Bell decided to return to London via Germany. At Munich, he spoke with Praeses Koch, Bishop Hans Lilje (Hannover) and Pastor Hans Asmussen (all from the Confessional Church) on 12th September. Bell then went on to Berlin. Here the Minister for Church Affairs, Dr Kerrl arranged a meeting with Hitler's deputy, Rudolf Hess. He and his wife received Bell at their home on 20th September. Bell raised the question of the independence of the Church, stressing the fact that "the Churches of the world had a great battle to fight against the things which were hostile to Christianity, and they wanted the full strength of the German Evangelical Church in this common fight".[103] Hess assured Bell that Hitler had no desire to meddle in the affairs of the Church. On 21st September Bell was Ribbentrop's guest. Here he met Kerrl, with whom Bell talked at length. Kerrl assured the English Bishop that the Confessional Church would have a full place in the life of the German nation. All that he had heard from Hess, Ribbentrop and Kerrl Bell regarded with much reserve. From Berlin Bell proceeded to Hannover where he met Bishop Marahrens on 23rd September. Marahrens, noted Bell, was "most courteous and charming", - a "very dignified man, rather of the old school, and the contrast between him and these modern men of Hitler must be very great".[104] Marahrens "spoke very gratefully" of the ecumenical relations and of the way in which they and Bell "had helped the German Church", and he strongly "wished to maintain these links".[105]

Bell had no doubt in his mind that he shared Marahrens wishes. Back in England Bell began his correspondence with Hess, reminding him of the questions Bell had raised in Berlin. Hess promptly replied expressing optimism, but very little of this was evident in the actual deeds of the State. By a decree of 3rd October Kerrl appointed a State Church Committee of eight members, headed by the seventy year old Dr Wilhelm Zoellner,[106] former General Superintendent of the Evangelical Church in Westphalia. This Committee was now to represent the German Evangelical Church. Not long after Zoellner took over the chairmanship of the State Church Committee, he issued an appeal for co-operation with the Committee and for loyalty to the State. Many (though not all) members of the Confessional Church, led by Pastor Niemöller, refused to answer Zoellner's call.

Bell had not written to Koechlin for a while. He did so on 21st October, telling Koechlin all about his own activities, and all that he had heard lately from Germany:

```
        The Palace,
        Chichester
        21 October 1935

        My dear Koechlin,
        We have not corresponded for some time and I
    write in haste now. I was in Germany last month. I
    had a very useful talk for an hour with Rudolph Hess,
    and I have been in correspondence with him since.
    He wants, it seemed to me, to have a reasonable and
    happy solution of the Church question, and I have
    put in the form of a Memorandum what I believe the
    fundamental issue to be. He has acknowledged this
    Memorandum with much gratitude. Praeses Koch knew
    that I was seeing him, and approved. Praeses Koch
    also asked me to see Ribbentrop and Kerrl if I could
    in Berlin. I did so and had nearly two hours with
    Kerrl, and a most friendly conversation. I reported
    all these conversations not only to Lilje at leisure
    but also to Bishop Marahrens on whom I called at
```

Hannover on my way back to England on September 21st . The fundamental issue as I stated it both to Kerrl and to Hess may be stated as follows: Does the National Socialist Government intend and wish to bring the Church under the hammer of the State and make it a State department from all practical points of view, or does it wish to give the Church a life and a place of its own, free to preach its Gospel and to live according to its faith? Most emphatically the answer from each was that there was no desire for a State Church or for a Church under the hammer of the State, but every desire for a Church able and free to live its own life.

Now I have just had a message from Berlin brought to me from Kerrl to the effect that a Joint Committee has been appointed on which Zoellner serves and others who represent both German Christians and the Confessional Church, i.e. not purely a Committee of neutrals but lacking, not unnaturally, the well-known leaders on both sides. The way in which this Joint Committee has been interpreted in our English papers is, in Kerrl's judgement and Ribbentrop's, unfair. I am told that the statement which was issued on Friday in the form of an appeal to the German Evangelical Church and signed by all the members of the Joint Committee, was approved by Marahrens and that Marahrens was present when it was drafted. Further, Kerrl had nothing whatever to do with the drafting of the statement, but was most happy when he saw its complete text. My informant tells me that Pastor von Bodelschwingh is working sympathetically with Kerrl, and he believes approves of the joint statement, but he is to verify this statement and let me know on Wednesday in London at Lambeth Palace where I shall be.

Now it is suggested that a reserved statement from somebody in England welcoming this step towards a solution should be made now. It is further said that if this step is a genuine step, as they believe, and it is disregarded or ignored, it is very discouraging to the National Socialist Government. It is also suggested that what would really be useful would be a statement intimating one's awareness of the new move but at the same time leaving it quite open to the writer - say myself - to criticise later developments if they are not in accordance with the spirit of this document.

I know one has to be very careful, so I do not wish to do anything rash. At the same time I want to be reasonably encouraging, as I feel sure you will appreciate. Kerrl and Hess, to whom for personal reasons I am in a position to write at any time now, have shown their goodwill and have been very reasonable in their conversations with me personally, and I believe that the fact that I have taken a little trouble to understand them has been a help in the present situation. So you will understand that there is something to be said for a bare recognition of their efforts if I can be satisfied that the efforts are genuine and that Marahrens and Co. would feel sympathetic to a short letter, say from myself, in *The Times*.

Let me know what you think, and the sooner the better. I can be reached at Lambeth Palace till Thursday night by air mall - otherwise Chichester.

Yours ever,

p.p. George Cicestr

(Dictated by the Bishop of Chichester but not signed owing to absence.)

Dr. Koechlin responded on 23rd October:

The Right Rev. the Lord Bishop of Chichester,
The Palace,
Chichester

My dear Lord Bishop,

I have been very glad to read you again and to hear from you what you very kindly tell me about your different important interviews in Berlin.

As to the advisability of an article to be written by you in *The Times*, I am a little hesitant and embarrassed to answer your question, as I have not been last months in very close touch with the German Church developments and as I have in fact not been in Germany since the Dahlem Confessional Synod just a year ago. From what I know and feel I might be allowed to bring before you the following.

I am convinced that some day the State had to lay a new constitutional foundation for the official

Church life in Germany. The old foundation of the constitution of Weimar and the new constitution of Wittenberg with the Reich bishop were broken and the basis of the all too well known Church elections of 1933, was on the one side impossible and on the other side hardly possible to be changed. The line of emergency Church law, taken in Dahlem, could not lead to a definite result without decisive co-operation of the State. I think also that Bishop Heckel was right in telling me that the new financial arrangements taken by Minister Kerrl were necessary, as the provisional arrangements inaugurated by Praeses Koch and others did not work sufficiently all over the place as to give to the State real guarantee that the Church taxes were used in an irreproachable way.

The move of the State in creating the Church-Ministry headed by Reichsminister Kerrl was, as I feel, a real programme.

The Ausschuss [the Committee] chosen and put into office by Minister Kerrl cannot, as I feel, be opposed to. The effect of the Reich bishop Müller being put aside was a happy one. The men chosen offer as a unit strong guarantees. It seems to be certain that the election of this Reichs-Church-Executive took place not only in accord with Bishop Marahrens, but also with the Bishops of Bavaria and Württemberg.

As to the appeal it was new to me to hear that Bishop Marahrens was present when it was drafted. I do not think however that your information, according to which Pastor von Bodelschwingh approved it also, can be right. He seems to suffer from a complete nervous breakdown, complicated by a light pneumonia obliging him to leave every kind of work for weeks and possibly months. He cannot at any rate have been in the picture in an effective and really authoritative way. The wording of the appeal seems on the whole to be a not all too unhappy compromise. It gives me however some concern to see a sentence like the following: "We stand by the rebirth of the Nation on the foundation of race, blood and soil".

This concession to national-socialist ideology does not give any hope for the distress of non-Aryan Christians. It has to be noted that Reich bishop Kerrl in two speeches soon after the issue of the appeal made very unclear and even dangerous statements. On 17 October he said in the German Academy for economic questions: "I do not stress on the State Church because I wish an evangelical Church coming out of innermost conviction by its own free will to our State and it has to come to it (!), if it wishes to live, because it has to deal with the same members of the Nation with which we have to deal with the fellowship of the blood into which God has placed us ... This Nation is marching with the Leader".

In a second speech addressed to the press, Kerrl has emphasised also that the appeal has made the very happy and definite distinction between Christian doctrine and Christian life, leaving the life to the State and the doctrine to the Church. He has added words on the German Faith Movement being really astonishing. He said that this Movement could not be called to be godless, that in the contrary faith came in it to birth and showed how much national-socialism was a religious movement staying every where for positive faith and life, also for positive Christendom. May be that he had to make concessions to the party ideology and party policy, going even a step further than the sentence of the Church appeal quoted above. At any rate one has to remember that Kerrl is not party leader and that important party leaders like Rosenberg[107] have a power he has not got in spite of his ministerial standing. Party interference of dangerous character are still very possible. For this reason I am glad to think that you intend to be as cautious as possible in any approval of the new German appeal, because I wonder if you ought to back the new authority and not wait for some clear facts giving the true interpretation of the wording of the appeal. I know that Bishop [Ernst Ludwig] Dietrich of Hessen, in spite of orders given to him, did not allow last Sunday confessional preachers to preach in their own parish and church and that he said quite clearly to have a promise of Minister Kerrl that if he should go his own way, nothing would happen to him. Dietrich has a very strong position in the party. In other counties the situation seems to be equally unclear.

Another important consideration to be born in

mind is that evidently Hitler needs peace in the Church and that his nearest friends like Hess and Ribbentrop see every interest in giving to the first steps of Kerrl and his Church-Executive as much weight as possible, even before the Church-Executive has come to act. They evidently have the greatest interest of having the authority of your approval on their side to be in a position to put in their papers words used by you in favour of the State efforts to bring about peace in the Church. Your name would become a weight on their side of the balance as it has been on the side of the Confessional Synod these last two years.

In view of all these facts I think the words "wait and see" have their full right and importance. I quite understand and approve of your wish to acknowledge in a fair way good steps made by official Germany in the Church question, but after all one has seen and heard in the years behind us, one would like to wait for more guarantees that a really acceptable solution has been inaugurated by these very first steps, as important as they may be. At any rate you ought in writing to be very clear in your interpretation of what has been achieved in Germany, including even a strong advice as to the tendency which the next steps ought to have. In this respect I am very glad to think that you are in the possibility of writing at any time to the Ministers Kerrl and Hess.

If I should hear important facts arising out of the situation, I would be glad to let them be known to you.

With my very best regards,
Cordially yours,
[A. Koechlin]

The opposition of some of the members of the Confessional Church to Zoellner's appeal had invited suppression of their activities by the State. Bell felt greatly distressed, and he wrote a forceful letter to Hess on 2nd December. "The imposition of a very severe censorship on all written and printed matter proposed for distribution by the Confessional Church authorities has been announced from police headquarters in Berlin: and further action of a very grave kind is announced as impending against the whole organisation of the Confessional Church. So stern an attack on an organisation which (as was stated in our conversation on September 20th) included the great majority of churchmen as members or sympathisers must appear to impartial observers as a hostile action taken by the State, and a denial of a corporate existence of its own to the Church, robbing the Church of freedom to preach the Christian teaching. I would, with the utmost respect, as well as with a readiness on my part to give any help in my power and with all earnestness, beg that this freedom may still be preserved".[108] Hess was noncommittal in his reply. It is, however, probable that Hess communicated Bell's remonstrance to Zoellner and, perhaps, even suggested that the Committee chairman might explain the situation to Bell.

That the Confessional Church was not united in its support of Zoellner became evident at its Synod, which met at Bad Oeynhausen from 17th-22nd February 1936. A group under Pastor Niemöller voted against, and another under Bishop Marahrens vote for co-operation with Zoellner. This dissent was exploited by Zoellner. He wrote an unusually long letter to Bell explaining the development within the German protestant Church. The letter was personally delivered to Bell by one prominent German Christian, Dr Wahl.

```
    D.Wilh.ZOELLNER,Wirkl.Geh.Oberkonsistorialrat
Generalsuperintendent Berlin-Charlottenburg 2
    Marchstrasse 2
    Chairman of the German Church Committee
    1 April 1936
    The   Right   Reverend,   The   Lord   Bishop   of
Chichester,
    The Palace, Chichester, Sussex, England

    My Lord Bishop!
    You   have   had   the   kindness   of   repeatedly
accepting   informations   on   occurences   within   our
German Protestant Church. Allow me to outline in
this letter the situation of the Church as it is
today when in my opinion an important stage in the
development within the German Protestant Church has
been reached.
    By a decree of the German  Minister for Church
Affairs   on   October   3,   1935,   with   the   material
previsions   of   which   you   are   probably   acquainted,
the German Church Committee (Reichskirchenauschuss
```

– RKA) whose chairman I am was entrusted with the task of directing and representing the German Protestant Church. The said decree created an absolutely new situation in our Church. For thereby the functions which according to the Constitution of the German Protestant Church were the Reich Bishop's and the Ecclesiastical Ministry's, viz. The direction and representation of the Church were transferred to the RKA. Accordingly the latter assumes the full rights of the Church government of the German Protestant Church, although the decree of October 3, 1935 provides that this shall be subject to limits concerning both time and matter, in as much as the Church government shall only be in the hands of the RKA up to the time when a definitely organised Church may be given the possibility of solving her own religious problems in full liberty and peace.

Here I must briefly characterise the German Church Committee's position regarding the State. The statement that we are a Church government appointed by the State is not to the point. It is not correct too, as is sometimes alleged, that the German Ministry for Ecclesiastical Affairs had assumed ex officio, on behalf of the State, the control of the entire ecclesiastical life, thus constituting a sort of supreme authority of the German Protestant Church. It is just the reverse. In the first instance the German Ministry for Church Affairs, on behalf of the State, has only undertaken the tasks that formerly were those of the "Kultusministerium" and the German Ministry for the Interior respectively. By its institution no new law regarding the relations of Church and State (StaatsKirchenrecht) has been created. With regard to the particular distressed condition of the Protestant Church, it is true, this German Ministry for Church Affairs has been set a limited special task, viz. The task of helpful legal redress for the restoration of order in the church. The direction and representation of the German Protestant Church has been placed into the hands of the Church Committees. These Committees consist of irreproachable churchmen – as a rule they are duly appointed and ordained ministers of God's holy word. Thus the members look upon themselves as men of the Church in the State, not as

men of the State in the Church. They perform their
duties in accordance with ecclesiastical standards
and constitute the Church government of the German
Protestant Church.

As churchmen we have welcomed this form of
legal redress offered by the State to the Church,
as it alone could furnish the basis for preventing
the impending schism which would divide the German
Protestant Church into two Churches, an official
"Reichskirche" and a Bekenntniskirche (Confessional
Church). To-day we can say that within the 4 ½ months
of our activities we have succeeded in largely
restoring order and authority within the German
Protestant Church. The RKA and the Territorial
and Provincial Church Committees appointed in
connection with it are the lawful holders of
authority in external and internal Church affairs,
a condition precedent to the success of their work.
In order to achieve the restoration of an orderly
state of affairs in the various spheres within the
shortest possible time and with complete success we
have so far appointed Committees corresponding to
the RKA for 6 Territorial Churches and within the
old Prussion Territorial Church for 7 more Church
provinces, which Committees have already succeeded,
partly by way of decrees issued by them in settling
the most urgent cases. For the Protestant Lutheran
Territorial Churches of Hannover and Brunswick
Church governments were instituted instead of
Committees in order to create legitimate bodies
for these territories. All these Committees consist
of trustworthy churchmen, among them many who came
from the Confessional Movement. The Hanoverian
Church government, for instance, is presided over
by Landesbischof Mararhrens.

This satisfactory progress of our work does not
deceive us as regards the fact that to this day there
exists a struggle of the various spiritual currents
within our Church, although we think that we have
definitely prevented a separation of the German
Protestant Church into two Churches. It is not easy
to outline these currents quite correctly. Besides
a numerically insignificant group of determined
"German Christians" there is a group which must
not be underrated of clergymen and congregations
who have kept aloof from Church policies and have

joined no group, without however having abandoned in any respect whatever the ground of the Church. The spiritual discussions within the Church are also quite materially influenced by the clergymen and congregations united in the "Confessional Church", only the latter reflect spiritual and ecclesiastical movements greatly differing from each other.

From the outset the attitude of the "Confessional Church" towards the work of the Church Committees has not been clear. Whereas at the beginning of our work individual members of the Confessional Church joyously agreed to become members of the Committees, and Landesbischof D. Marahrens declared on December 6, 1935, that he together with his Hanoverian Council of Brethren agreed to cooperate with and support the Church Committees, the attitude of the majority of the "Confessional Church" was reserved, temporising and often negative. Even the 4th Synod of the Confessional Church which met at Oeynhausen from February 18 to February 22, 1936, has not really passed beyond this divided attitude of the "Confessional Church". For, whereas in the first theological statement made by the Synod, which contained a confessional statement in writing, an agreement was arrived at as to the organisation and the duties of a genuine Church government, opinions differed widely when the practical problem had to be solved whether the work of the Church Committees should now be rejected unconditionally and from the outset or whether the individual measures taken by them should be tested on hand of Scripture and Creed, the attitude to be observed conforming to the result of such test. The Synod's final resolution purporting that up to the definite reorganisation of the Church the bodies of control appointed by the Confessional Church "shall test on hand of the Creed the measures taken by the Church Committees and fraternally advise the congregations and clergymen on the attitude to be observed by them", has not been adopted unanimously by the entire Synod. For a third part of the members of the Synod (just the representatives of the moderate South-German opinion) had to depart before the conclusion of the Synod for reasons connected with their official duties. A further scanty third part had placed their personal diverging opinion on record in connection with the respective propositions in the theological statement. One of these members who made a separate statement is the Präses of the Confessional Synod, D. Koch, Oeynhausen. Some of these statements purported a radical NO, others a readiness to co-operate with the Committees. Accordingly two things are apparent:

1. The Synod has not been able to pass a resolution binding upon all, but is dissenting in itself.

2. The theological statement regarding the attitude of the Confessional Church towards the Committees is contradictory in itself, as it tries to couple the two views - the rejection and the recognition of the Committees. But even this statement, which at the conclusion demands a further testing of the Committees' acts by the controlling bodies of the Confessional Church, and accordingly not their rejection on principle, has been rejected by part of the members as being too strong. Therefore the report in the foreign press that at Oeynhausen 90% of the Confessional Church had declared against the Committees is absolutely incorrect. If the attitude of the Synod towards the Committees shall be expressed in numbers it may be stated without exaggeration that most representatives of the Councils of Brethren of Old Prussia reject the Committees, it is true, whereas a large majority of the Councils of Brethren of South Germany and of the rest of Prussia are prepared to co-operate with them. This state of things was given expression in the fact that the Vorläufige Kirchenleitung ("Provisional Board of the Confessional Church"), of which Landesbischof D. Marahrens, Präses D. Koch, Oberkirchenrat Breit, etc. are members, resigned at the meeting of the Synod. The remaining radical group have appointed a new provisional board consisting of three members, all of them representatives of the radical opinion of the Old-Prussian Councils of Brethren. This committee cannot be considered any longer a joint representation of the ecclesiastical circles hitherto united in the "Confessional Church". The attitude, by no means uniform, of these circles is illustrated inter alia by the fact that just a few days ago it has been possible, after some

difficulties which existed at first, had been overcome, to organise in the particularly difficult province of Westfalia a Church Committee consisting of four members presided over by a leading member of the "Confessional Church".

Recapitulating I may point out that for many years I myself in my ecclesiastical office, have defended a central prevalence of the Creed. Therefore I have always fully sympathised with the "Confessional Movement", but I must disagree when from a movement within the Church, arising out of a momentary situation in a fight, and justified by it, the false thesis is deduced that the creation of a separate "Confessional Church" was concerned. There are not – this is the clear result of the development in the Church during the last six months – two Protest Churches in Germany but there is one Church, with a variety of ecclesiastical currents but with one legitimate Church government.

The Church government bears and exercises the responsibility and the representation of the entire Church. Of this responsibility I, as chairman of the RKA, am aware also as regards ecumenical relations, and I am certain that the uniformly organised representation of the German Protestant Church has restored an essential clearness also for the ecumenical relations. I am happy that the German Protestant Church, as a member Church of Life and Work again can and will provide for its ecumenical representation in full ecclesiastical independence.

I am inclined to hope that also on the part of the Churches ecumenically connected with us this new situation will be fully appreciated, and the more so as there is now no longer any occasion for the doubts which temporarily were raised within the ecumenical community against a Church government of past days.

I have caused these statements to be translated into English for your convenience; a copy of the translation is enclosed herewith.

I remain, my Lord Bishop,
with sincerest regards,
Yours very truly,

D. Zoellner

Before Bell would answer, he wisely thought that he should seek Koechlin's opinion. So Bell dispatched a copy of Zoellner's letter to Koechlin for his comments. Koechlin answered on 28th May.

28 May 1936
The Right Rev. the Lord Bishop of Chichester,
The Palace,
Chichester

My dear Lord Bishop,
The letter you have written to me on April 29th and the letter of Dr Zoellner were constantly in my thought during these last weeks. Without showing to him Dr Zoellner's letter, I had yesterday an interchange of thoughts and views with Karl Barth, who, as you will imagine, is still in close contact with the German Confessional Church and had only a few days ago here in Basle a short visit of Pastor Niemöller. I had also the opportunity of discussing the whole problem confidentially with another personality in closest contact with the Church life of Southern Germany and especially near to Bishop Wurm. As the result of these conversations I might state the following:
First I am not quite clear how far Dr Zoellner is correct in stating that the "right of directing and representing the Church" has passed into his own hands. The Kirchenausschüsse [Church Administrative Committees], as far as I know, are legally limited to regulating the organisational functions of the Church life without power of any spiritual direction of the Church. The Reichskirchenausschuss and the other Ausschüsse are institutions "for time", limited to the date of autumn 1937 or, and even if they can guarantee earlier the normal functioning of organisational Church life before that date, bound to leave their place earlier. It is theoretically a fact that Reich bishop Müller has not been legally forsaken, neither the Bishops created by him. There is of course some kind of understanding, probably approved and even desired "for time" by party and state according to which Bishop Müller and his men are living a private life, but ready at any time, without any legal change being necessary,

to resume their former functions. The Reich bishop still is signing his books and letters with "Reich bishop ". Bishop Koch and Dietrich are going about visiting parishes and allowed to do so by party-authorities in spite of all remonstrance of the Reichskirchenausschuss.

I do not wish to say that one might expect the Reich bishop probably resuming one day again his functions, but the possibility exists and evidently State and party at least do not wish to render such a possibility impossible.

It is certainly a fact that the Reichskirchenausschüsse have gone further than the limits legally traced to their activity and have very largely tried to direct and represent the German Evangelical Church. They certainly succeeded in many parts of Germany to bring about order and more peace, but it is equally a fact that very often when they tried to change impossible situations, agreeable to local State and party authorities, their power at once failed to get the desirable result. I know personally the President of the Hessen-Nassau Landeskirchenausschuss, who, forced to follow the Bishop Dietrich to do what he, the President, desired to make impossible, and being obliged by the State to act against the Confessional Church, has become a broken man asking his friends to think of him in their prayers as of a man being a captive of the State, because in fact he is, as Zoellner is, a State employee.

The Oecumenical Movement would be mistaken in accepting definitely the Reichskirchenausschuss of Dr Zoellner as being the definite legal authority directing and representing the German Evangelical Church. However it might in fact certainly be the case that this Reichskirchenausschuss has the largest power of all German Church authorities and that for the moment it has taken the place of the old Reichskirchenregierung of Reichsbishop Müller through which the Oeccumenical Movement was until now connected with the German Evangelical Church as a whole. Heckel with his Aussenamt [Foreign department] is certainly now dependent from Zoellner.

For this reason I feel that the Oecumenical Council ought to accept the situation as such, deal with Zoellner instead of Heckel, but with all the reservations necessary to guarantee the possibility of another attitude if the situation should change again in Germany.

This possibility exists, seems even to be very probable. Hitler in one of his great addresses of March said, as different trusted men have heard through the radio, that the national-socialist movement was bound to go his way over "parties, states (Länder, i.e. Bavaria, Baden etc.) and confessions". In the reprint of the address these words were left out. But the meaning of the Führer in this respect is very evidently clear. The school policy, the growing power of Rosenberg, the development of the Hitler youth, the programme of the new national-socialist leader-training castles (Ordensburgen) are illustrating this fact. And there seems hardly to be any one, even in the Reichskirchenausschüsse, who does not know that the decisive fight between Church and State, Gospel and national-socialism is still to come. It is nearly for all concerned only a question of tactics, if the Church might come into a better position for this fight in regulating with the help of the Reichskirchenausschüsse its situation, or if the way of Niemöller is the better one. In judging this situation, one has at least to bear in mind that the Reichskirchenausschüsse in the last analysis and in spite of the personal integrity and view of the men leading them, are instruments of the State.

As long as the attitude of the State towards the Church is as unclear as at present, I think the Oecumenical Council has to be careful not to identify definitely the Reichskirchenausschüsse, being institutions of the State, with the Church itself.

As to the Confessional Church, we have to take into account the fact that the Churches of Bavaria, of Württemberg, of Baden, even of Hannover have not left the Confessional Church, even though Bishop Marahrens is working with Dr Zoellner. The interpretation of the decisions of Oeyenhausen may be different here and there and the practical actual attitude towards the new Government of the Confessional Church might be different too. The fact is that Bishop Marahrens and his provisional

Church Government has passed over peacefully and completely the power and papers of the former provisional Church Government to the new Church Government instituted in Oeynhausen. It is equally a fact that the great Lutheran Churches, though they have come to a closer connection with each other ("der lutherische Pakt") have not instituted any sort and form of Church Government.

If Württemberg and Bavaria do not place themselves under the new Church Government of the Confessional Church, they do not either place themselves under the Reichskirchenausschuss, maintaining their complete independence of an intact Church.

One might say that the different circles belonging to the Confessional Church are partly moving forward towards the Reichskirchenausschüsse giving to the so called efforts of the State a fair chance and hoping in doing so to find their own chance. Others refuse to do it for reason of principle or reason of tactics. Those going forward, go forward partly one step, partly two and three steps, but all of them without an exception take care to leave the bridge behind them intact so that they might go back and lean upon the Confessional Church as soon as a new decisive fight has to be fought through. One might even say that for the sake of the whole Church it is urgently necessary that at least one wing (radical or extreme, as it may be called) is maintaining strictly the principle of the freedom of the revelation of God in the Gospel against the totalitarian claim of the State even over the Church.

Psychologically and politically it is natural that as long as the State is seeming to understand and to help the Church, the front of the Confessional Church is becoming less compact, but it is to be expected that with every new attack of the State either on the Prussian side or in Munich or Stuttgart, the confessional front will become united again.

For this reason it would be a great mistake if the ecumenical Movement would not any more stand to the decisions of Fanö. We might before long have in Germany again a situation very similar to that with which we were confronted in 1934 and it could be for the Confessional Church and for the German Evangelical Church as a whole of greatest importance if the Oecumenical Council and yourself on its behalf, based on official decisions taken and maintained, act as you have done these last two years.

May I add one further aspect illustrating the situation. The German foreign missions are refusing absolutely to place themselves under the Reichskirchenausschuss, but are maintaining their very close contact with the Confessional Church without being organisationally and fully part of it. The Youth Movement is taking a similar attitude. Missions and the Youth Movement especially are under greatest pressure coming from the State. The missionary Societies with their literature and with other aspects of their work are in constant difficulties. The Reichskirchenausschüsse cannot help them. They are even a danger for them. Their hope is in the existence of the Confessional Church. I think they would not understand if the Oecumenical Council would give up its relationship with the Confessional Church of Germany.

Hoping to be able to give you more information after my interview with Pastor Riethmüller and my short visit in Stuttgart next week, I am yours very sincerely,

[A. Koechlin]

Bell thanked Koechlin for his "extremely valuable letter" and wrote to tell him how he shared the same views:

The Palace,
Chichester
5 June 1936

My dear Koechlin,
I am most grateful for your extremely valuable letter of May 28th about Dr Zoellner. What you say harmonises very much indeed with my own *prima facie* view. I have had one or two opportunities of talk with Germans in this country, and I had an indirect idea of the views of Pfarrer Maas from a Non-Aryan German teacher who has just come over. But your quotation from Hitler's speech in March is most

significant, and what you say about the meaning of the Führer with regard to Confessions, as well as Parties and States, is very clear.

Somehow or other I think our Administrative Committee must make it clear to Zoellner that while for certain limited administrative purposes communications may be made with him, there must be no sort of final committal of the Universal Council, nor must there be any abandonment of the stand taken at Fanö. Nor must there be any discontinuance of the relations which we have had and enjoy with the Confessional Church.

The way of putting all this, with the necessary courtesy and the essential limitations, will require much thought. I should be most grateful for anything you can tell me after your interview with Pastor Riethmüller and your visit to Stuttgart.

With all best wishes, and warmest thanks,
Yours ever,
George Cicestr

Bell was now in a better position to answer Zoellner's letter.

The Palace, Chichester
23 June 1936

Dear Dr Zoellner,

I am now in a position to write to you in reply to your very important and courteous letter of April 1st in which you were kind enough to give me an outline of the situation within the German Protestant Church in view of the fact that in your opinion an important stage had been reached in the development within that Church.

Once again I would thank you for that letter, and assure you of the deep interest with which I have read it.

The Administrative Committee of the Universal Christian Council for Life and Work met in Paris last week, and though most unhappily I was not myself able to be present at the Session, I have received a personal report from M. Henriod who has since stayed with me in Chichester. Moreover as he had enjoyed the great advantage of personal conversation with yourself in Berlin, and had various opportunities of acquainting himself with the developments at first hand, I am in a much better position to reply than I was at Easter. I may say that copies of your letter were in the hands of members of the Administrative Committee well before the Meeting. It is in the light of all these facts that I now send you an answer.

The Administrative Committee and the officers of the Universal Christian Council, in between the Meetings of the Council, are bound to be guided by any Resolution which may have been passed setting out matters of principle, should any situation arise to which such principle might be applied. On no occasion have principles been laid down with such clearness as on the occasion when the situation in the German Evangelical Church was considered at the last Meeting of the Council, held at Fanö in August, 1934. A resolution of great importance was passed, and by this Resolution the Council and its various sub-Committees are bound, until any other decision is taken by the Council itself. This Resolution, amongst other things, expressed the Council's desire "to remain in friendly contact with all groups in the German Evangelical Church". It also instructed the Administrative Committee to follow up the principle which the Resolution set forth.

In the Resolution at Fanö the Council refrained from expressing a judgement with regard to the legitimacy of the different Church organisations then in existence. The Administrative Committee, in considering questions relating to the representation of the German Evangelical Church at oecumenical gatherings, and notably at the Oxford Conference on Church, Community and State, is not in a position to adopt any different procedure. The manner of representation must be decided within the German Evangelical Church itself, as these questions involve the constitution and authority of the Church. I entirely realise the extraordinary difficulties of the immediate situation, and of coming to a conclusion satisfactory all round with regard to the composition of a delegation representing the German Evangelical Church. I also realise that much has happened since 1934.

The members of the Administrative Committee are very much alive to the struggle of the various spiritual currents within the German Evangelical

Church to which your letter alludes. I appreciate further the statement which your letter of April 1st makes, that the Church Committee over which you preside has been entrusted by the State with "a limited special task, viz. the task of helpful legal redress for the restoration of order in the Church". Nor do I overlook all that you say with regard to the steps that have been taken and are being continued, and the hope that in due course a definite reorganisation may be achieved in the Church after a manner and following a method which will be welcome to all. But the very careful exposition in your letter to me of the various difference which are still unreconciled, makes it impossible to regard the present position as more than a provisional position, or as more than, to use your own words, "an important stage in the development".

Accordingly the Administrative Committee, in loyalty alike to the facts known to it and also to the Resolution adopted at Fanö, cannot cease to maintain the connection with the Confessional Synod of the German Evangelical Church which was there deliberately authorised and endorsed by the Council. In a very special section of the Fanö Resolution the Council assured its brethren in the Confessional Synod of the German Evangelical Church of its prayers and heart-felt sympathy in their witness to the principles of the Gospel, and of its resolve to maintain close fellowship with them. That Resolution must give us our direction to which we are obliged to adhere.

It seems to me however that this very fact lends great force to the suggestion which M. Henriod made personally when in Berlin, viz. that an agreement should be reached, in which the Confessional Synod would play its full share, for the adequate representation of the German Evangelical Church in oecumenical work. I would, with very great respect, and yet with serious conviction, beg you to respond to this earnest suggestion.

With regard to the Meeting at Chamby itself, I am very greatly cheered to learn from M. Henriod that you have every intention of coming yourself. I hope very much that a full representation of the different currents in the Evangelical Church may be present at Chamby, in view of the grave importance

of the matters to be discussed, and the laying
down of the programme for the Oxford Conference.
We rely much on your own help, and the help of your
colleagues, in the whole task of preparation for
the Oxford Conference. We also wish definitely that
those who are identified most closely with the work
of the Confessional Synod should come to Chamby,
and we wish definitely that they may be represented
under conditions and in a way in accordance with
their own conscientious convictions. The members of
the Universal Christian Council are usually chosen
by the Sections, though the Council has power to
co-opt a certain number of consultative members. In
the judgement of the Administrative Committee it
ought to be possible in these circumstances, by the
exercise of goodwill on all sides and by an effort
of mutual understanding, to bring it about, without
implicating the Council in controversies internal
to the German Church, that the Council at the next
meeting, which will be concerned principally with
the preparations for the Oxford Conference, should
have the advice and help of persons representing
different parties, within the German Evangelical
Church, who will be able to make the largest and
richest contribution to the life and thought of the
oecumenical movement.

I need hardly add that the work of Chamby will
be constructive work, with the Oxford Conference
almost entirely in view, and I should myself hope
that matters of controversy may be avoided.

I remain, with sincerest regards,
Yours very truly,
George Cicestr

Bell had made it abundantly clear to Zoellner that he wished that
"those who are identified most closely with the work of the Confessional
Synod should come" to Chamby, where the Administrative Committee
of Life and Work were to meet from 21st-25th August to discuss not
only the German position, but also the programme of the international
Church conference to be held at Oxford in July 1937. Would Zoellner
meet Bell's wishes? Bell wanted to know more about Zoellner and sought
Koechlin's assistance. Koechlin supplied the needed information, for
which Bell was most thankful.

The Palace,
Chichester
8 July 1936

My dear Koechlin,
I am most grateful for your very interesting
and important letter of July 3rd . What you say about
Zoellner's position in the oecumenical relations
is a real surprise. When Wahl came over on April
1st with the letter he certainly led me to think
that Zoellner was now the authority for oecumenical
relations, and that Heckel was under him. So it is
most extraordinary to learn that Heckel has got rid
of Müller without coming under Dr Zoellner. This
seems a quite unprecedented affair. Henriod thought
that Heckel had in fact written Zoellner's letter
to me. This I believe was not the case, for the
letter was written by a much younger man who has
been in touch with Confessional circles but is now
with Zoellner.
I am also very much interested in what you
tell me about the Lutheran Pact being part of
the Confessional Synod still, and looking towards
Praeses Koch as its head. I wonder how he would
justify however the distinction between the
Confessional Synod itself and the Executive of
the Reichsbruderrat? Your mention of Bishop Wurm's
very great reserve, especially in connection with
Zoellner's association with Dr Rehm, is also very
interesting. I am sending herewith a copy of my
reply to Zoellner, so that you may see exactly what
I said. Please keep the letter. I have heard from
Krummacher since and enclose a copy of his reply.
I am delighted to hear that you are now the
permanent representative of the Swiss Churches in
the Oecumenical Council, and hope to come to Chamby.
That will be a very great pleasure and help.
Yours ever,
George Cicestr

Zoellner seemed to be obliging. He himself came to Chamby.
Also present at the meeting were Bonhoeffer, Koch and Bishop Otto
Dibelius[109] (all distinguished representatives of the Confessional Church).

Bell talked to each of them separately, explaining how important it was to be united, and to have a single, yet representative German delegation at Oxford. After much discussion it was agreed that the German delegation would compose of: 1/3 the Confessional Church, 1/3 the Lutheran Church and 1/3 the State Church Committee. Bell was satisfied, so was the Administrative Committee. Zoellner was not so happy with what he had agreed to, and he only realised that he could not keep his promise after having been thoroughly reprimanded by Kerrl on his return to Germany. The difficulties were now reported to Bell. He thought that his personal intervention might ease the situation. So he decided to visit Germany from 28th January to 1st February 1937. Zoellner told him frankly that he could not fulfil the Chamby agreement. From Koch and Dibelius Bell learnt that the position of the Confessional Church had gone from bad to worse. Koch was even being charged with high treason. Dibelius now seriously doubted whether he or his colleagues would be going to Oxford at all. Bell was decidedly distressed to hear all this. After his return to England he wrote to Hess on 15th March and to Ribbentrop on 6th April hoping that an acceptable solution would be found to determine the composition of the German delegation to Oxford. The response was ambiguous. Not only that. The members of the of the Confessional Church were being continually persecuted, some arrested, others forbidden to preach. Then came shocking news. Koechlin reported to Bell that the passports of all the delegates of the Confessional Church (among them Dibelius and Niemöller) chosen to attend the Oxford conference had been confiscated on May 24th. Bell expressed his sadness in his letter to Koechlin.

```
        The Palace,
        Chichester
        28 May 1937
        Private.


        My dear Koechlin,
        Very many thanks for your letter of May 26th. I
        know Dr von Thadden and am very glad to know first-
        hand from you what he has said. I am afraid the
        situation is very serious. As a matter of fact I
        had a letter a fortnight or so ago from Karl Barth,
        telling me that Niemöller was in grave danger, and
        urging me to take action. I asked Karl Barth for
```

details of the danger, but he has not yet replied. Only I at once got into touch with Ribbentrop and von Blomberg, and have heard from Graf von Durckheim, Ribbentrop's right-hand man. The last named tells me that Niemöller has not been arrested, nor has Dibelius, but suggests that they are trying to be martyrs. He writes also (though he marks the letter confidential) that the prospects of a German delegation coming are exceedingly remote. I am following it up with him, for he has promised to send me more details when he has found out more.

But in the meantime Henriod, who was in Berlin in the earlier part of the month, is coming to England next Tuesday or Wednesday, and I am hoping to arrange a meeting between him and Oldham and Sir Walter Moberly and myself, and any other person who is knowledgeable and available. The Germans whom Henriod saw are very anxious to keep in continuous touch with England by a succession of short visits. They also want us to say something, but not at once. I think they want us to say something when it is finally settled that a German delegation is prohibited. It is possible that it may be well for one or two individuals to say something, but I think the most authoritative statement must be made at Oxford.

I am inclined, to suggest on Friday night - and on this I should very much like your reaction - that the Oxford Conference should send a special delegation immediately after Oxford to Berlin, to see the Church leaders and to speak to them, not only in a private way but in a public way, though not necessarily asking for any public answer from them. My thought was possibly that if this seemed a reasonable line of policy, a few people should, well before the Oxford Conference, think out the character of such a statement, and then that a Committee should be appointed at Oxford with regard to the absence of the German delegation, this Committee being able, if so disposed, to make a recommendation for such a delegation to the Oxford Conference. Whether we could have a session of a Section of the Conference in Berlin rather than the delegation, I do not know. But there is something to be said for an adjournment to Berlin to deal with this special point. I wonder what you would think of any statement indicating a recognition on the

part of the members of the Conference of a sense
of the real reasonableness of some of the political
desires of the German people, quite apart from the
Nazi regime.

I entirely agree with what you say about Bishop
Heckel who must certainly not be allowed to come
if others do not come; and what you say about the
Committee of Thirty-five. I wonder what will be the
position of Martin Dibelius and others who are
officers or Chairmen of Commissions. Will they be
allowed to come to the Conference?

Yours ever,

George Cicestr

On 1st July Niemölller was arrested. The Oxford Conference met from 12th to 26th July (1937), without the participation of the delegation of the German Evangelical Church. A very sad moment for Bell. But he would not give up or keep silent. "Silence [he told Archbishop of Canterbury] would be conceived as a betrayal".[110] Together with Koechlin Bell drafted a Message to the German Church. The Message, adopted unanimously by the Conference, acknowledged the afflictions of the Confessional Church, upheld the right to preach the Gospel and appealed to Christians all over the world to pray for their German brethren. The Nazis were furious. Koechlin reported to Bell on 3rd August that orders had been given by the State that "the Message was not to be published in any paper, including Church papers".[111]

The persecution of the members of the Confessional Church continued with more severity. A large number of them had by now been so bullied by the State authorities that they acquiesced and swore allegiance to Hitler and his Reich. But not everyone succumbed to State intimidation. Niemöller was secretly tried in February 1938, found guilty, and then sent to Dachau concentration camp. Others followed. And yet, the Confessional Church, though decidedly weakened, would not totally submit to the dictates of the Nazi State. At the time of the dismemberment of Czechoslovakia in September 1938 it issued a Service of Intercession for Peace, calling for prayer for those "whose country is threatened by war".

Niemöller isolated, it was now Dibelius who kept Bell informed on what was happening in Germany. A fuller insight was given by Koechlin. For this Bell was as ever grateful:

The Palace,
Chichester
14 January 1939

My dear Koechlin,
I am very grateful for your letter of 11th
instant. I have often thought of you during these
last months and of our time together, especially
in Berlin at Easter. How much has happened since
then. I am looking forward very much to seeing you
in Paris at the end of the month.
I am very grateful for the message from
Dibelius. Professor Dodd was here last Sunday, and
the full explanation of what was in Dibelius' mind
is a real help, for it was not absolutely clear from
the correspondence, though Dodd and I both thought
that what comes out clearly in your letter, was the
wise and the desired course. All shall be done, I
feel certain as Dibelius desires in the terms of
your letter.
With all warmest remembrance from us both to
you and your wife,
Yours very sincerely,
George Cicestr

Bell naturally welcomed news and views from Bonhoeffer. On 13th
March 1939 Bonhoeffer wrote to Bell to tell him that he wished to see
the Bishop to discuss with him "so many things":

My dear Lord Bishop,
May I just let you know that I have arrived in
London last night. I am so happy to be here once
again for a short time, and I am looking forward
very much to seeing you soon. A friend of mine,
Pastor Bethge,[112] has come with me and wishes to
bring you a special message from the Provisional
Administration. There are so many things which I
should like to discuss with you, that I should be
very grateful, if you could let me know when and
where 1 could see you. I have found the Leibholz's[113]
well and full of gratitude for all your goodness
and help. It makes me so happy to know that. — I am
afraid the political situation is just now becoming
more tense and precarious. In deep gratitude for

```
all you are doing for us.
     Yours very sincerely,
     Dietrich Bonhoeffer
```

Bonhoeffer again wrote to Bell on 25th March, giving him in detail the chief purpose of his visit to Bell. The letter is a testimony of great confidence that Bonhoeffer had in Bell's personal involvement and in his wisdom:

```
     Westbrook, Westwood Park, London S. E. 23
     25 March 1939

     My dear Lord Bishop,
     Dr. Rieger just tells me that Visser't Hooft[114]
will come to London next week and stay with you at
Chichester. I also understand that the next weekend
does not suit you well for our visit to Chichester.
May I now ask a great favour from you? Would you
kindly tell Visser't Hooft that I am very anxious to
see him during his stay in London? Any time except
Wednesday when I have to be at Oxford would suit me
well. Would you also be so kind as to let me know
any time when I could see you once more before I go
back to Germany? In order not to take too much of
your time when we meet I should like to put before
you the two questions which I am very anxious to
discuss with you before my return to Germany. The
first question concerns the Confessional Church,
the second one is very personal. Please excuse my
troubling you again and again and my placing one
burden after another on your shoulders.
     With regard to the position of the Confessional
Church we feel strongly in Germany that - mainly
owing to travelling difficulties - the relationship
of our Church to the Churches abroad is not as it
ought to be. The responsibility which is placed
upon us makes it more and more necessary to have
a permanent exchange of opinion and the advice
of other Churches. We are fully aware of and
gratefully appreciate what is continually being
done for us from individuals to individuals. But
I think, we must try to go a step further and to
come to some sort of regular co-operation with and
to a better representation of the Confessional
Church at the ecumenical movements. If we are
```

not going to make a decisive step forward in this direction I am afraid we shall very soon be cut off entirely from our brethren abroad, and that would at any rate mean a tremendous loss to us. What I therefore think we should try to get, is a man who could devote all his time to establishing the necessary contacts, to co-operating in the ecumenical meetings and conferences, learning and contributing. I think we failed in earlier years to give our full assistance in advice and fellowship to the Russian Christians; now a similar situation is clearly developing in Germany. Do you not think, my Lord Bishop, it is urgently necessary to avoid a similar failure? Frankly and with all due respect, the German representative in Geneva simply cannot represent the cause of the Confessional Church. So there is a real vacancy which must be filled sooner or later. This is the first question which I should like to raise and to discuss with you before I go home again to see the men of the Brethren Council. I have also an idea in my mind for the eventual financial difficulties.

The second point is of entirely personal character and I am not certain if I may bother you with it. Please, do take it quite apart from the first point. I am thinking of leaving Germany sometime. The main reason is the compulsory military service to which the men of my age (1906) will be called up this year. It seems to me conscientiously impossible to join in a war under the present circumstances. On the other hand, the Confessional Church as such has not taken any definite attitude in this respect and probably cannot take it as things are. So I should cause a tremendous damage to my brethren if I would make a stand on this point which would be regarded by the régime as typical of the hostility of our Church towards the state. Perhaps the worst thing of all is the military oath which I should have to swear. So I am rather puzzled in this situation, and perhaps even more because, I feel, it is really only on Christian grounds that I find it difficult to do military service under the present conditions, and yet there are only very few friends who would approve of my attitude. In spite of much reading and thinking concerning this matter I have not yet made up my mind what I would do under different circumstances. But actually as things are I should have to do violence to my Christian conviction, if I would take up arms "here and now". I have been thinking of going to the Mission Field, not as an escape out of the situation, but because I wish to serve somewhere where service is really wanted. But here also the German foreign exchange situation makes it impossible to send workers abroad. With respect to British Missionary Societies I have no idea of the possibilities there. On the other hand, I still have the great desire to serve the Confessional Church as long as I possibly could.

My Lord Bishop, I am very sorry to add trouble to your trouble. But I thought, I might speak freely to you and might ask your advice. You know the Confessional Church and you know me a bit. So I thought you could help me best. It was with regard to this matter that I wanted to see too.

Please excuse this long letter. I hope to see you soon. Leibholz asks me to thank you for your letter to Dr Lindsay.

In sincere gratitude I am, my Lord Bishop,
Yours sincerely,
Dietrich Bonhoeffer

Bonhoeffer wrote again on 13th April to thank Bell "for the great help you gave me in our talk at Chichester":

13 April, 1939
My dear Lord Bishop,
Before returning to Germany I just wish to thank you once again for the great help you gave me in our talk at Chichester. I do not know what will be the outcome of it all, but it means much to me to realise that you see the great conscientious difficulties with which we are faced. I will let you know as soon as I see the situation clearly. Thank you for all sympathy for our cause.

In sincere gratitude I remain, my Lord Bishop,
Yours ever
Dietrich Bonhoeffer

Bell did not only feel "sympathy for our cause", he publicly manifested his support for the Confessional cause. On 1st July, the first anniversary of Niemöller's arrest, Bell preached at St. Martin-in-the Fields. Through Niemöller's wife, who was allowed to visit her husband once a month, Bell sent letters and other information to Niemöller. Some British politicians, including Lord Cecil, thought that Bell's actions might even harm his German friends. No, assured Bell, in his letter to Cecil on 3rd July (1939): "My action for Pastor Niemöller is very definitely desired and warmly welcomed by N.'s own personal friends, and particularly by his wife, with whom I am in constant touch".[115] Niemöller's wife held the view that "the worst thing that could happen to N. is that he should be forgotten by people outside Germany".[116] His friends in the Confessional Church, wrote Bell, "have no doubt that in the case of the Confessional Church victims, speaking is the right policy".[117]

The spectre of war had now appeared. Hitler intended to destroy not only the German Church but the whole of Europe as well. War was now imminent. What would the Confessional leaders do? Bell had managed to arrange for Bonhoeffer to go to America in June, where he could work as a pastor for the German refugees. Bonhoeffer spent a month over there, but his conscience would not let him prolong his stay. In a moving letter to Bell Bonhoeffer explained his reasons. He was, he wrote, duty bound to work for the Confessional Church at home in Germany. Bonhoeffer thanked Bell "for all help and friendship and real understanding in the past and in the future", and assured him: "We shall never forget you during the coming events".

```
London, S. E. 23
22 July 1939

My dear Lord Bishop,
When you were in London on Thursday I asked
Hildebrandt[118] to tell you that I had already come
back from USA and that I am on my way to Germany.
Unfortunately, he forgot to tell you. Now I can only
write a few words of explanation and to say "good
bye" to you. I shall leave on Tuesday morning.
    On my arrival in New York Dr Leiper[119] very
kindly offered me the post of a refugee pastor
(I mean a pastor for the refugees) in New York.
This post was to be connected with lectures in
various places. Of course, I was rather surprised
about this offer and told Dr Leiper, that I had
```

promised to the Confessional Church to come back at the latest after a year unless the political circumstances would make that impossible. So it was just a question of loyalty whether I could accept a post which by itself would make my return doubtful or even impossible. I discussed the problem with my friends very thoroughly and decided to decline the offer for three reasons: I was bound by my promise to go back next year; there were many Non-Aryan brethren who are much more entitled to such a post; I had got my leave of absence for another purpose.

It was a difficult decision, but I am still convinced, I was not allowed to decide otherwise. That meant early return to Germany. Kindly enough, I was invited by Dr Coffin and Van Dusen to stay at Union Seminary as long as I wanted. But when news about Danzig reached me I felt compelled to go back as soon as possible and to make my decision in Germany. I do not regret my trip to USA, though, of course, it had been undertaken under different presuppositions. I have seen and learned much in the few weeks over there and I am looking forward to my work in Germany again. What sort of personal decisions will be asked from me I do not know. But nobody knows that now.

My passport expires next spring; it is therefore uncertain when I shall be in this country again. Let me thank you today for all help and friendship and real understanding in the past and in the future. We shall never forget you during the coming events. I thank you for what you have done for my brother-in-law and his family. It has meant everything to them. Will you allow me to leave them in this country with the confidence that they may approach you whenever they need advice and help? Of course, their future is unsettled, too, and it will require much patience and much energy before they can start afresh. Nevertheless I am confident that they finally will not suffer more than they can bear.

May I ask you to convey my best regards to Mrs Bell?

I remain, my Lord Bishop, in sincere gratitude,

Yours ever,

Dietrich Bonhoeffer

4

"The Church at all costs to remain the Church"

With the outbreak of war on 1st September direct contact between Bell and the Confessional leaders in Germany became ever more difficult. Bell again sought Koechlin's assistance. A citizen of now neutral Switzerland, and living in Basle, Koechlin's help proved indispensable. Bell wrote to him on 11th September to ask if he would act as an mediator between himself and the Confessional leaders in Germany. Bell also requested Koechlin to communicate to "our brothers in the Confessional Church" that his "affection and fellowship for them is, as indeed goes without saying, unchanged and unbroken".

```
         The Palace,
         Chichester
         11 September 1939


         My dear Koechlin,
         You and I have not exchanged letters for
    sometime but I have constantly thought about you,
    and when Markus Barth was here for a weekend your
    name naturally came up. This is just intended to
    say that I do very much want to keep in touch with
    you during this time of war. I also should heartily
    welcome any means of friendship and fellowship
    with our brothers in the Confessional Church. I
    do not know whether this will be possible through,
    for example, your mediation, but anything that you
    think I can do on my side I shall be only too happy
    to do. And I do want you to know this. My affection
    and fellowship for them is, as indeed goes without
    saying, unchanged and unbroken.
         The new Bishop of Tinnevelly, Stephen Neill,
    was here yesterday. I think you met him at the
    Madras Conference. He is a quite first-rate man.
    I had heard much about him but had never met him
    before. We had a long talk and he was most anxious
    to do anything he could on the spot, for the German
    missions in India. He is hoping to see the Secretary
    of State for India, Lord Zetland, before he returns
    to India, which is quite soon on account of the
    war, and I have told him that he ought to see Paton.
```

He thinks, and of course I agree, that everything
possible should be done to enable their work to
continue.
    Yours ever,
    George Cicestr

Koechlin responded on 17th October. The response was "most welcome" to Bell. In his letter of 9th November to Koechlin Bell referred to the release of German pastors, interned in Britain after the outbreak of hostilities. The internees, German citizens, included not only non-Aryan Christians, but as well pastors, members of the Confessional Church. This development greatly distressed Bell. It embarrassed him so much the more since he had just recently sent a letter to all German refugees sharing with them "a word of special remembrance and sympathy at this sorrowful time". There was no cause to be afraid, he had assured them. There would surely be problems, "resulting from war conditions", but these would be worked out, and not to be forgotten. "We are brethren in adversity. This trouble draws us closer together than before. May God reconcile the nations now at war; may He assuage the suffering which will be so heavy on both sides, and may he give us peace".[120]

The internment problem had to be solved, and without much delay. With the support of Archbishops of Canterbury and York Bell approached the Home Office and obtained the release of the interned pastors. Bell then insisted that the Home Office establish an Advisory Committee to look into other pending cases. This was done. A member of this committee, Dr William Paton,[121] visited various camps and reported on the circumstances under which the internees were living. Bell himself was permitted to see these camps and to talk personally to the inmates. It was important that this information should reach Germany through Koechlin.

    The Palace,
    Chichester
    9 November 1939

    My dear Koechlin,
    Very many thanks for your most welcome letter
of 17th October. It took ten or fourteen days to
arrive. It Is a real pleasure to maintain personal
contact with you. I do hope we shall keep the

correspondence continuing during the war. I am very glad you were able to tell a trusted friend about my feelings towards the Confessional Church and am much cheered by his own emotion and feelings as a result. I am also very much interested to know of the possibility of greater freedom where the army has taken control.

We had a most moving service for refugees in St John's Church, Westminster on October 28th. It was very largely attended. Two German Pastors, one Aryan and the other non-Aryan took part, and a Methodist and myself. There was one sermon in English by me and another in German. The strong desire was expressed that such services should be continued and this will be done. A prayer fellowship was started, bearing refugees especially in mind, and I hope it will have a wider ambit as well.

You will be glad to know that the Home Office has released five of the six German Pastors who were interned. They heard their appeals before those of any other Germans and indeed gave them priority over a number of others. They could not have been more considerate. These, of course, are the official German Pastors. I have seen them all since their release and they are most grateful. The non-Aryan German Pastors who have come over to England have all, I think, been freed from all restrictions, with one or two cases pending, and are regarded as "friendly aliens".

With all warmest regards from my wife and myself to Mrs Koechlin and you,

Yours most sincerely,
George Cicestr

Now that the war was in full swing, and spreading, what was the Church to do? This occupied Bell's mind. He made known his views in an article entitled, "The Church's Function in War-Time", published in The Fortnightly Review of November 1939. The function of the Church, Bell wrote, was "at all costs" to "remain the Church". The Church "ought to declare both in peace-time and war-time, that there are certain basic principles which can and should be the standards of both international social order and conduct". The Church "must not hesitate, if occasion arises, to condemn the infliction of reprisals, or the bombing of civilian populations, by the military forces of its own nation. It should set itself against the propaganda of lies and hatred. It should be ready to encourage a resumption of friendly relations with the enemy nation. It should set its face against any war of extermination or enslavement, and any measures directly aimed to destroy the morale of a population".[122]

What Bell expounded in his article as his own credo, he set about putting into practice. Bell explained his views in detail in his speech in the House of Lords on 13th December 1939. (He had taken his seat in the House of Lords on 27th July 1938.) Bell pleaded for a negotiated peace. He was not, he admitted, speaking as a pacifist, nor was he asking for peace "at any price", but for peace by settlement, settlement of the "problems of frontiers and nationalities which will reduce friction to the minimum". He was asking for agreement on disarmament and on the reorganisation of international economic relations.

Just two weeks later Bell rightly thought that his credo was being acknowledged by the allocution which Pope Pius XII delivered on Christmas Eve 1939. The Pope set out Five Peace Points. The first Point was the most significant. It said among other things that a "fundamental postulate of any just and honourable peace" was "an assurance for all nations great and small, powerful or weak, of their right to life and independence" The second Point spoke of general disarmament, the third signified the importance of creating "some juridical institution which shall guarantee the loyal and faithful fulfilment of the conditions agreed upon, and which shall in case of recognised need, revise and correct them". The fourth Point stressed "the real needs and the just demands of nations and populations, and of racial minorities". In his last Point the Pope asserted that the best regulations were "foredoomed to failure" unless the peoples and those who govern them developed "that sense of deep and keen responsibility which measures and weighs human statutes according to the sacred and inviolable standards of the law of God".

To Bell this "noble and generous appeal" by the Pope represented "an immense step forward" It also presented "a basis on which the different sections of the Christian Church could agree to press forward". What was now wanted was "application and expression".[123] With these two maxims Bell set about his task.

Bell raised the matter of the refugees once more in the House of Lords on 12th June 1940. An indiscriminate internment of aliens, he told the House, could not be "in all circumstances either necessary or right". A large group of aliens of German and Austrian origin, who regarded Nazism with horror, and who had been driven out of the their countries because of the persecution suffered there and who had sought refuge in Britain had been interned. That was most improper, asserted Bell. He urged the Government that "there should be local tribunals in the camps set up now, which should have the power to order the release of persons of indubitable integrity and loyalty". A number of peers, Lord Cecil and Lord Noel-Buxton among them, supported Bell. The Duke of Devonshire, speaking for the Government, shared Bell's anxieties.

At this moment an extraordinary event took place in Britain. Cardinal Arthur Hinsley,[124] the Roman Catholic Archbishop of Westminster, founded in August 1940 a peace movement called The Sword of the Spirit. Essentially based on the Pope's Five Peace Points the new movement aimed at uniting all men of goodwill towards the restoration of a Christian order of justice and peace. Prominent Catholics, such as Barbara Ward,[125] Christopher Dawson[126] and A.C.F. Beals[127] worked for the movement.

Bell very much welcomed the Cardinal's initiative. So did the Archbishop of Canterbury. The results were momentous. On 21st December 1940 a letter over the signatures of the Roman Cardinal and the two English Archbishops appeared in *The Times* endorsing the Pope's Five Peace Points. In May 1941 two interdenominational meetings were organised at the Stoll Theatre, London. The one on the 10th on "A Christian International Order" was chaired by Cardinal Hinsley. Bell was one of the principal speakers, delivering one of his finest speeches.[128] At a time , he maintained, when civilisation was being seriously threatened the Church must intervene. The other meeting on "A Christian Order for Britain", chaired by Archbishop of Canterbury, Lang,[129] was held on the 11th. The Archbishop also spoke forcefully. He firmly believed, he said, that "the lasting result of these meetings may be that Christian citizens, while frankly recognising and respecting the differences which still divide them, may find a new unity in thinking and acting together for the making of a way of life national and international , which will in some measure, however partial, reflect the Spirit of Christ and the Rule of the Kingdom of God".[130] Cardinal Hinsley also spoke in the same spirit: "Our unity must not be in sentiment and in word only; it must be carried into practical measures. Let us have a regular system of consultation and collaboration from now onwards, such as his Lordship the Bishop of Chichester has suggested, to agree on a plan of action which shall win the peace when the din of battle is ended".[131]

Large crowds attended the Stoll Theare meetings, although on the night of 10th-11th May both Westminster Abbey and the Houses of Parliament were hit by the German bombs.

The Sword of the Spirit was a Roman Catholic movement. The Church of England would co-operate with it, but not be an integral part of it. After much discussion Bell and Hinsley agreed on 24 June 1942 that there would have to be parallel movements, the Catholic Sword of the Spirit and the non-Catholic Religion and Life. The two would hold joint actions on the Christian social teachings, but no joint religious services.

Bell dedicated his time and energy to other, now equally, important things. One such thing was the problem of conscientious objectors. They needed legal help. And Bell intervened wherever he could.

What Bell did, and how and with whom he worked, we learn a great deal from the letters he wrote and received. The following letters enclosed here (Annex 3) speak for themselves, and our knowledge of the circumstances is the richer.

Annex 3

1) Arthur Wragg, the artist, to George Bell, 2 November 1939.

2) George Bell to Arthur Wragg, 4 November 1939.

3) George Bell to Stephen Hobhouse, 22 April 1940.

4) George Bell to Stephen Hobhouse, 15 June 1940.

5) George Bell to a friend, regarding Arthur Wragg, 26 November 1940.

6) Archbishop of Canterbury to George Bell, 11 February 1941.

7) Archbishop of Canterbury to George Bell, 15 February 1941.

8) George Bell to Archbishop of Canterbury, 19 February 1941.

9) George Bell to Walter Cawley, 26 April 1941.

10) George Bell to Archbishop of Canterbury, 15 May 1941.

11) George Bell to Archbishop of Canterbury, 30 May 1941.

12) Lord Noel-Buxton[132] to George Bell, 5 August 1941.

13) George Bell to Archbishop of Canterbury, 6 August 1941.

14) George Bell to Lord Noel Buxton, 16 August 1941.

15) Chairman, The Sword of the Spirit, to George Bell, 25 August 1941.

16) Lord Noel Buxton to George Bell, 1 September 1941.

17) Secretary, Central Board for Conscientious Objectors to George Bell, 8 September 1941.

18) Rev. William Paton, World Council of Churches, to George Bell, 23 September 1941.

19) George Bell to Professor R.W. Chambers,[133] 24 September 1941.

20) Secretary, Central Board for Conscientious Objectors, to George Bell, 2 October 1941.

21) Dorothy Morgan, Solicitor, to George Bell, 5 October 1941.

22) Miss Ellis to George Bell, 16 December 1941.

23) George Bell to Miss Ellis, 18 December 1941.

24) George Bell to Archbishop of Canterbury, 6 February 1942.

25) George Bell to Canon G. L. Prestige,[134] 4 July 1942.

26) George Bell to Norman Sykes,[135] 8 July 1942.

27) Henry Andrews to George Bell, 21 September 1942.

28) George Bell to the Lord Bishop of London,[136] 5 November 1942.

29) George Bell to Christopher Dawson (no date).

Polperro,
Cornwall.

Nov 2nd 1939.

Dear Dr Bell,

I hope you will forgive my troubling you when I can see you are so active; your protest regarding our "freedom" in today's press, together with some encouragement (via Christopher Hassall) regarding my last book "Seven Words," has prompted me to ask whether you would be kind enough to spare me a few words for the jacket of still another book called "Thy Kingdom Come". This book is on the same plan as "Jesus Wept" (1934) only more up-to-date. At the moment I cannot send a copy as it is not printed yet — but I wanted to be able to print something of yours (commending it!!!) because I anticipate the book being entirely ignored by the Press, & yet I feel that it has, perhaps, a little to say before we are all gagged entirely.

The book is strongly pacifist, but it also comments (as forcibly as my drawings are able to) upon the peace which led to here. For instance the first drawing shows the figure on the Cross obliterated by newspaper-cuttings, like blankets blown by the wind. The shape of the figure is visible underneath such words as "Boom in Armaments Shares",

"A Strong Britain Means Peace" etc etc. The words opposite this drawing are "Behold the Son of man is betrayed into the hands of sinners." The contrast of poverty amidst plenty, of the pawning of posterity against the selfishness of the present, of suppression of good by smugness, and of liberty lost by idle thinking — all form subjects for the rest of the drawings. There are four more hopeful pictures. The first end-paper shows the dawn of man's realisation of God — early man & woman clinging to each other as a comet passes over their cave-dwelling ("Then began Men to call on the name of the Lord") in an earthly fear & wonder. The last end-paper shows the spirit of Man humbled, kneeling on the world as it spins through the universe and upon whom streams the light of love & reason through the pierced hand of Christ ("I came that they might have life, and have it more abundantly.")

All the other drawings are supported (or contradicted) by evidence of cuttings from Press, Reports, statistics, etc.

A few words would help enormously — but only if you are not too busy, or really feel you would ever regret it! (Very clumsy this — but I want you to easily refuse).

Very sincerely,
Arthur Wragg.

4th November, 1939.

Dear Mr. Wragg,

        I really feel it an honour to receive such a
request from you.   I admire your work very much.   I
shall be most happy to write something for the jacket
of your new book "Thy Kingdom Come".   You will let
me see it in due course, no doubt, and it would be
kind if you could tell me when you expect it to be
visible in proof at any rate.   I wonder who is
publishing it and are you having someone to write an
introduction as well?   Anyhow I am at your service.
I am very glad we have Christopher Hassall as a
mutual friend.

        With all kind regards,

                        Yours sincerely,

Arthur Wragg, Esq.,
Polperro,
Cornwall.

22nd April, 1940.

Dear Friend,

     I am very grateful for your letter of 12th April,
and for letting me see Der Quäker.   I am delighted
that your efforts should have been crowned with success
so far as Evelyn Underhill's article was concerned.
I am also very glad to see what the periodical itself
contains in various ways.   I am sending this back to
you via my Pastor friends at St. Leonards, so it may
take a few days in transit.

     I do not know whether you heard the Broadcast by
Onlooker last Friday.   I unfortunately missed it myself,
but one of my refugee friends, who was a distinguished
German Professor tells me that it was a magnificent
defence of the refugee and up to the highest traditions
of this country.   I saw the Clerk of the Aliens Department
at the Police Station in Brighton this morning.   He was
very cheering about the attitude of the public in Brighton,
and said there was no trace of agitation against the refugees
here.

                    Yours sincerely,

Stephen Hobhouse, Esq.,
Failand,
St. Catharine's,
Broxbourne, Herts.

15th June 1940.

My dear Hobhouse,

I am much interested to read the memorandum about William Law and Christain literature in Germany. I do congratulate you, both on the references to your book, and on being able to secure this book from Germany itself.

Most of our pastors are now interned, including Hildebrandt. But I am sending your letter to Pastor Kramm of Oxford, who should be able to answer the questions.

So far as Heiler is concerned, he is not a member of the Confessional Church. He is a great friend of mine. Some years ago he was ordained in Switzerland in a rather curious way, and he now regards himself as a priest of the Catholic tradition, and, before the war, used to celebrate Mass in his own house. His ecclesiastical position is, to put it mildly, eccentric. He was transferred from his post at Marburg some time before the war, when the changes in the universities took place. I think he was to go to Greifswald, but he fell ill, and another arrangement was made by which he was transferred to a chair in another faculty at Marburg.

I am very glad your refugees are all right.

Stephen Hobhouse, Esq.,
Failand,
St. Catharine's,
Broxbourne,
Herts.

Re Arthur Wragg 285

22 The Droveway,
Hove.

xxxxxxxxxxxxxxxxx
xxxxxxxxxx
xxxxxxx
xxxxxxxx
Preston 2518

26th November 1940

My dear Inman,

I wonder if you could find time to read the enclosed letter from an artist, Arthur Wragg. He is quite a young man, about 35 I should think, a great friend of Dick Shepherd. You may know some of his work. He produced "Illustrations to the Psalms" with a preface by Dick Shepherd, also "Seven Words from the Cross" with a preface by Laurence Housman, and "Thy Kingdom Come," and some others. He is an artist who is very good technically and has a dramatic gift for linking up the contemporary scene with the gospels. He has been doing some work for the Cambridge Press lately.

It is his great ambition to illustrate the Life of Christ, placing Christ in the middle of the present life. I did just wonder whether you would think that any publisher would consider his proposal, viz., to give him a salary of £5 per week in return for the copyright and the original drawings, as advance royalties. I think he might well produce the kind of book which would create a great stir and mean a good deal. He is intensely real. I was wondering whether the proposal he makes, or some adaptation of it, would be feasible. I really feel he is an inspired man and I should enormously like to help him to do this work.

I expect you could, if you wanted to, form an opinion of him. You could get him to come from Polperro, where Mrs. Bell and I stayed with him for a night in January, and bring some of his work with him. It did just strike me as a chance, seeing that you are in Devonshire. Anyhow, you will not mind my telling you about him.

If you read his letter, you will see that he has been asked to be their War Artist, bythe Friends' Peace Committee, and would like to be the Church of England War Artist. I wish we could have a War Artist attached to the Church of England. It would be a fine idea. He told me some time ago how much he would like to draw the effects of the war on ordinary life, evacuation, air raids, and all sorts of other things.

I think you will be interested to hear that, rising out of the Sussex Churches' Art Fund, I have got into

touch with the artist, Duncan Grant, who lives with Clive Bell
at Firle.   He is eager to paint the walls of a beautiful
little Church, next to Firle, called Berwick.   The Rector is
keen and Vanessa Bell, and her son and her daughter (all artists)
are preparing a scheme of decoration which I am to look at.
I am very much hoping that this may come off, and I rather think
we shall be able to get the help of local people interested in
Duncan Grant, to pay what is necessary.

            The mural painting for Bishop Hannington Church
is making good progress.

            The scheme for lending modern pictures to
Churches is also about to start.   I have got fifteen or
sixteen Churches in the scheme.

            We had a meeting of the Finance Committee
yesterday which is very pleased with the Twelve Good Causes
Calendar, and I am most grateful for all your help with that.

                        Yours ever,

OLD PALACE,
CANTERBURY.

Confidential.   11th February 1941.

My dear George

        Pray forgive my delay in writing in answer
to your letter of February 5th. I have been very busy and it
is a constant difficulty to do business from two places.

        You ask whether I can write to Cardinal
Hinsley about the Sword of the Spirit. It is a somewhat
delicate matter. I have some reason to suspect that those who
at present are very busy in putting the Roman Church in this
country forward as the one really active agency on the Christian
side of patriotism, are making the most of this Sword of the
Spirit and comparing it with the apparent inactivity of the
Church of England. I have no doubt that our Roman friends
would be eager to enlist as many Anglicans as possible in the
work of this Association under Roman leadership. Accordingly
I am very clear that anything that Anglicans do should be done
quite apart from belong to this particular organisation, admirable as it
may be. However I have no objection to writing to the
Cardinal on the lines which you suggest and will do so and
will let you know his reply.

The Right Reverend
    The Lord Bishop of Chichester.

183

O 1925:41

Personal

OLD PALACE,
CANTERBURY.

15th February 1941.

My dear Bell

About the Sword of the Spirit, I wrote to the
Cardinal as you suggested and I had better simply send you his
reply which please return when you have considered it or,if
you think fit,copied it.   I have acknowledged it.
You will see that, as I expected, it is really quite frankly
a Roman Catholic organisation and though it permits persons
of other communions who accept its aims to become Associate
Members, such persons will obviously be identifying themselves
with an organisation which is naturally on a definite Roman
Catholic basis.   I do not think it would be possible to
encourage Church people in these circumstances to join it.
But I have told the Cardinal that I assume that the Sword of
the Spirit will be an organisation with which any organisations
of the Church of England with similar aims might co-operate.
This, I think, is the utmost that can be done in the matter.

Cosmo Cantuar

The Right Reverend
The Lord Bishop of Chichester.

184

19th February 1941

My dear Lord Archbishop,

Many thanks for your letter of the 15th February,
enclosing the reply from the Cardinal, which, as you kindly
permitted, I have copied. It certainly does not carry us
very far. It does not seem that the Cardinal is altogether
seizing the point. It is realized that the Sword of the
Spirit is a Roman Catholic organization with Associate
Members, non-voting, belonging to other Communions. Is
it authorised, as a Roman Catholic organization, to be the
representative organ of the Roman Church for collaboration
from time to time with non-Roman Communions in this country,
in social and political action? What one would like to
realize would be this. If the Commission on the Christian
Faith and the Common Life is the organ for collaboration
between the Church of England and Free Churches in this
country in the social and international field, so the Sword
of the Spirit is the Roman organization, and from time to
time the two bodies might associate with one another for
definite projects. But I think perhaps we can extract
as implicit in what the Cardinal says in his letter to
Your Grace, and in accordance with its spirit.

Yours affectionately and dutifully,

His Grace The Lord Archbishop of Canterbury

26th April 1941

Dear Sir,

Mr. Richard Gooding has given me some particulars of Reginald Jenkins, and he tells me that you could give further details. Isshould be very glad if you could give me the facts with regard to his case, from your knowledge of them.

Could you tell me the home address, and age of Mr. Jenkins, and his former employment? I understand that he appeared before a local Tribunal on August 9, 1939; was this at Cardiff? And who was Chairman of that Tribunal? I understand that he was then given non-combatant duties with a recommendation for the R.A.M.C. Mr. Gooding tells me that the London Appeal Tribunal upheld this decision in December 1939. Does that mean that Mr. Jenkins applied for unconditional exemption, and that was refused in August, and that he appealed and that his appeal was unsuccessful, yet the Appeal Tribunal agreed that he should be given non-combatant duties and recommended him for the R.A.M.C. When did he join up? Did anything happen between December 193 and June 18, 1940 when he was summoned for a medical examination? Can you tell me on what date he was arrested in Cardiff, and why the recommendation for the R.A.M.C. was disregarded and the A.M.P.C. substituted?

I very much wonder what steps Mr. Jenkins has taken to put his case before higher authorities. For example, has it been represented to his M.P.? And does the Rev. Mark Pierce, who is his Minister, support the case unreservedly?

Yours faithfully,

Walter Cawley, Esq.

186

15th May 1941

My dear Lord Archbishop,

I am delighted to hear how well the Stoll Theatre meeting went on Sunday, in spite of all the difficulties caused by the terrible experiences of Saturday night.

I had a talk with the Cardinal at the time of the Saturday meeting, and he volunteered the statement that the plan which I put forward in my Penguin Special, about a Christian consultative body at Rome, could not, in present circumstances, be achieved as Rome was no longer the Pope's city. On the other hand, he said that it could, and should, be achieved in England, and that he wanted just such a Council started in this country. This conversation was before his final words, which he said it anticipated. In case Your Grace has not seen the exact text of his final words, I quote them -

> "We must leave no doubt that we strive to be citizens of the heavenly Kingdom wherein is peace through the life of Divine love. On this common ground we all stand united. Our unity must not be in sentiment and in word only: it must be carried into practical measures. Why should we not have a regular system of consultation and collaboration from now onwards, such as His Lordship The Bishop of Chichester has suggested, to agree on a plan of action which shall win the peace when the din of battle is ended?"

I think this is important, and a big step forward. The two officers of The Sword of the Spirit, Miss Ward and Mr. Beales, are in close touch with me about possibilities, and are going to talk or write to me on the subject, to see how effect can be given to the project of what Mr. Beales calls "A Christian Council

187

of Action."

This is only to let Your Grace know, at the earliest possible stage. I will, of course, immediately let you know anything I discover.

Yours affectionately and dutifully,

His Grace
The Lord Archbishop of Canterbury

30th May 1941

My dear Lord Archbishop,

I have today seen Miss Barbara Ward about the
possibility of a Joint Council.   I told her that I had
seen Your Grace, and gave her, in general terms, the
import of what you had said to me.   I made it quite plain
that the setting up of a Joint Council could not be the
work of any voluntary organisation such as the Sword of
the Spirit;   and I said Your Grace was convinced that it
must come from the Heads of the Churches; and I added
that you were inclined to feel that the most natural way
of forming the Council would be to start with the four
signatories of the joint letter.

It was a great relief to me to find that Miss Ward
had talked to the Cardinal, and that, quite independently,
the Cardinal and his advisers had reached an identical
conclusion.   They also thought that it was not a matter
for the Sword of the Spirit, but that it was a matter
which the four signatories to the joint letter should set
on foot.   Indeed, it seemed to be the Roman view that
the Council might consist of quite a small number of people,
i.e. the four signatories, together with possibly three or
four additional members.   There would have to be a
Secretary or Secretaries, for, if the Council was to get
things done, using voluntary help in the main, it would
certainly need a whole time secretariat in one form or
another.

Then came the question, "What about the next step?"
I said, and Miss Ward agreed with me, that it would seem
to me most appropriate that the Archbishop of Canterbury
should write to the Cardinal and suggest that the
signatories should meet and discuss the matter.   I believe
that if Your Grace were willing, after hearing from the
Archbishop of York, to take this step, the whole thing
would start.

I took the opportunity of showing Miss Ward, in the

Report of the Oxford Conference, the reference to Your Grace's
expressed wish as President of the Oxford Conference, that
the Roman Church which then stood apart, would one day come
into collaboration.

Our whole talk was most friendly, and I think it was
most useful.

Yours affectionately and dutifully,

His Grace The Lord Archbishop of Canterbury

Comeragh Court, Hook Heath, Woking.

~~48 COWLEY STREET~~
~~WESTMINSTER~~
~~S.W.1~~

5th August, 1941.

My dear Bishop,

I was told at the recent Peace Council
Conference that you held a strong opinion
against any possible discussion of terms
with Hitler, not only now but at any time,
even when Hitler might be driven to offering
attractive terms.   I feel it may interest
you to know that this view of your opinion
was expressed.   I hope some day we may
have a talk about this problem. Meanwhile,
may I ask you to read the enclosed?

Not long ago, I found that Arnold
Toynbee, who has knowledge and influence, was
of the opinion that if Hitler was driven to

accepting terms representing German failure, it
would be unwise to insist on dealing with some
other authority, because failure would lead to
his fall at the hands of spontaneous German
feeling, so that his fall would be more final
than if it were insisted on by us in the first
place.

Yours sincerely

Noel Buxton

6   August   1941

My dear Lord Archbishop,

　　I saw Bishop Mathew on July 30 at the Athenaeum, and
we had a good talk about the Joint Consultative Council.
I told him of your great readiness to do everything possible
to follow up the letter to the Times, and to co-operate in
setting up a Joint Council on the lines we had discussed.

　　Since my last talk with him one or two things had
happened of which he was anxious I should inform Your Grace.
I think I shall put the difficulties which have arisen most
clearly if I state them in the following way:-

　　The Archbishops of Liverpool and Birmingham were
approached informally with regard to a Joint Consultative
Council of Roman Catholic and Anglican Bishops and Free Church
Leaders, such a Council to discuss possible joint action in
the social field, and in the field of natural law.   Before
the Archbishop of Birmingham replied, the Archbishop of
Liverpool wrote, deprecating the formation of a formal organ
of opinion, and suggesting rather that Anglican, Roman Catholic
and Free Church experts in sociology might meet and report
back.   For this reason it seems wisest to proceed by way
of direct communication between Lambeth and Archbishop's House,
Westminster, each side taking such advice as seemed best.
This would in no way exclude informal consultation between
other leaders.

　　Further, with regard to the subject matter which might
come before any Joint Consultative Council which might be
set up in future, the Catholic Education Council would require
that matters dealing with education should be left in their
hands and in those of the Standing Committee of the
Catholic Education Council and the Roman Catholic Bishops.

　　These were the two points of which Bishop Mathew wanted
to tell me.

　　The difficulty felt by the Archbishop of Liverpool means,
I am afraid, that it will hardly be possible to take

immediate steps for the formation of the Joint Consultative
Council on the lines originally proposed, though, from what
Bishop Mathew tells me, I hope that the delay may be only
temporary.   In the meantime, the original group of the
four signatories holds the field.   They are the hinges on
which, in any case, the large Council would depend, as well
as the persons who would, naturally, sign any further
statement on some social or similar question which it might
be agreed to publish.   Each member of the original group
would also be perfectly free to consult such others of his
own communion as he wished from time to time, if it were
thought desirable to consult on some particular subject.

In this way, if not in so ample a form as previously
envisaged, the group of the four signatories would, in
practice, do the work of a Joint Consultative Council.
And when I asked Bishop Mathew if he thought the way was
open for Your Grace, if you were so disposed, to write and
ask the Cardinal whether the group of the four signatories
might be regarded as a Consultative Body, with power for each
of the signatories to consult experts and others on any
matters on which a common discussion was desired, he replied
that, in his opinion, it would be an excellent thing to do.

I hope very much that I have made the position clear,
and that Your Grace may feel able to write along these
lines to the Cardinal.

Yours affectionately and dutifully,

His Grace The Lord Archbishop of Canterbury

```
------------------
-----------------
------------
```

The Palace,
Chichester.

16   August   1941

My dear Lord Noel Buxton,

   I was very glad to have your letter of August 5,
and the most interesting confidential memorandum.
I don't know who quoted "my strong opinion" against
any possible discussion of terms with Hitler.   I
have expressed my grave doubts, from the point of view
of practical politics, as to it being possible to
contemplate our Government negotiating with Hitler.
I have also, no doubt, said that I should find it
extremely difficult to contemplate Hitler as a person
with whom negotiations could be conducted, because
of his record.   But, though I should judge such a
possibility of negotiation extremely doubtful, I
should not go so far as to say that no negotiations
about peace could take place with Hitler, at any
time, in any circumstances.

   What you say has a great deal of force in it.
But I believe that our wisest course is to press
as strongly as we can the kind of peace aims which
Roosevelt and Churchill have now, at last, issued;
and to show that we mean business in putting them
forward.   If such peace aims were really to be
carried through, it would surely mean that Hitler's
victims outside Germany would be set free, and that
the Hitler regime in Germany would be ended.   For these
terms pre-suppose the final destruction of Nazi tyranny,
and that applies in and out of Germany.   At the same
time, we would have, in fairness, to admit in
accordance with Point 3 of the Declaration, that, if
Germany really freely chose (which is surely impossible)
Hitler, it could do so.

               Yours very sincerely,

Sword of the Spirit

President : HIS EMINENCE CARDINAL HINSLEY.
Vice-President : CHRISTOPHER DAWSON.

All Communications to the Hon. Secretary :
MISS BARBARA WARD.

108, GLOUCESTER PLACE,
LONDON. W. I.
Telephone : WELBECK 7595.

25th August, 1941.

My Lord Bishop,

I feel I should write and thank you for the generous letter which appears over your signature in the "Church Times". As you know, I have lately been elected to the office of Chairman of the Executive Committee of the Sword of the Spirit, and in any event I should have sought an opportunity to send you greetings.

As I do not consider that I have any special competence in settling the terms of our proposed co-operation, I think it will be wise for the negotiations to be continued by the very competent minds and hands who already have the conduct of the matter on our side.

None the less, I shall welcome an opportunity of meeting you sometime when you are in London and renewing the very friendly relations you were so good as to extend to me at and after the meeting at the Stoll Theatre.

Allow me to add, with my thanks the expression of my very high regard,

Yours sincerely,

Richard O'Sullivan

Chairman.

The Rt. Rev. the Bishop of Chichester,
 Bishop's Lodging,
  22 The Droveway,
   Hove, Sussex.

Upshire,

Waltham Abbey.

1st September, 1941.

My dear Bishop,

Many thanks for yours.

I am grateful for your trouble in telling me your view
in regard to terms with Hitler, and I am glad to be able to inform
anyone who speaks of your opinion. It interests me very much that
you feel we can strongly support the Atlantic policy.   I feel
drawn to Anglo-American action and even the world control which the
Declaration implies, but I feel doubtful whether we ought to abandon
the hope of a more ideal world-grouping, not only because it is an
ideal, but because an oligarchical domination can hardly be durable
in the long run. Secondly, the Atlantic policy requires an absolute
knock-out. While it may prove that a situation similar to that of
the Lansdowne episode will arise, and a compromise be far preferable
to a prolongation aimed at knock-out, leading to a repetition of
the history of 1919 onward.

I agree with you that there is a snag in the Declaration
as to nations choosing their own Government. We know little of
feeling in Germany, but I gather that attachment to the present
régime may very well continue.

Yours Sincerely,

Noel Buxton

197

CENTRAL BOARD FOR CONSCIENTIOUS OBJECTORS

6 ENDSLEIGH STREET, LONDON, W.C.1

Telephone : EUSton 5501

Chairman: FENNER BROCKWAY
Vice-Chairman: STEPHEN J. THORNE
Treasurer: ISAAC GOSS

Organising Secretary:
A. JOSEPH BRAYSHAW
Public Relations Officer:
STUART MORRIS
Secretary: NANCY BROWNE

The Rt. Rev. the Bishop of Chichester,
Bishop's Lodging,
22, The Droveway,
Hove.

September 8th, 194

Dear Dr. Bell,

I have heard recently that you have been kind enough
to interest yourself in conscientious objectors who are being
prosecuted because they refuse to undergo medical examination for
the Army. I first heard through a Mr. Stanley Jackson, unknown
to me, to whom I sent some literature which he passed on to you,
and I have to-day had a visit from the Prison Visitor at Lewes who
hopes to see you on the same subject shortly.

The purpose of this letter is to tell you that if there
is any way in which I can help you in giving you further informatio
I will gladly do so.

At this present moment we know of 207 men who are
actually in prison because of their conscientious objection. 21
of these men are serving court-martial sentences, one is doing a
month for refusing to fire-watch and the remainder have refused to
be medically examined. 48 of the latter are serving a sentence of one ye

If I may speak on behalf of conscientious objectors I
do not think they wish to complain against the penalties they may
have to suffer because of their views. They really are prepared to
suffer for their convictions though the majority are not anxious
to be "martyrs" and they naturally deplore being removed from useful work.

But what conscientious objectors are very anxious to
avoid is the "cat and mouse" treatment which took place in the last
war being applied to men in this war who refuse medical examinatio
The Government insisted on retaining the right to operate such
treatment when the National Service Act 1941 went through Parliamen
though there was opposition both in the House of Commons and the
House of Lords.

If there is any way in which you can get the Government to
reconsider the threat and make a declared intention not to put
such men in prison repeatedly it would be a great day for us.
There are, I am sure, quite a few in the House of Lords who would
support you.   I can think of the Bishop of Birmingham, Lord
Ponsonby, Lord Arnold, Lord Faringdon etc.

I hope you will forgive me for bothering you with additional
correspondence.   Please don't bother to reply to this letter.
I am only anxious to assure you that the majority of the conscientious objectors are not asking to be let off lightly, but they
are asking that they should not be sent to prison repeatedly for
the same offence.

If you need any more information or would like to see me when
you are in London I should naturally love to see you.

I hope you are fixed up with secretarial help now.

Yours sincerely,

Nancy Browne.

TELEGRAMS:- "INMISCO, KNIGHTS, LONDON"

TELEPHONE:- SLOANE 1435.

WORLD COUNCIL OF CHURCHES

(In process of formation)

PROVISIONAL COMMITTEE
*(Constituted by the World Conference
on Faith and Order and the Universal
Christian Council for Life and Work)*

Chairman of Provisional Committee:
THE ARCHBISHOP OF YORK

Chairman of the Administrative Committee:
M. LE PASTEUR MARC BOEGNER, D.D.

General Secretaries:
REV. W. A. VISSER 'T HOOFT, D.D.
REV. WILLIAM PATON, D.D.

Secretary in America:
REV. H. S. LEIPER, D.D.

EDINBURGH HOUSE

2 EATON GATE

LONDON, S.W.1

WP/SM

September 23rd, 1941

The Rt Rev. the Lord Bishop of Chichester,
The Bishop's Lodging,
22 The Droveway,
HOVE

My dear George,

Thanks for your letter. I am dictating this in bed, as I have a little bronchial trouble which I must kill off as soon as I can.

I have recently had long talks with Beales and with Miss Ward and am well-informed about the 'Sword' situation. I have also seen Miss Ellis and realise that it would be foolish to regard the Sword as the only possible bridge between Romans and other Christians. I wish you had kept the rest of us informed of your own negotiations, for, when I spoke with Beales, I realised that he and, I presume, also the committee of the Sword, were under the impression that what they called the 'Chichester Memorandum' had the general agreement of the non-Roman churches. I was bound to tell him that this was not so but I added that I had not myself seen the Chichester memorandum except in the form in which you put it before a few of us assembled for another discussion. I told him in particular that I thought that the Free Church attitude was very difficult and that it was quite useless to proceed without genuine knowledge of what the attitude of the separate bodies actually was.

I think the basic facts are these: (a) I agree with you that we must not throw away the possibility of Protestant and Roman Catholic co-operation. I attach enormous importance to this; (b) the constitutional action of the Sword has

200

erected a very serious barrier; (c) I believe it to be
impracticable for an Anglican-Free Church parallel to the
Sword to be started. It would lack the freshness of the
original proposal, it would be open to the criticism of all
the people who objected to the constitutional line taken
by the Sword and who will say that the other churches are
merely being obedient to the Roman fiat, and I have not
yet heard who is supposed to run it. (d) Beales agrees
with me that the ideal thing is for the Sword to change its
constitution and to have a single organisation in which
people of all churches can be full members. We should
therefore take action now which will help towards that end.
(e) The Commission of the Churches which is now, I hope, to
be merged with the Council on Christian Faith and the Common
Life, ought to have a personal membership. This I hope
will be agreed at the coming meeting and will be vital for
the whole work of co-operation in the country, of which this
business of Roman Catholics, Sword, etc., is only a small
part. (f) My own proposal therefore is that the Commission
should collaborate with the Sword, if necessary having a
common committee with it, for the purpose of arranging joint
meetings and I hope that this will be proposed and carried
through at the meeting next week.

    Certainly the thing must not be allowed to drift and
nobody so far as I know desires that that shall happen. The
chief difficulty in the way is that the matter is being tackled
by too many people who refrain from informing each other about
their activities. Beales has asked me to put something on
paper to him even before the Commission meeting and this I
hope to do as soon as I am well. He was very pleased with
the line I suggested to him.

                    Yours ever,

[signature]

Later. Out of bed.

On reading this it sounds
acid. I am very sorry not near
that. But there is danger of both being
at cross-purposes.

24 September 1941

I am in very close touch with the Executive of the
Sword of the Spirit, and am in correspondence with
Cardinal Hinsley about co-operation between them and the
Church of England and the Free Churches.   The Commission
of the Churches, on which the Church of England and the
Free Churches are represented under the Chairmanship of
the Archbishop of York, meets in Oxford next Tuesday.
The relationship of the Sword to the Commission is on
the agenda, and the position is a very difficult one for
some of the strong men on the Commission are not being very
helpful.   I am very anxious to see a national movement,
and not two rival movements,for so-operation.   I see that
you are a member of the Sword.   I wonder whether,
supposing an Anglican division or an Anglican and Free Church
division of the Sword were to be created, you would be
willing to give it your support, and, best of all, take an
active part on an Executive.

I am going to Oxford, and shall have the Sword of the
Spirit's latest point of view after their Executive meeting
this Friday.   It would be a very great gain if I were able
to say that you would take part, an active part, in an Anglican
Sword completely parallel and on equal terms with the Roman
Sword.

                    Yours sincerely,

Professor R.W. Chambers

202

CENTRAL BOARD FOR CONSCIENTIOUS OBJECTORS

6 ENDSLEIGH STREET, LONDON, W.C.1

Telephone : EUSton 5501

2nd October, 1941.

The Rt. Rev. The Bishop of Chichester,
The Bishop's Lodging,
22, The Droveway,
Hove, Sussex.

Dear Dr. Bell,

Thank you for your letter of September 26th.
Although our Executive Committee did not feel able to alter
its opinion with regard to the advisability of the appeals
being lodged by Robert Copping and H. Parudominsky, I was
asked to get in touch with Miss Morgan and for the purposes
of her information sent to her the report of the only case
in which a conscientious objector in similar circumstances
has appeared before Quarter Sessions.   In that instance a
sentence of one month's imprisonment only was passed, and
we thought it might be of some value to Miss Morgan to have
this information in her possession.

Yours sincerely,

Nancy Browne
Secretary.

NB/DS

TEL. Nº 53.

F. W. MORGAN,
SOLICITOR & COMMISSIONER.

DOROTHY MORGAN,
SOLICITOR

10. Wellington Place,
Hastings.

5th. October 19 41.

My Lord Bishop,

Mr.Copping's Appeal against the 12 months' term of imprisonment imposed upon him by the Brighton Bench last month, came before the Recorder of Brighton,(Sir Charles Doughty K.C.) on Thursday last.

Unfortunately the Appeal was lost.

I had instructed Mr.Geoffrey Lawrence. He made an excellent and eloquent speech,but the Recorder was obviously out of sympathy with Conscientious Objectors,and he took the line,(Which could not be shaken,) that the sooner that Copping and others like him changed their views the better. The Recorder intimated that he thought that a term of imprisonment was the most likely means of bringing about a change of mind,and said that he could see no reason why the length of the sentence should be reduced.

The result was disappointing,but Copping was grateful to Counsel,and told him he was satisfied that he had said all that could be said.

I wish that I had been able to report otherwise.

I beg to remain my Lord,

Yours faithfully,

Dorothy Morgan

The Right Reverend the Lord Bishop of Chichester,

Hove.

Sussex.

111

I go back to Oxford on Friday.

1 Sudeley Street.
W.C.1.

No. 1, MAGDALEN GATE HOUSE.
OXFORD.
TEL. 48392.

Dec. 16th 1941.

Dear Bishop.

I was so very sorry not to see you at the Cardinal's reception yesterday. There was much cheering when the Cardinal mentioned your name, but you did not seem to be present. The Bishop of Sodor was there.

I have no further news about the Christmas letter so I cannot say whether or no anything will be forthcoming. It is a very difficult situation. The Pope will make his broadcast on Christmas Eve but he will hardly be likely to be in a position to say anything very fresh.

I have been turning something over in my mind and I wonder how it will commend itself to you. We are faced with a world wide war with at the present moment 2 non Christian nations gaining victories. We English people have no guarantee that peace when it comes will establish a new world on Christian foundations if we win. There is a very beautiful prayer by the present Pope, part of which I copied for the Archbishop of Canterbury in which he prays that our Lord will show His Power to heal the sorrows & assuage the anger in the world.

would it not be possible for them to be some
consultation ^about the New world & its foundations^ between sincere Christians
of the different nationalities represented
here, many of them from sorely stricken lands.
You would perhaps think first of the
prominent Ecclesiastics of which there are
a good many. a united mind on the
essentials with the one thought of furthering
Christ's Kingdom - out of that something
might grow to help bring in our sincerity
of purpose A New world order under
the mind of Christ.

"The sword of the Spirit." more meant. has a very
strong spiritual dynamic - one felt that
yesterday but it cannot appeal to
stricken souls in Russia or Germany who
are denied the practice of their religion.

We want something linked to Heaven
itself to lift our poor human efforts up
& bring some hope & healing to us
at Christmas time. I would have written
this Bishop of Gibraltar but he is out of town.
Is there a germ of an idea in this?
I don't think it should be pro allies alone.
If possible Spain, Portugal who are suffering
so acutely from famine should be linked into
this world order. The Apostolic Delegate could help there.
Yours very sincerely Edith M Ellis.

206

112

18th December, 1941.

Dear Miss Ellis,

Very many thanks for your letter. I confess to
being a little puzzled about the Cardinal's reception.
I have heard from one or two people who were there
of the kindly way in which my name was received when
the Cardinal mentioned it in his speech, and I am
myself much touched by this. I have a very great
regard and indeed affection for the Cardinal. But I
was not asked to the reception, and I hope he did not refer
to me as a guest who was present or expected to be
present. What troubles me is that he may have thought
that an invitation reached me, and that I was rather
discourteous in not replying. I should not in fact have
been able to come to the reception. The Bishop of London
lives in London, and that is obviously a different affair.
I don't want to suggest that I was expecting to be invited,
for I was not at all; but it would distress me if an
invitation was thought to have been sent and neglected !

I am looking forward very much to the Pope's
broadcast on Christmas Eve. I have heard no more about
the Christmas letter, and I think very likely it is
off.

The conversations with the Sword are going happily.
There are also some interesting conversations going on
in which Dr Paton and the Rev. W.T. Elmslie are concerned,
between Protestants of different nationalities, under the
auspices of the Commission of the Churches. But I don't
see the way clear to a united statement at the present
moment.

Yours sincerely,

6th February, 1942.

My dear Lord Archbishop,

To-day the Joint Committee of the Commission of the
Churches and the Sword of the Spirit met to hear the
result of the meetings of the Council on the Christian
Faith and the Common Life with the Sword of the Spirit
about Christian co-operation and the proposed Statement.
All the members were delighted to learn that the
Council had warmly approved the document, and that the
Sword of the Spirit had done the same.

It would make all the difference if this Statement
which represents a big step forward, could be announced
in a way which would let the public at large see what
an important event it was. We were all at the Committee
this morning exceedingly anxious that your Grace should
preside over a meeting of representatives of the different
Churches, and should make a public announcement of what
had been achieved, copies of the Statement being simultaneously circulated to all in the hall, the press of course
being invited.

Representatives of the various Churches would be
invited to the meeting, which might consist of two or
three hundred persons and might take place in Lincolns
Inn Hall. The invitations would go out in the name of the
Joint Committee of the Commission of the Churches and the
Sword of the Spirit, asking people to meet your Grace and
the Cardinal in view of an important pronouncement to be
made. We should hope that you would say something to call
attention to the document, and, if you felt so disposed,
read the document itself, after which the Cardinal would
say something on his side, and I hope Dr Berry as Moderator
of the Free Churches, something on his side. It would make
obviously a real impression on the public if it could be
done in this way. There was a general feeling that the
mere issuing of the statement to the press would be quite
insufficient.

The week commencing March 15th was thought to be a very
appropriate week, and the most suitable day Thursday, March 19th

at 3.30 or 4 o'clock. Tea would be served so that
there would be something informal as well as formal
about it.   I do hope this may be possible. If that
date is impossible, could your Grace offer another day ?

                    Yours affectionately and dutifully,

4th July, 1942.

My dear Prestige,

I was grateful for the encouragement
of your report in The Church Times on the
Church Assembly resolution approving of the British
Council of Churches.

I wonder whether you could give a
little space some time to the co-operation between
the Church of England and the Free Churches and the
Roman Catholic Church. The recent statement
issued by the Joint Committee of Religion and Life
and the Sword of the Spirit received very considerable
publicity in the Roman press. But the Church press
did not say very much about it. I know, or hope I
know, the dangers. But I am impressed by the
opportunity of collaboration between our Church and
the Roman Catholics in the practical field.

I am not asking for anything special at
the present moment, but if you could keep your weather
eye open for opportunities of encouraging this
co-operation, it would, I believe, be doing a real
service to the Church.

Yours ever,

Sent also to the Rev. E.C. Ratcliff.

8th July, 1942.

My dear Sykes,

The Joint Committee on Christian Co-operation
(consisting of Romans, Anglicans and Free Churchmen)
is charged with the preparation of a pamphlet
on the attitude of the different Churches to
religious freedom.   As a first step towards that
I have been asked to collect any official Church
of England statements on religious freedom which
could be quoted as authoritative.

It is a little difficult to know where to
look for these. There is Jeremy Taylor, and
there are no doubt other Anglican divines who
deal with the subject. But I wonder whether
they could be considered really authoritative, or
whether there are official statements put out ad
hoc at any time, to which the Church of England
could now point as setting a standard ?   I can of
course look up the Lambeth Conference reports, but
I doubt whether that will get us very far.

Any help you can give me will be very greatly
valued. I am writing also to Ratcliff.

Yours ever,

IBSTONE HOUSE,
IBSTONE,
Nᴿ HIGH WYCOMBE,
BUCKS.

Sept 21, 1942.

My Lord,

I write to thank you as a private
person for the beautiful sermon which
you preached yesterday in Westminster
Abbey at the service of intercession
for the people of Yugoslavia, and to
express the hope that this sermon will
be printed. If it is not your intention
that the sermon should be printed,
would you, I wonder, be willing to
send it to me so that it may be
copied here and then returned to you?

You will understand
my feelings when I suddenly heard
you read a passage from my
wife's book "Black Lamb and
Grey Falcon." My wife herself

was not at the service. She was in the train to Manchester, where she is today giving the Margaret Ashton lecture to a Manchester University audience on the subject of 'Slav women in the war.' I had come up to town in order to join in the worship at the intercession service.

I was deeply moved when you made special mention of Bishop Nikolai, who had impressed us as a very great man. The church slava at Ochrid, at which I had the honour of sitting next to Bishop Nikolai at the feast in the porch, remains with me as a true religious experience. My wife forced herself to finish

TURVILLE HEATH 310

IBSTONE HOUSE,
IBSTONE,
Nᵣ HIGH WYCOMBE,
BUCKS.

the book when she was ill, so that it might be a testament in case an operation, which she had to undergo in February 1941, went wrong. The last pages, including the passage read by you, were added when she was convalescing. She pressed into it the best that was in her, and it will be a great happiness to her when she hears about the service from me tomorrow. A copy of your sermon would be an honoured treasure for her son and for his children to remember that you so singled out his mother on such a day and such an occasion.

I remain, my Lord, with a
renewed expression of gratitude
and of profound respect
Yours
Henry M. Andrews.

(husband of Rebecca West)

CHICHESTER 2161

THE PALACE,
CHICHESTER.

5th November, 1942.

My dear Bishop,

Religious Liberty

I am very sorry I cannot come to the meeting of the Joint Committee tomorrow. I have work that I have got to do in the Diocese. I got my Examining Chaplain, Norman Sykes, on to the question of the Church of England and religious freedom. He tells me that he knows of no official statements on this subject. In fact, the position of the Church of England till the Toleration Act was that everyone was required to confirm. There are a number of statements in Anglican divines and some of these statements could be put together and in Dr. Sykes' opinion these would be valuable as authoritative statements of Anglican opinion, but he also says that the nearest one could get to anything authoritative would be in some resolution of the Lambeth Conference

Though I do not say the Lambeth Conferences from 1867 onwards contain nothing about religious freedom, I have not been able in the index of the Report of the Conferences to find anything on the subject. I think that the Free Churchmen will be much better able to produce statements of religious freedom. In the Lambeth Conferences one does find appeals not to proselytise, especially in connection with our relations with the Eastern churches, e.g. the encyclical letter of 1888. Intimations of a similar character are also to be found in connection with proposals usually emanating from the Church of Ireland to link up with Protestants in Spain so that I think one could therefore quote Lambeth Conferences as warning against proselytism. Recommendat 66 and 69 of the Lambeth Conference of 1908 emphasize the imports of courtesy and deprecate a setting up of a new organised body in regions where a Church with apostolic ministry etc. is already in existence.

The subject of religious freedom is, however, directly touc on in some Lambeth Conference reports in relation to missionary freedom and particularly in connection with Governments. Thus Lambeth Conference 1920 adopted the following Resolution :-

"Whereas from time to time restrictions on Missionary Freed have been imposed by Governments, we desire to reaffirm the dut; which rests upon every Christian man and woman, of propagating the Faith of Christ, and to claim that any restrictions should I of a strictly temporary nature only, so that freedom of opportunity to fulfil this spiritual obligation may be afforded to Christians of all nationalities."

The report of the Committee on missionary problems to the same Conference also contains passages referring to missionary freedom which bear on our problem and lie behind the resolution quoted above. But it is perhaps important to remember that the Lambeth Conference of 1920 had present in the minds of the Bishops the difficulties arising out of the last war as illustrated by the following paragraph on page 92 of the Lambeth Conference 1920 report in the report of the sub-committee :

"In the present state of international relations there is a real danger that missionaries may be tempted to forward the commercial and political aims of their own nation, and we emphatically declare that such action lies entirely outside the scope of their proper functions."

I am sorry that apart from the authoritative teaching by Anglican divines of which there is a good deal, Anglican formularies or statements of teaching seem to afford little material on the subject of religious freedom. I have no doubt that the Free Churchmen will have many statements, indeed they have asserted freedom continually in the older days against the established church.

This question of religious freedom has, of course, come vividly to the fore in recent years and members of the Church of England have taken an active part in ecumenical conferences where forthright expressions about religious freedom have been issued.

Yours ever,

The Rt. Rev. the
Lord Bishop of London.

My dear Dawson,

        Very many thanks for your letter which
finds a wholehearted disciple in me. The question
really is what are we to do on the spiritual line
which, as you so rightly insist, is the only line
which matters. I have been wondering whether we could
not get some help from the experience of the Germans
in the Confessional Church and in the Catholic Church.
I know the Confessional Churchmen, of course, much
better than the Catholics, so I make a proposal with
regard to them on which I should greatly value your
reaction, if possible by return, as next week I am
presiding over a conference in London of the Confessional Pastors.

        We have a fellowship called "Christian
Fellowship in Wartime" one of the principal points
of which is to help the German Pastors now in England -
there are about twenty of them - to pass on their experience in conflict with the totalitarian regime in
Germany to Christians of this country. Some of the
Pastors by the simplicity of their preaching and their
great sincerity made most profound impressions upon
audiences of the most different kinds particularly
working class audiences. We have them stationed in
different parts of England and they really do speak
the Word of God, sometimes in church, sometimes to
mixed gatherings of clergy and ministers, sometimes
in workmen's cottages or in church halls. The testi-
monies which we got as to the impression they make is
remarkable in places where they have had at first to
overcome the ordinary British prejudice about Germans
in wartime.

        At our Pastors' Meeting next week I am
proposing to devote some of the time to getting out
of them what they conceive to be the lesson from their
experience and the churche's experience in Germany.
For us in England or, if you like, in Europe, the Confessional Church is now submerged in Germany, but they

                                           p.t.o.

and the Catholics were the one body which stood up
against Hitler. We in the rest of Europe have had to
stand up against a spiritual enemy or at least to
deal with the spiritual ill. Can we learn about methods
from them ? For example from their system of Bible
reading, prayer circles, brotherhood councils and the
like. The Pastors have often reminded me that it was
in the places where this simple bible witness had been
most cherished, that the resistance of the Confessional
Church was at its strongest.

      Do let me know whether this wakes an answer-
ing chord in your heart.

                       Yours ever,

Christopher Dawson, Esq.,
Boars Hill,
Oxford.

5

"Germany and National Socialism are not the same thing"

George Bell had written to Alfons Koechlin on 11th September 1939 that his "affection and fellowship" for the Confessional Church were "unchanged and unbroken". Bell meant it and kept his word. He carried on his correspondence with Koechlin on the fate of the Confessional Church, and this communication helped Bell to act to promote its cause. The following letters confirm Bell's intense desire not to leave his friends in the lurch:

1) Bell to Koechlin, 8 December 1939.

```
From The Bishop of Chichester.
Wartime Address
ST. Martin's Vicarage,
Brighton 7
8 December 1939
```

```
My dear Koechlin,
    Your letter of November 20th gave me the greatest
pleasure, and I do most heartily appreciate the
very generous words which you use. I was surprised
and delighted by the honour which Basle University
has conferred upon me. The Theological Faculty of
Basle has an eminence in the whole world altogether
of its own; to be associated with Basle in this most
honourable way is to have a relationship of which
any man might be proud. I am exceedingly proud that
it should have been paid to me at this very time,
and in the very midst of war. I value what you say
regarding me as belonging to you at the end of the
terrible battle-lines, deeply concerned and ready
for spiritual help wherever it can be given.
    I am very much interested to hear what you tell
me about the Confessional Church, and your recent
contact with a student close to Pastor Albertz. The
Archbishop of Canterbury always asks me whenever I
see him what news I have, and I was glad to be able,
the other day, to give him this last news, though
it is sad news.
```

What a heavy task falls upon your shoulders now with regard to the Basle Mission and the whole world wide missionary responsibility in which you take so energetic and devoted a share. These days are tragic days and testing in every sort of way.

I am very glad the Archbishop of York has decided to summon the Provisional Committee to meet in a neutral country on February 1st and 2nd. I hope most earnestly that nothing will turn up to prevent such a meeting. Bishop Berggrav has cabled to say that he is coming to London today. I had a long letter from him on Wednesday suggesting Anglo-Scandinavian and German-Scandinavian conferences in different places at an early date. He will, no doubt, have something to say about these when he comes. But those conferences were proposed at a meeting in Oslo on November 22nd and 23rd when Professor Gulin of Finland was present, with the three Primates. But Finland has become a victim since then. I expect that Berggrav's visit is more immediately concerned with Finland and Norway than with the general oecumenical task.

My wife joins in warmest greetings to you and your wife and Elisabeth,

Yours most sincerely,

George Cicestr

2) Bell to Koechlin, 19th April 1940.

From The Bishop of Chichester.
War-Time Address: St Martin's Vicarage
22 Franklin Road, Brighton
19 April 1940

My dear Koechlin,

I was very glad to receive your letter of the 26th March and to read your news and your judgements. Even since you wrote the situation in Scandinavia has got so much worse and such terrible things have happened.

I, too, have often thought of our time together in Holland. I learnt much then, and such opportunities give one a wonderful chance of sharing feelings and judgements. I certainly came away a wiser and a spiritually richer man. I have often thought of your words with regard to the remarks I myself made on the responsibilities of churchmen when governments have taken such deep and costly decisions. You are a very wise and far-seeing man.

Most unfortunately I was hundreds of miles away from home when Berggrav came back from his visit to Berlin. I had a letter from him but he did not seem to have got much in Berlin or been allowed to have much free conversation with church leaders; though I think he had a very full talk with Weizsäcker. I am told, however, since then by Canon Thompson Elliott of the World Alliance, that he was much more sanguine about what Germany said as to peace possibilities and that he was disappointed by the British attitude. I do not know myself anything about this at first-hand. I wonder whether you have heard anything, especially since Norway was invaded? *The Daily Telegraph* of April 17 said that he had joined the "Puppet Government" at Oslo and had broadcast urging Norwegians to make peace. I cannot believe that this represents his attitude. I think that *The Telegraph* (so far as I can judge from *The Times*) has misrepresented the administration at Oslo as a Puppet Government. It seems to be a care-taking administration under Governor Christensen and not under any German control. If Bishop Berggrav made a broadcast, I should imagine it was to encourage and comfort the people and urge them to have patience. If you have news, do please tell me.

I was glad to have your news of the Confessional Church and also of the attitude taken in Berlin with regard to the friendly character of church leaders and reliance on our doing our best to help German prisoners. What you reported about Peters was therefore encouraging on that score.

I have enquiries from time to time from Archbishop Eidem as a result of enquiries to him from Heckel, and I replied to the best of my ability. I think the arrangements for spiritual ministrations to the prisoners in various camps are pretty regular and sound. One of the German Pastors has been for some time ministering to the women prisoners and has now been authorised to minister to certain camps for men prisoners.

Pastor Wehrhan has had to be re-interned. He was one of the Pastors who were released on

representations made to the Home Office, but he
behaved so indiscreetly that they had to re-
intern him. I think that he will probably be re-
patriated.

In the meantime, you will be interested to know
that the German Church Committee has offered the
post of German Priest in his Church in London to
Pastor Busing. He is a refugee married to a non-
Aryan wife, a quite admirable man, and he has made
it understood to the Committee that he will welcome
refugees at the Church and he will indeed be a most
useful centre of spiritual help to Germans of all
kinds.

I can imagine how difficult the position in
Switzerland must be. I do trust that you and Mrs
Koechlin and the family keep well and are standing
the strain. May all good be with you. Please let me
hear again.

Yours ever,
George Cicestr

3) Bell to Koechlin, 9th May 1940 (see Annex 4).

Apart from Koechlin the person who kept Bell abreast of progress
in the German situation was Bonhoeffer's brother-in-law, Dr Gerhard
Leibholz, who had taught International Law at the University of
Göttingen. Leibholz, a Jew, who had left Germany in 1938, with his
wife (Bonhoeffer's sister) and two daughters, lived now in England,
but maintained close contacts with Bonhoeffer and his colleagues in
Germany. The detailed and clear-sighted information supplied by
Leibholz earned him Bell's gratitude. Leibholz himself was quite active
in Britain. He wrote articles, drafted various memoranda, lectured at
learned institutions. Bell of course helped him in all this, especially in
establishing contact with British academicians. Bell and Leibholz became
close friends. The letters printed below bear witness to this fact.[137]

1) Bell to Leibholz, 15th November 1939.

The Palace,
15 November 1939

My dear Leibholz,
Very many thanks for your letter and for the
news of Dietrich. Yes, I got your article about the
German Church question, and was very glad to have
it, and liked it, and also the letters which are
always a pleasure to receive.
I hope you and your wife and the two girls are
well. I shall be very much interested to hear when
you have more news of Dietrich. He cannot, as you
say, be an Army Chaplain,
Yours ever,
George Cicestr

2) Bell to Leibholz, 24th January 1940.

From the Bishop of Chichester.
War-Time Address:
St Martin's Vicarage
Brighton
24 January 1940

My dear Leibholz,
I am ashamed of myself for not having written
before now to thank you for your kind and most
welcome letter. I am greatly interested to hear of
the invitation which you received from Oxford before
Christmas to lecture about questions of democracy.
I very much wonder whether you have actually gone
forward with them. It would be an interesting
experience if you were able to get the time for the
work, with the other things you have to do.
I was talking the other day to the Professor
of International Law at Cambridge, he would be glad
to see you. He said that in England little work has
really been done on the subject of canon law. He
wondered whether some of the German scholars who
had come to this country were interested in that
subject. I said I did not know but that I would
bear it in mind, and I mentioned your special lines
as known to me. He is of opinion that canon law
had much more to do with English law than English
lawyers usually acknowledged, and that there is
a good deal of research work waiting to be done
in this field. I thought I would just mention this
matter in case it was of interest to you. (...)

Yours very sincerely,
George Cicestr

3) Bell to Leibholz, 30th October 1941.

From The Bishop of Chichester.
The Bishop's Lodging
22 , The Droveway, Hove, Sussex
30 October 1941

My dear Leibholz,
Very many thanks for your letter. I do hope
that Magdalen College will come to a favourable
decision.

I entirely agree with your view on the comments
from Geneva on Dr Paton's book. I remember your
letter to me after the Atlantic Charter very well. I
am also entirely with you in what you say endorsing
the comments, and have written to Paton strongly in
that sense myself. Thank you also for the cutting
from the Swedish paper, and the comments on the
Bishop of Münster.

I am much interested to hear about your course
of lectures on Christianity and Politics, and I
do hope that you will give this course. Is it
not possible that the lectures might be printed
afterwards? In any event it would be most healthy
and helpful that you should give them.

I had a letter from Dietrich the other day; he
wrote very cordially from Zürich, and is full of
courage and hope. I trust that you and your wife are
cheered both by his reports from Germany and by his
confidence, which I share, in a happy future for you
and your wife and children. These months of waiting
are difficult and trying, but I most earnestly hope
and believe that the valley through which we are
passing at this moment, and through which you are
also passing, will not be a long or an endless one,
but will lead to the day.
Yours very sincerely,
George Cicestr

4) Bell to Leibholz, 26th December 1941 (see Annex 4).

5) Bell to Leibholz, 24ᵗʰ March 1942.

```
From The Bishop of Chichester.
The Bishop's Lodging
22. The Droveway, Hove, Sussex
24 March 1942
```

My dear Leibholz,

I am deeply interested in getting your two letters, and to know that your lectures have been accepted for publication by S.P.C.K. in the Christian News Letter series. This is a great encouragement and will be of great interest to the readers.

I respect and appreciate your hesitations with regard to letting your name appear on the title page; you and your wife are naturally very careful not to do anything which would hurt any members of your or your wife's family, but particularly Dietrich, who is in an exposed position. I take it from what you say that the lectures show a very clear antagonism to the National Socialist State. That is to say that what you have written for this book will be much more antagonistic and outspoken than any articles or essays which you have hitherto published in this country. It may, on the other hand, be the case that this book says in a more extended form what you have already said. What I mean is that to my mind so much depends on the amount of additional antagonism and strong criticism which your book will convey, over and above what your essays have conveyed. If your book is simply an enlarged edition of criticisms you have previously made, or in accord with criticisms you have previously made, then I do not think you should, worry over much about your name appearing on the title page of the book; for the Nazis would assuredly have seen your essays, and no one in Germany, so far as you know, has suffered on that account. I know that a book is a much bigger affair than an essay, and it must be the case of course that more attention is focussed on a book than on an essay. Nevertheless, it does seem to me to be a question rather depending on the strength of your criticisms, and how far the book is what might be called a strong attack on the Nazi system rather than a piece of research work, with an approach which, while of course practical, is in the main academic.

Suppose however that you feel that the book is, and would be taken by the Nazis to be, a strong attack on the Nazi State, then you know more about the Nazi reaction and how that would be likely to affect Dietrich and others, than many people here can know. Naturally you would wish to avoid hurting Dietrich. If, knowing the Nazis as you do, you feel that there is a very grave risk to his safety as a result of the publication of your book in England, then I think people here would thoroughly appreciate your unwillingness to let your name appear on the cover.

There is always, of course, the possibility that the Nazis would unearth the author's identity, even though he did his best to disguise it. But I do not think one ought to consider that risk as a very serious one. I take it that some German refugees who write on purely political subjects in this country have some experience as to the effect on their relatives in Germany of what they have written and published. There may be such refugees in Oxford, who could tell you personally about this:, and you might find their experience very valuable.

I expect the Editors of the series would be rather disappointed at not having your name – if you decide, in view of the risk, not to publish it. But in that case, I should be inclined to adopt a pseudonym. Don't make the book entirely anonymous, but adopt a name. That is much better than anonymity, and presents the writer as a personality to English readers. I believe Sebastian Haffner, for example, is a pseudonym. Why should you not have a pseudonym of your own?

It looks to me as though Hodgson's preface, which is excellent, would not need much if any change, as no University is mentioned, if you adopt a pseudonym.

Yours very sincerely,
George Cicestr

On the basis of the information Bell was receiving from his trusted German friends the Bishop of Chichester was more than ever convinced that the British Government was totally wrong in accusing the whole

German nation of Hitler's crimes. This accusation had been made publicly by Alfred Duff Cooper,[138] on 23rd April 1940, and by Sir Robert Vansittart[139] in a series of broadcasts on the BBC Overseas programme. This policy was harmful, warned Bell. It discouraged all those Germans, loyal to the Confessional Church, who had been and were opposing the Nazi rule. There were many in Germany (Bell declared in his speech on 10th May in the Stoll Theatre), "silenced now by the Gestapo and the machine-gun, who long for deliverance from a godless Nazi rule, and for the coming of Christian Order in which they and we can take our part". Was there "no trumpet call to come from England, to awaken them from despair?"[140] In his book, *Christianity and World Order*, published in July 1940, Bell argued further that the world conflict at the moment was "essentially a spiritual conflict". It was not "totalitarianism versus liberal democracy" nor was it "Germany versus Western civilisation". It was "Godlessness versus Christianity". The longer the war continued the more difficult it would be to "get that better order", the bitterness would become greater. It would be "unreal to ignore the fact" that neither side had "any conception of ending the war except through its own victory." ... "Yet here is the Universal Church with its members, Catholic and Protestant, also subjects of the warring nations. Here is a great reality which stands for what is super-national and supernatural. It claims a transcendent gospel which gives a meaning to life. And the bonds between the members of this Universal Church should be the strongest bonds of all, and should have a relevance to temporal life. It cannot therefore be wrong for Christians in one belligerent country to seek such opportunities as may be open to discover through neutral channels, in every way possible, from fellow-Christians in another belligerent country, what terms of peace would be likely to create a lasting peace, and not lead to a further poisoning of international relationships".[141]

Bell understood how much his views were being shared by the fellow Christians in Germany, and thus continually emphasised the fact that Germany and National Socialism were "not the same thing".[142]

When Bonhoeffer read *Christianity and World Order*, he wrote to tell Bell that he had "had the great pleasure and satisfaction to read your newest book". But so far no "trumpet call" had come from the British official circles to "awaken" the German opposition from despair.

Bell was also now publicly suggesting that night-bombing of the civilians be abolished. In a letter to *The Times* on 17th April 1941 he wrote, how "barbarous" it was "to make unarmed women and children the deliberate object of attack", and asked it were not "possible for the British Government to make a solemn declaration that they for their part will refrain from night-bombing (either altogether or of towns with civilian population) provided that the German Government will give the same declaration? If this single limitation were achieved it would at least make a halt in the world's rushing down to ever-deeper baseness and confusion".[143] Very few paid attention to Bell's interventions, and the few who did were the noted writers like Bernard Shaw,[144] or distinguished scholars like Gilbert Murray.[145] Equally disappointing was the response, when Bell pleaded for relief for the starving peoples of the German occupied territories.

At this very time an entirely unexpected, but equally dramatic event occurred far away from England at the end of May 1942. Bell had been asked to go to Sweden. Why and what happened there Bell tells us fully in his own words:[146]

> (...) Early in 1942 air communications were restored between Britain and Sweden under Government auspices, in a limited way. The British Ministry of Information was anxious to use the opportunity to resume contacts between different departments of British and Swedish culture. Sir Kenneth Clark, the Director of the National Gallery [1934-45], and T.S.Eliot, the poet, were among those who were thus enabled to re-establish connections with art and literature. It was thought desirable to send someone who could renew personal relations with members of the Churches. And as I had many friends in the Church of Sweden, I was invited to undertake this task.
>
> I arrived a little before 3 a.m. on May 13, at the airport of Stockholm, in an aeroplane with a Norwegian pilot and 2 crew, and no other passengers. During the first fortnight I travelled to different parts of Sweden, and met many old friends, and saw many new faces. In the course of my travels I learned far more about what was happening in the world than there was any possibility of learning in Britain. But the first 14 days, enthralling as they were, did nothing to prepare me for my dramatic encounter

with a German Pastor, on May 26, in Stockholm.

I was staying at the time with Mr Victor Mallet,[147] the British Minister, at the British Legation. That night Nils Ehrenström, a young Swedish pastor, Dr Hans Schönfeld's assistant in the Research Department at Geneva, took me to the Student Movement House where he introduced me to the Secretary, Mr Werner. There, to my amazement, I found Dr Schönfeld himself, fresh from Geneva via Germany. He had come expressly to meet me, the news of my visit having been published in the press. He was clearly suffering under great strain. After warm words of welcome, he spoke first of what he and his colleagues at Geneva were doing. He gave me copies of sermons composed by German Army chaplains for English prisoners of war in Germany, circulated by the office of the German Evangelical Church, of which Dr Eugen Gerstenmaier was head. He spoke of the work of the YMCA and of the Student Movement. And then, after a while, he reached what was most clearly the object of his visit. He told me about a very important movement inside Germany, in which the Evangelical and the Roman Catholic Churches were playing a leading part. There was, he said a block of Christians belonging to both confessions who were speaking strongly of three human rights – the right of freedom, the right of the rule of law, and the right to live a Christian life. The movement included trade unionists and working men. These working men challenged him and Dr Gerstenmaier about the Christian attitude, and asked "How will your Churches face a National Socialism?" And he went on to describe a gradual development of Christian groups in military circles, and the civil service, as well as among the trade unionists. There was, he said, a growing movement of opposition to Hitler, and men were on the look out for a chance to attack him. He spoke of the recent refusal of a number of officers to continue serving in Russia, and how the developments of the previous winter had opened men's eyes – but no lead had been given. And he spoke of a plan for a federation of European nations with a European army under the authority of an executive which might have its headquarters in one of the smaller countries. He added that many Germans were convinced that they must make great sacrifices of their own personal incomes to atone for the damage Germany had done in the occupied territories.

The likelihood of a British victory was not very great, he said, but on the other hand the Opposition was aware of impending revolt inside the Nazi Party; of Himmler[148] and his followers against Hitler. The first stage would be the overthrow of Hitler by Himmler and the SS, when the Army would take control of Germany. But - here was Schönfeld's question - would Britain and the United States be willing to make terms with a Germany freed from Hitler? There was no confidence at present that Britain would act differently from the way in which it had acted at Versailles. Although a successful coup by Himmler might be of service to the opposition, its members were under no illusion as to the essential preliminary being the elimination of Hitler and Himmler and the Gestapo, and the SS. They also realised that another essential preliminary was the withdrawal of German troops from all occupied territory, with a view to its being taken over by a European authority. But - (they asked) - would the British encourage the leaders of such a revolution to hope for negotiations if the arch-gangsters were removed? The alternative, as he and his friends saw it, was further chaos - with Bolshevism increasing.

I reported the essence of the conversation to the British Minister when I got back to the Legation. He was interested, and told me to go on listening, but not to encourage my visitor; he thought that what Schönfeld said might possibly be a "peace-feeler".

Three days later, on the afternoon of May 29, I saw Schönfeld a second time. Ehrenström and Werner were again present. There was more discussion about the resistance movement. Schönfeld emphasised the reality of the Church opposition, and quoted General Superintendent Blau in Posen and Bishop Wurm as particularly striking examples of the leadership, and also Hanns Lilje. All those opposed to Hitler, he said, were agreed about the necessity of a Christian basis of life and of government, and very many were looking to the Church leaders for help and encouragement. He spoke also of the significance of the Churches' opposition in Norway and Holland.

Our conversation on this occasion lasted about an hour. I asked Schönfeld to put what he had told me in writing, and he promised to do so.

That evening I went to Upsala to stay with Archbishop Eidem. I told him of our talks. He had no doubt of Schönfeld's sincerity, or of the great strain from which he was suffering. But when we walked together next morning, May 30, he said that he thought Schönfeld was too wishful in his thinking, and found a relief in pouring out to sympathetic ears.

But the next day, Sunday, May 31, was crucial. I went that morning to Sigtuna, where I was met by Mr Harry Johansson, Director of the Nordic Ecumenical Institute. I lunched with Dr Manfred Björquist, head of the Sigtuna Foundation, and his wife. Then, to my astonishment, after tea, arrived a second German pastor, Dietrich Bonhoeffer. He had known nothing of Schönfeld's visit (nor Schönfeld of his). He came with a courier's pass made out by the Foreign Office in Berlin, through the help of General Oster, who had planned the whole journey with Bonhoeffer's brother-in-law, Hans von Dohnanyi, and Bonhoeffer himself. We told him of the conversations with Schönfeld, who was not present when Bonhoeffer appeared. I then suggested that Bonhoeffer and I might talk together in private, and he and I left the rest and withdrew into another room.

He gave me messages for his sister in England. He said that his seminary had been dissolved for the second time, in 1940. The Gestapo had forbidden him to speak or preach or publish. Nevertheless he had been working hard by day at his book on Ethics, and in preparing Memoranda for the Brethren's Council, and by night had been engaged in political activity. There had been some danger of his being called up for military service, but he had approached a high officer in the War Office, a friend of the Confessional Church, who had told him "I will try and keep you out of it".

Turning then to my conversations with Schönfeld, I emphasised the suspicion with which my report would be met by the British Government when I got home. And I said that, while I understood the immense danger in which he stood, it would undoubtedly be a great help if he were willing to

give me any names of leaders in the movement. He
agreed readily – although I could see that there
was a heavy load on his mind about the whole
affair. He named Col. General Beck, Col. General
von Hammerstein, former chief of the General Staff,
Herr Goerdeler, former Lord Mayor of Leipzig,
Wilhelm Leuschner, former President of the United
Trade Unions, Jacob Kaiser, Catholic Trade Union
leader. He also mentioned Schacht,[149] as an ambiguous
supporter, a "seismograph of contemporary events".
He emphasised the importance of Beck and Goerdeler.
A rising led by them should be taken very seriously.
He also said that most of the Field Marshals and
Generals (or those next to them) in the Commands
of the Home Front, were reliable – von Kluge, von
Bock, Küchler, and though not so likely to come into
prominence, von Witzleben.

Our private talk then ended. Schönfeld
arrived, and he, Björquist, Johansson, Ehrenström,
Bonhoeffer and I joined in general conversation. It
was impossible, Schönfeld said, to tell the numbers
of those in the opposition. The point was that key
positions were held by members of the opposition on
the radio, in the big factories, in the water and
gas supply stations. There were also close links
with the State police. The opposition had been
in existence for some time; it was the war which
gave it its opportunity, and it had crystallised
in the autumn of 1941. If the Allied leaders felt
a sense of responsibility for the fate of millions
in the occupied countries, they would consider
very earnestly the means of preventing great
crimes against those peoples. And as to Russia,
Schönfeld reminded me that the German Army held
1000 miles of Russian territory. Stalin could, he
considered, be satisfied on the boundary question
if the Allies would give a guarantee to the Soviet
Government. High German officers, he said, had been
impressed with the Soviet elite, and believed in
the possibility of an understanding.

Here Bonhoeffer broke in. His Christian
conscience, he said, was not quite at ease with
Schönfeld's ideas. There must be punishment by God.
We should not be worthy of such a solution. Our
action must be such as the world will understand
as an act of repentance. "Christians do not wish

to escape repentance, or chaos, if it is God's will to bring it upon us. We must take this judgement as Christians". When Bonhoeffer spoke of the importance of the Germans declaring their repentance, I expressed very strong agreement with him. I also spoke of the importance of the Allied armies occupying Berlin. Schönfeld agreed to this, but with the proviso that they occupied Berlin not as conquerors but to assist the German Army against reactionary or hostile forces. The question was asked whether the British would favour the return of a Monarchy in Germany. A possible monarch was Prince Louis Ferdinand, who had been brought over from USA by Hitler after the death of the Crown Prince's eldest son, and was now living on a farm in East Prussia. He was known to Bonhoeffer, and was a Christian, with outspoken social interests.

All this was communicated to me, with a view to my passing it on to the British Government. The resistance movement's aim, I was again told, was the elimination of Hitler, and the setting up of a new bona fide German Government which renounced aggression and was based on principles utterly opposed to National Socialism. This new German Government would wish to treat with the Allied Governments for a just peace. But it was urged that it was of little use to incur all the dangers to which the Resistance movement was exposed in fulfilling its aim, if the Allied Governments were going to treat a Germany purged of Hitler and his colleagues in exactly the same way as they proposed to treat a Hitlerite Germany. I was therefore asked to make enquiries, and, if possible, to let the two Pastors know the result. It was suggested that should there be any wish on the part of the British Government for preliminary private discussion, Adam von Trott, a friend of Sir Stafford Cripps'[150] son, would be a very suitable person.

I again emphasised the reserve with which my report would be met, and the probability of the Foreign Office taking the view that the whole situation was too uncertain to justify any action on its part. But it was agreed between Bonhoeffer, Schönfeld, Johansson and myself that, if at all possible, the following method of communication should be adopted:

1. If the Foreign Office made no response to my report, I should send a cable to Harry Johansson, Sigtuna, saying simply: Circumstances too uncertain.

2. If the Foreign Office were sympathetic, but unwilling to commit itself, the message should be: Friendly reception.

3. If the Foreign Office were willing to authorise some person from the British Legation or the Foreign Office, or a British churchman from London, to discuss possibilities, the message should be: Paton can come. (The use of the name Paton, a well known British Churchman, did not mean either that this particular person or that a churchman would be chosen, but was simply for convenience.)

It was further agreed that if the Foreign Office proved willing to authorise some person unspecified to discuss possibilities, the following replies, according to circumstance, should be sent either by Johansson from Sigtuna or by Visser't Hooft from Geneva, naming the kind of representative preferred, and the date before or on which the meeting would take place:

a) If the representative of the Resistance movement wished the person authorised to be a diplomat, a cable would be sent to me at Chichester as follows: Please send manuscript before July 20.

b) If a churchman were preferred to a diplomat at this stage, the cable would say: Please send manuscript before July 20. Emphasise religious aspect.

c) If for some reason it was not possible for the representative of the Resistance movement to send anyone to Stockholm, but only to authorise a Swedish third party, who would in fact be Ehrenström, to make further enquiries in London, the cable would say: Please arrange to see Strong July 20.

I should explain that the month to be named in the cable was, for security reasons, to be a month later than the month actually intended - so that July 20 meant in fact June 20. But it is certainly curious that the date actually agreed on in our conversations as the code date was July 20 – though in a fair copy made later, in order to give more time it was changed to July 30. In any case the exact date on which any meeting in Stockholm or London could take place depended on circumstances, which could only be made clear after I had reported to the Foreign Office.

Next day, June 1, I returned to Stockholm, staying at the British Legation. In the afternoon I saw Johansson, who told me that Björquist refused to allow Sigtuna to be used for purposes of communication between Chichester and the Resistance movement, as inconsistent with Sweden's political neutrality. This meant that messages would have to be sent through Geneva.

I saw Bonhoeffer again the same day, for the last time. He gave me messages for his brother-in-law, Dr Leibholz, and asked me to tell him that Hans (meaning von Dohnanyi) was active in the good cause. I was also given, I think by Schönfeld, a short written message of greetings from Helmuth von Moltke,[151] simply signed James, for his friend in England, Lionel Curtis of All Souls College, Oxford. In the evening I dined quietly with the British Minister and Mrs Mallet and had a long talk about the Sigtuna conversations.

The day closed with the receipt of two personal letters, one from Schönfeld enclosing the full text of the Statement which I had asked him to prepare, and one from Bonhoeffer. Both pastors spoke of what our meetings had meant, whatever the outcome.

"I cannot express what this fellowship you have shown to us means for us and my fellow Christians who were with us in their thoughts and prayers", wrote Schönfeld. The following is the text of the Statement, which Schönfeld delivered to Bell:

Statement by a German Pastor at Stockholm
31 May 1942

I.

The many opposition circles in Germany who had beforehand no real contact with each other have crystallised during the last winter into active opposition groups working now closely together as centres of a strong opposition movement to the whole Nazi régime on the European Continent.

There are three main groups of action preparing definitely to overthrow the Nazi régime and to bring about a complete change of power.

1. Essential parts of the leadership in the Army and in the central State administration.

(In the Army they include key men in the Highest Command [OKW] for the front troops, Navy and Air forces, as well as in the Central Command of the Home Military forces; also in the State administration the liaison men to the State Police forces largely in opposition to the Gestapo.)

2. The leaders of the former Trade Unions and other active liaison men to large parts of the workers.

(Through a network of key men systematically developed during the last six months they control now key positions in the main industrial centres as well as in the big cities like Berlin, Hamburg, Cologne and throughout the whole country.)

3. The leaders of the Evangelical Churches (under Bishop Wurm) and of the Roman Catholic Church (the Fulda Bishop Conference) acting together as the great corporations and as centres of resistance and reconstruction.

By their close co-operation these three groups of action have formed the strong opposition movement which, in the given situation, would have sufficient power to overthrow the present régime because of their control over large masses now having arms in their hands, and, as regards the workers, at their disposal.

II.

The leaders of these key groups are now prepared to take the next chance for the elimination of Hitler, Himmler, Göring, Goebbels, Ley and Co., together with whom the central leaders of the Gestapo, the SS and the SA would be destroyed at the same time, especially also in the occupied countries.

This change of power would not lead to the establishment of a military clique controlling the whole situation but to the coming into power of a government composed of strong representatives of the three key groups who are able and definitely prepared to bring about a complete change of the present system of lawlessness and social injustice.

Their programme is determined by the following main aims:

1. A German nation governed by law and social justice with a large degree of responsible self-administration through the different main provinces.

2. Reconstruction of the economic order according to truly socialistic lines; instead of self-sufficient autarchy a close co-operation between free nations, their economic interdependence becoming the strongest possible guarantee against self-reactionary European militarism.

3. A European Federation of free States or Nations including Great Britain which would co-operate in a close way with other federations of nations.

This Federation of Free European Nations to which would belong a Free Polish and a Free Czech Nation should have a common executive, under the authority of which a European Army should be created for the permanent ordering of European security. The foundations and principles of national and social life within this Federation of Free European Nations should be orientated or re-orientated towards the fundamental principles of Christian faith and life.

III.

The internal circumstances are becoming now peculiarly favourable to a coup d'etat by the Army and the other combined forces of the Opposition. It would help and quicken this process toward the change of power along the lines mentioned above (see II) if the Allies would make it clear whether they are prepared for a European peace settlement along the lines indicated. If otherwise the Allies insist on a fight to the finish the German opposition with the German Army is ready to go on with the war to the bitter end in spite of its wish to end the Nazi régime.

In the case of agreement for a European peace settlement as indicated, the Opposition Government would, after a coup d'etat, withdraw gradually all its forces from the occupied and invaded countries.

It would announce at once that it would restitute the Jewish part of the population at once to a decent status, give back the stolen property, and co-operate with all other nations for a comprehensive solution of the Jewish problem.

It would be prepared to take its full share in the common efforts for the rebuilding of the areas destroyed or damaged by the war. It would declare itself at once disinterested in any further co-operation with the Japanese Government and its war aims, being prepared, on the contrary to place at disposal its forces and war material for finishing the war in the Far East.

It would be prepared to co-operate for a real solution of the Colonial problem along the lines of a true mandate system in which all member nations of the European Federation should participate together with the other nations or federations of nations concerned.

It is to be expected that representatives of the SS will offer the elimination of Hitler in order to secure for themselves power and a negotiated peace.

It would be a real support for the start of the whole process towards the change of power as indicated if they would be encouraged in any way to go on.

It would help the opposition leaders to mobilise and to lead all the other forces of the Army and the nation against Himmler and the SS leaders against whom the bitterness and hatred is greater than against anyone else.

In regard to the Russian Problem.

1. The opposition groups have no aims to conquer or to get for Germany parts of Russia as a colonial area.

2. They hope it may be in the future possible to co-operate in a really peaceful way with Russia, especially in the economic and cultural field.

3. But they are not convinced that the totalitarian methods of revolutionary brutal warfare would be changed without very effective guarantees, even when the totalitarian régime in Central Europe would have been abolished.

4. They would regard the building up of an Orthodox Russian Church by the renewal of Christian faith in Russia as a real common basis which could further more than anything else the co-operation between Russia and the European Federation.

Bonhoeffer in this moving letter to Bell expressed his gratitude and hope:

1 June 1942

My dear Lord Bishop,
Let me express my deep and sincere gratitude for the hours you have spent with me. It still seems to me like a dream to have seen you, to have spoken to you, to have heard your voice. I think these days will remain in my memory as some of the greatest of my life. This spirit of fellowship and of Christian brotherliness will carry me through the darkest hour, and even if things go worse than we hope and expect, the light of these few days will never extinguish in my heart. These impressions of these days were so overwhelming that I cannot express them in words. I feel ashamed when I think of all your goodness and at the same time I feel full of hope for the future.
God be with you on your way home, in your work and always. I shall think of you on Wednesday. Please pray for us. We need it.
Yours most gratefully,
Dietrich

Bell left Sweden on 9th June, and reached home on 11th June. A week later, on 18th June he went to see the head of the Department concerned at the Foreign Office, Mr Warner, at whose suggestion he wrote to the Foreign Secretary, Anthony Eden.[152]

The Bishop's Lodging,
22 The Droveway, Hove
18 June 1942

Dear Mr Eden,
I have just got back from Sweden with what seems to me very important confidential information

about proposals from a big opposition movement in
Germany. Two German Pastors, both of them well
known to me for 12 years or more (one of them an
intimate friend) came expressly from Berlin to see
me at Stockholm. The movement is backed by leaders
of both the Protestant and Catholic Churches. They
gave me pretty full particulars, and names of
leading persons in the civil administration, in the
labour movement and in the Army, who are involved.
The credentials of these pastors are such that I
am convinced of their integrity and the risks they
have run.

I ought to say that I was staying at the British
Legation, and told Mr. Mallet all about it. He
thought the matter important enough to justify me
in asking if I might see you and tell you personally
what the pastors had told me. The information is
a sequel to the memorandum you have already seen,
brought from Geneva by Visser't Hooft of the World
Council of Churches, and having to do with von
Trott.

I have also today reported to Mr. Warner on my
visit to Sweden and given him some information as to
the visit of the pastors. It is his suggestion that
I am writing direct to you, and I should be very
grateful if you could receive me. I will bring my
papers with me. I could come any time on Saturday,
or from 3 p.m. onwards on Monday. From Tuesday to
Friday I have some engagements which I cannot break
in my diocese. I do not know whether you will be at
West Dean this week-end. If so, and it suited you,
I could easily come over after tea on the Sunday.
Yours very sincerely,
George Cicestr

**Bell also wrote to Leibholz about his meeting with Bonhoeffer in
Sweden:**

From The Bishop of Chichester.
The Bishop's Lodging
22. The Droveway, Hove, Sussex
Private
20 June 1942

My dear Leibholz,

Very many thanks for your letter and its welcome back.

To my great surprise I saw Dietrich at the end of my stay. He had come over specially as a courier with a 48 hour visa in order to see me. We talked very much on very important matters. I told him your news, of which he was very glad. He was very well. He said that Hitler's health was unfortunately very good; the uncle of whom he spoke in his letter was the war, not Hitler. His Seminary had been closed twice, and he had been forbidden by the Gestapo to preach or speak. He is at work now on a book and in connection with the Brethren's Council and at nights on political work.

I told him about your book, and your question as to publishing it anonymously. He wanted to know what was its exact subject, and whether there were things in the contents of the book which in themselves might cause difficulties for relations. We might get a word about this when we meet at Cambridge. He asked me to say Hans was very well and continuing his work on the right side. Of course he sent his sister and you and the girls his warmest love. It was a real delight to see him, as you can imagine. His coming was entirely unexpected. I had heard of his passing through Sweden on his way to Norway before I arrived (also as a courier), but Archbishop Eidem thought he had gone through as a soldier, and I could not find any way of communicating with him in any case. But he heard that I was in Stockholm, and so arrived.

Yours ever,
George Cicestr

Eden received Bell on 30th June. Bell gave Eden a full account of his experiences and conversations.[153]

(...) I emphasised my long-standing personal relations with the two pastors, and my association with them, and with Bonhoeffer in particular, before the war, in strong opposition to Hitler and all he stood for. I described the character of the opposition, and the questions put, and gave Mr Eden all the names which Bonhoeffer had given me.

Mr Eden (my diary notes) was much interested. He appreciated the fact that I had warned the pastors that the British Government was likely to be very reserved in its attitude, as opinion in Britain tended to blame all Germans for tolerating the Nazis for so long. Mr Eden himself seemed more inclined to think it possible that in some curious way the pastors, without their knowledge, were being used to put out peace feelers. He said that peace feelers had been put out in Turkey and Madrid. He must be scrupulously careful not to enter into even the appearance of negotiations with the enemy, and be able to say truthfully that this was so, both to Russia and to America.

Bell handed Eden the Statement, which Schönfeld had prepared for him, and his own "Memorandum of Conversations". Bell also told Eden that the pastors would be "waiting for some sort of reply" from Bell. Eden "promised to consider the whole matter and write later". The text of Bell's "Memorandum" read as follows:

Stockholm 1942
Secret
Memorandum of Conversation

I.

Two German Pastors came from Berlin to see the Bishop of Chichester in Stockholm at the end of May, 1942. They arrived independently, one of them only staying 48 hours. The Bishop saw them both individually and together on four separate days. They are men very well known to the Bishop, and have collaborated with him for many years in connection with the ecumenical movement, the World Council of Churches, and in different stages of the German Church struggle. One lives in Switzerland, but pays constant visits to Germany. The other lives in Berlin, and is one of the leaders of the Confessional Church; he has been forbidden by the Gestapo to preach or speak.

Their purpose was:

A. To give information as to the strong, organised opposition movement inside Germany, which

is making plans for the destruction of the whole
Hitler régime (including Himmler, Göring, Goebbels,
and the central leaders of the Gestapo, the SS and
the SA), and for the setting up of a new Government
in Germany of

    1. Representatives of certain strong anti-
Nazi forces in the Army and central State
Administration.

    2. Former Trade Union leaders.

    3. Representatives of the Protestant and
Catholic Churches, pledged to the following
policy:

      a) Renunciation of aggression.

      b) Immediate repeal of Nürnberg Laws, and
co-operation in international settlement of
Jewish problem.

      c) Withdrawal by stages of the German forces
from occupied and invaded countries.

      d) Withdrawal of support to Japan, and
assistance of Allies in order to end the war in
the Far East.

      e) Co-operation with the Allies in the
rebuilding of areas destroyed or damaged by the
war.

    B. To ask whether the Allies, on the assumption
that the whole Hitler régime had been destroyed,
would be willing to negotiate with such an new
German Government for a peace settlement, which
would provide for:

    1. The setting up of a system of law and social
justice inside Germany, combined with a large degree
of devolution in the different main provinces.

    2. The establishment of economic interdependence
between the different nations of Europe, both as
just in itself, and as the strongest possible
guarantee against militarism.

    3. The establishment of a representative
Federation of Free Nations or States, including a
Free Polish and a Free Czech Nation.

    4. The establishment of a European Army for the
control of Europe, of which the German Army could
form a part, under central authority.

    II. Character of the Opposition

    The opposition has been developing for some

time, and had some existence before the war. The war gives it its chance, which it is now waiting to seize. The opposition crystallised in the Autumn of 1941, and might have seized an opportunity in December, 1941, with the refusal of many officers to go on fighting in Russia. But no lead was given. Hitler's last speech, openly claiming to be above all laws, showed the German people more and more clearly the complete anarchy of the régime. The opposition has full confidence in the strength of the German Army, and is ready to go on with the war to the bitter end if the Allies were to refuse to treat with a new Government controlling a non-Hitlerite Germany, after the overthrow of the whole Hitler régime; but it believes that to continue the war on the present or on a greater scale in such circumstances would be to condemn millions more to destruction, especially in the occupied countries.

It also believes that a fight to the finish would be suicidal for Europe. Hence its desire first to destroy Hitler and his régime, and then to reach a peace settlement in which all the nations of Europe shall be economically interdependent, shall be protected against aggression by the possession of an adequate European military force, and shall be in some way federated. The opposition, while having some hesitations with regard to Soviet Russia, has the hope (as a result of impressions made by some of the high Russian officers on some of the German officers) of the possibility of reaching an understanding.

III. Organisation of the Opposition

The opposition is based on members of the State Administration, the State police, former Trade Union chiefs, and high officers in the Army. It has an organisation in every Ministry, military officers in all the big towns, Generals in command or holding high office in key places very near the Generals. It has key men armed in the broadcasting centres, in the big factories, and in the main centres of war and gas supply services. It is impossible to tell the numbers of the opposition. The point is that key positions everywhere are held by members of the opposition, and that key positions in Germany itself are of chief importance.

The following names were given as those of men who were deeply involved in the opposition movement:

Generaloberst Beck: Chief of General Staff before the Czechoslovak crisis in 1938. Aged 60.

Generaloberst von Hammerstein: Chief of General Staff before Beck.

Goerdeler: Ex-Price Commissar, former Lord Mayor of Leipzig. Civil Front Leader.

Leuschner: Former President of the United Trade Unions.

Kaiser: Catholic Trade Union leader.

All the above are said to be strong Christian characters, and the most important of all are Beck and Goerdeler.

Certain other persons of a less clear Christian character would be available, such as Schacht. Most of the Field Marshals are reliable, especially von Kluge, von Bock, Küchler and possibly Witzleben. Whether a member of the opposition or not, was not stated, but the question was asked whether England would favour a monarchy in Germany, in which case Prince Louis Ferdinand was possible. He had been fetched from the United States by Hitler after the heroic death of the Crown Prince's eldest son. He had been working in a Ford factory as a workman, and now lives on a farm in East Prussia. He is a Christian, has outspoken social interests, and is known to one of the two German Pastors. The leaders of the Protestant and Catholic Churches are also closely in touch with the whole opposition movement, particularly Bishop Wurm of Württemberg (Protestant) and Bishop von Preysing of Berlin, acting as the spokesman of the Catholic Bishops. (At the same time it should be said that included in the opposition are many who are not only filled with deep penitence for the crimes committed in Germany's name, but even say "Christians do not wish to escape repentance, or chaos, if it is God's will to bring it upon me".

IV. Action of the Opposition

The opposition is aware of impending revolt inside the Nazi party, of Himmler and his followers against Hitler; but while a successful coup by Himmler might be of service to the opposition, the complete elimination of Hitler and Himmler and the whole régime is indispensable. The plan of the opposition is the achievement of a purge as nearly simultaneous as possible on the Home Front and in the occupied countries, after which a new Government would be set up. In the securing of a new Government, the opposition realises the need of an effective police control throughout Germany and the occupied and invaded territories; and it appeared that the help of the Allied Armies as assistants in the maintenance of order would be both necessary and welcome, all the more if it were possible to associate with the Allied Armies the Army of a neutral power in the maintenance of order.

V. Enquiries by the Opposition of the Allied Governments

The above being the policy and plan of the opposition, the question arises as to what encouragement can be given to its leaders with a view to setting the whole process in motion and the facing of all the dangers involved. As examples of encouragement, such enquiries as the following are made:

1. Would the Allied Governments be willing to treat with a new bona fide German Government, set up on the lines described in A of Section I above, for a peace of the character described in B of Section I above?

(The answer to this might be privately given to a representative of the opposition through a neutral country.)

2. Could the Allies announce now publicly to the world in the clearest terms that once Hitler and the whole régime were overthrown, they would be prepared to negotiate with a new German Government which renounced aggression and was pledged to a policy of the character described in A of Section I above, with a view to a peace settlement of the

character described in B of Section I above?

VI. Means of Communication

Arrangements have been made by which any reaction in important British quarters which the Bishop of Chichester might be able to obtain could be communicated through a neutral channel. The British Minister in Stockholm was fully informed at the time of the tenor of the conversations. On his advice the Bishop warned the two German pastors not only that the American and Russian and the other Allied Governments would necessarily be concerned, but that the Foreign Office might take the view that the situation was too uncertain to justify any expression of opinion on its part. On the other hand, if it were thought desirable to obtain further elucidation, a confidential meeting could be arranged at Stockholm between a German representative and a representative of the Foreign Office or other suitable person.

Bell wrote to Leibholz again on 10th July, telling him that he had not heard from Eden since his interview with him on 30th June, and that he hoped that the Foreign Secretary was "giving careful consideration to the matters I laid before him".

From The Bishop of Chichester.
The Bishop's Lodging
22. The Droveway, Hove, Sussex

10 July 1942

My dear Leibholz,
Ever so many thanks for your kind letter of 8th July.
I am very much pleased and very glad that you thought that my report on my experiences in Sweden was so useful and realist. I entirely agree with you that the highly political character of the whole question by no means relieves Christians from doing what they can to find positive solutions. I have heard nothing from Mr Eden since my interview with him on June 30th. I hope that he is giving careful consideration to the matters I laid before him. I

hope indeed that other members of the Cabinet may also have been informed of what I told him.

I should very much like to see Mr Winant, but I am not quite sure what would be the best way of setting about it. I feel that I do not want to get things tangled and should be much happier if I had heard something from Mr Eden. But I will see what can be done and I realise that one has to act fairly quickly.

Many thanks for sending me the table of contents with the foreword. It is an extraordinarily interesting table of contents and deals with the very things that we most ought to be considering in relation to Christianity and politics. There does not seem to me, from the table of contents, the least sort of reason why the book should not be published under your own name. I am sure that Dietrich would be of the same opinion. I do very greatly appreciate the words which you have inserted in your preface about myself though I feel very unworthy of what you so kindly say.

I shall be in Oxford on Thursday at Balliol for a Conference on what are called Peace Aims, in which the Archbishop of Canterbury will be taking part, and if there is a moment of free time in which to get hold of you - I am afraid it is rather doubtful - I will do so.

All warmest greetings to your wife and the children.

Yours ever,
George Cicestr

The Foreign Secretary wrote to Bell on 17th July.

Foreign Office, S.W.1
Personal and Private
17 July 1942

Dear Lord Bishop,
When you came to see me on June 30th, you were good enough to leave with me a memorandum of your conversations with two German pastors whom you met in Stockholm at the end of May, together with the record of a statement by one of the pastors.

These interesting documents have now been given

the most careful examination, and, without casting any reflection on the bona fides of your informants, I am satisfied that it would not be in the national interest for any reply whatever to be sent to them.

I realise that this decision may cause you some disappointment, but in view of the delicacy of the issues involved I feel that I must ask you to accept it, and 1 am sure that you will understand.

Yours sincerely,
Anthony Eden

Eden's completely negative reply was "a disappointment" to Bell, and he told this to Leibholz.

From The Bishop of Chichester.
The Bishop's Lodging
22. The Droveway, Hove, Sussex
24 July 1942

My dear Leibholz,
Many thanks for your two letters. I have tried to find the reference to Goebbels in the *Daily Telegraph*, but unfortunately I could not find it. I will have another look later on. I very much appreciate what you say about Prussia; it was very useful to have this at the back of my mind when I was attending the Peace Aims Conference in Oxford. It was a very good conference indeed.

I am sorry to say that I have had a reply from Mr Eden, which, though it shows a real interest in what I told him, and in the memoranda I left with him, and throws no doubt on the trustworthiness of the source, takes the line that it would not be in the national interest to make any reply. This is a disappointment.

With all best wishes,
Yours very sincerely,
George Cicestr

Bell also expressed his frustration in a lengthy reply to Eden:

25 July, 1942

Dear Mr. Eden,

Many thanks for your letter of the 17th July. I am very glad that after most careful examination of the documents which I left with you, you feel that no reflection can be cast on the bona fides of the two German pastors. I must of course bow to your decision that it is not in the national interest to make any reply to them personally. But I do greatly hope that it may be possible for you in the near future to make it plain in an emphatic and public way that the British Government (and the Allies) have no desire to enslave a Germany which has rid itself of Hitler and Himmler and their accomplices. I found much evidence on many sides in Sweden, in addition to my information from the two Pastors, of the existence of a sharp distinction between the Nazis as such and a very large body of other Germans. It is the drawing of this distinction (with its consequences) by the Government in the most emphatic way which is so anxiously awaited by the opposition.

I have read your Nottingham speech with great attention and with much sympathy. I appreciate all you say about our resolution to continue to fight against the Dictator powers until they are all finally disarmed and rendered powerless to do further injury to mankind. I appreciate to the full your words about the recent atrocities, and your statement that these atrocities represent the policy of the German Government, and your declaration of a resolve to exact full and stern retribution. All these words are dearly intended to show the consequence of the determined British and Allied policy to have no truck with the Nazis. But if you could at some convenient opportunity make it plain that the infliction of stern retribution is not intended for those in Germany who are against the German Government, who repudiate the Nazi system and are filled with shame by the Nazi crimes, it would, I am sure, have a powerful and encouraging effect on the spirit of the opposition. I cannot get out of my mind the words which the Norwegian Minister used in a private conversation with me in Stockholm about the reality of the German opposition. The opposition, he said, hates Hitler but sees no hope held out by the Allies of any better treatment for the Anti-Nazis than for the Nazis. "It is either this (i.e. Hitler) or slavery. We hate this, but we prefer it to slavery". And I see that Goebbels has just been intensifying his propaganda in the German home front to the effect that the Allies are determined to destroy Germany. I do not believe that Lord Vansittart's policy is the policy of the British Government. But so long as the British Government fails to repudiate it, or make it clear that those who are opposed to Hitler and Himmler will receive better treatment at our hands than Hitler and Himmler and their accomplices, it is not unnatural that the opposition in Germany should believe that the Vansittart policy holds the field.

Mr. Churchill said in his first speech as Prime Minister in the House of Commons on May 13th, 1940 that our policy was "to wage war against a monstrous tyranny never surpassed in the dark and lamentable catalogue of human crime", and that our aim was "victory at all costs". If there are men in Germany also ready to wage war against the monstrous tyranny of the Nazis from within, is it right to discourage or ignore them? Can we afford to reject their aid in achieving our end? If we by our silence allow them to believe that there is no hope for any Germany, whether Hitlerite or anti-Hitlerite, that is what in effect we are doing.

    I am,
    Yours very truly,
    George Cicestr

The pastors had now to be informed about Eden's negative stance. So on 30th July Bell cabled to Visser't Hooft at Geneva the following message: "Interest undoubted, but deeply regret no reply possible. Bell".

Eden answered Bell's letter on 4th August.

    Foreign Office, S.W.1
    4 August 1942
    Confidential

    My dear Lord Bishop,

Thank you very much for your letter of July 25th about the German problem.

I am very conscious of the importance of what you say about not discouraging any elements of opposition in Germany to the Nazi régime. You will remember that in my speech at Edinburgh on May 8th I devoted quite a long passage to Germany and concluded by saying that if any section of the German people really wished to see a return to a German state based on respect for law and the rights of the individual, they must understand that no one would believe them until they had taken active steps to rid themselves of their present régime.

For the present I do not think that it would be advisable for me to go any further in a public statement. I realise the dangers and difficulties to which the opposition in Germany is exposed, but they have so far given little evidence of their existence and until they show that they are willing to follow the example of the oppressed peoples of Europe in running risks and taking active steps to oppose and overthrow the Nazi rule of terror I do not see how we can usefully expand the statements which have already been made by members of the Government about Germany. I think these statements have made it quite clear that we do not intend to deny to Germany a place in the future Europe, but that the longer the German people tolerate the Nazi régime the greater becomes their responsibility for the crimes which that régime is committing in their name.

Yours sincerely,
Anthony Eden

Bell replied on 17th August.

Private
as from: The Bishop's Lodging
22 The Droveway Hove, Sussex

17 August 1942
Dear Mr Eden,
Very many thanks for your letter of August 4th about the German problem, which has been forwarded to me in Scotland.

I much appreciate what you say about your consciousness of the importance of not discouraging any elements of opposition in Germany to the Nazi régime, and your reference to the very important speech which you made in Edinburgh on May 8. I also see the force of your point that the opposition in Germany should be ready to take similar risks to those taken by the oppressed peoples in Europe. The German opposition would probably reply that there is a difference, in view of the fact that the oppressed peoples have been promised deliverance by the Allies, and that Germany has not exactly been promised that. At the same time I fully see the point has got to be rubbed home that the opposition Germans themselves must do their part in opposing and overthrowing the Nazi rule.

Certainly the pastors and their friends in Germany are fully alive to the grave character of the responsibility borne by the German people for the crimes committed by the Nazis in their name. The hopes of a return to a German State based on respect for law and the rights of the individual, after the overthrow of the Nazis, and of a place for a reformed Germany in the future Europe, ought to be powerful factors in making the opposition declare itself more and more plainly.

Yours sincerely,
George Cicestr

The silence of the British Government, Bell felt, "was a bitter blow to those for whom the pastors stood". Yet they had not given up their hope, as was avowed by Bonhoeffer in his letter from Switzerland to Bell at the end of August:

28 August 1942
My Lord Bishop,
I have just received a letter from my sister in which she tells me that she has met you after your long journey. I am so glad to know that you have returned safely and that you have already seen many people. Since I wrote you last not much has changed here. Things are going as I expected them to go. But the length of time is, of course, sometimes a little enervating. Still I am hopeful that the day might not be far when the bad dream will be over

and we shall meet again. The task before us will
then be greater than ever before. But I hope we
shall be prepared for it. I should be glad to hear
from you soon. Wednesday has for many of my friends
become the special day for ecumenical intercession.
Martin [Niemöller] and the other friends send you
all their love and thanks. Would you be good enough
to give my love to my sister's family?
       In sincere gratefulness,
       I am yours ever,
       Dietrich

Bell was pleased to receive some news from Bonhoeffer. It exalted
Bell's spirits as well and mobilised him to undertake further initiatives
towards encouraging the Confessional Church in Germany. The cause
was not entirely lost because of Eden's negative attitude. On the contrary.
Bell went on insisting that the British Government must distinguish
between Germany and the Hitlerite State. Even Stalin was prepared
to do so. And Bell was planning to put the question in the House of
Lords, that since the Soviet Government had declared that they were not
contemplating the destruction of Germany, but the destruction of the
Hitlerite State, would the British Government make the same distinction
in their war aims? Bell disclosed his thoughts privately to Leibholz. The
letters to Leibholz tell us more about Bell's intentions:

1) Bell to Leibholz, 4 December 1942.

       The Palace,
       Chichester
       4 December 1942.

       My dear Leibholz,
       Very many thanks for the Christian News-Letter
which I am delighted to have, and also for your
former letter of the 8th November. I am reading the
Christian News-Letter during the week-end and will
let you have any thoughts that it arouses.
       I am very glad to have the message from
Dietrich. I have written to Pastor Suta. I have
also written much more fully, in the hope that the
news will get round to Dietrich, to Harry Johansson
at Sigtuna. I am glad to say that Bishop Brilioth

spent a good many hours with me at Chichester when he was over from Sweden, and I gave him a careful account of the important talks I had, of which you know. I very much hope that he may see some of our friends in Sweden, so that they may know what I have tried to do.

I wonder whether you have seen Fraenkel's book, *The Other Germany*, which is just out ? It contains in summary form seven Questions and Answers which were broadcast early in July in the BBC German News Service, giving far more definite and satisfactory answers about the Government policy to a Germany in which Hitler has been overthrown than have ever been made public in this country. I have been able to get the original text of these Questions and Answers, and am seeing Lord Cranborne about them in the hope of being able to ask a question in the House of Lords - to see whether they are a correct representation of the policy of His Majesty's Government.

Please give my best remembrances to your wife.
Yours very sincerely,
George Cicestr

2) Bell to Leibholz, 11th December 1942:

The Palace,
Chichester
11 December 1942

My dear Leibholz,
I was very glad to get your News-Letter Supplement. I took it, and Christianity, Politics and Power away with me to read on a journey to Birmingham yesterday, and I have now read both the Supplement and the book. I am immensely impressed with both, but of course with the book particularly, as a full and clear statement of the position. I am a learner from you, but I agree whole-heartedly with you. I am sure that the position which you put before your readers is one which ought to be put forth on a large scale by the Churches just now wherever they can find an opportunity. There are two points on which I should very much like you, if you have time, to expand a little.

First, it would be extremely important to define in a clear way a statement of principles on which Christians could agree and could issue. On page 63 you speak about the continuous contribution of Christian thought, with special concern for the order of social life, etc. On page 64 you deal with the relations which should exist between the nations. You give certain illustrations of the points on which agreement could be found and sated, and you deal with the point at the beginning of the chapter - on the final issue at stake. What I feel that we badly need is a platform on which Christians of different Churches should unite, and on which they could collaborate with others sympathetic to the Christian tradition, comparable for force and clarity with the Facist Decalogue given on page 180 of Oakshott's *Social and Political Doctrines of Contemporary Europe* (Cambridge Press), and Hitler's Twenty-Five Points given on page 190 of the same book. There are probably similar brief statements of the Communist position. The Ten Points of Christmas, 1940 - the Pope's and the Oxford Conference, give something of what I mean. But I think they want to be put a little more sharply on the one hand, and possibly (though here collaboration with non-Christians raises a difficulty) in a rather more religious framework. Long ago Archbishop Söderblom pressed for a moral creed on which the Christian Churches could unite. But nobody has really tackled this. I mentioned it once in a letter to Madariaga, after reading a letter of his to *The Times*. He was sympathetic but really non-committal. I think Professor Vincent Smith of Oxford would be more sympathetic to this. I wonder if you know him ?

The kind of combination which I would like to see would be that of the statement of the Principles of Natural Law given by the Catholic Bishops in Germany earlier (I think) this year, in their protest to the State, and reproduced either in one of the Spiritual Issues bulletins of the M.O.I, or in the C.N.L., and the Ten Points of Christmas 1940. Does this wake any spark in your mind?

The second point concerns your brief analysis of power in your second chapter. I wonder whether there are ways in which the element of spiritual power, used I agree for political purposes, could be further drawn out for creative work in connection with the task, Christianity and politics? I am writing a longer letter than I intended. But there is one other matter of which I want to tell you, for I am sure it will interest you. I enclose a copy of a leaflet scattered by the R.A.F. at the beginning of last July, and widely disseminated on the BBC German News. I was able to get hold of it through Heinrich Fraenkel, who gives a brief summary in his new book, published by Lindsay Drummond and called *The Other Germany*. When I came to this chapter (at the end) in which the Questions and Answers are summarised, I at once saw how very important they were, and asked him if he could get me the original text in full. He did, and I got them translated. I have given notice two weeks' running to ask a question in the House of Lords as to whether the Answers to these Questions are a correct representation of the policy of His Majesty's Government. I postponed asking the question, at Lord Cranborne's request, pending a talk with him. I had this talk, and it was arranged that I should ask the question last Wednesday. But he rang me up again to ask for postponement and I am to see Mr Eden. There is great reluctance to give any publicity to these Questions and Answers in this country. This makes me very anxious. The Answers seem to me to give a far clearer and more satisfactory description of what our war aims should be than any we have yet heard. I am hoping to see Mr Eden in the next three or four days.

I am so glad you have heard from Dietrich. With all warmest remembrances to your wife and yourself,

Yours very sincerely,
George Cicestr

3) Bell to Leibholz, 17th December 1942.

The Palace,
Chichester
17 December 1942

My dear Leibholz,
I saw Mr Eden on Tuesday about the R.A.F. leaflet. He said that he was now in charge of political

warfare, and that the leaflets were distributed according to a plan, and that he had made it an absolute condition that the contents of the leaflets should not be canvassed in Parliament or elsewhere. A debate on the contents of a particular leaflet would be in his judgement most mischievous from the point of view of the general political warfare campaign. 1 replied that what had pleased me about the answers to these Questions was the clear distinction between Hitlerite Germany and the other Germany, a distinction which was not anything like so evident in his or the Prime Minister's public statements; that I was not wedded to the contents of this leaflet, but that I did very much want to get a statement made which showed that His Majesty's Government was acting on that policy and was ready to tell Germany so officially.

He did not object to my raising a debate on this subject in the House of Lords, and when I said that one way of doing it might be to call attention to the remarks made by Stalin on Russia's war aims at the end of his speech of November 6th, and to ask whether the intention to destroy the Hitlerite State but not Germany, the Hitlerite army but not the German army was also the policy of His Majesty's Government, he said that he thought he could probably say yes to that, and liked the idea. I said that I would like to do that. He told me to take the matter up with Lord Cranborne, who would consult him. My idea would be to ask the Question towards the end of January, as the House only resumes sittings about January 17th .

I have drafted a Question as follows: "To call attention to the passages in M. Stalin's speech of November 6th in which he drew a distinction between Germany and the Hitlerite State, the German armed forces and the Hitlerite army, and said that Russia did not contemplate the destruction of Germany and the German army, but the destruction of the Hitlerite state and the Hitlerite army (and their leaders) and to ask whether His Majesty's Government made the same distinction in their war aims; and to move for papers".

However, before writing to Lord Cranborne, I want to ask you whether the form in which the Question is put could and would, be twisted by Goebbels so as to make it appear that I or the Church of England had turned Communist. In my speech I should make my attitude absolutely clear to a quite different effect. The advantage of using Stalin's remarks as a peg on which to hang a question is that it is very difficult for His Majesty's Government to refuse to make the same distinction. If I were to make my question broader, without reference to Russia' s war aims, it would be easier to give a vaguer reply. And even if I did put a more general question, without mentioning Stalin, I expect I should have to mention the distinction drawn by him as an illustration in my speech. One of the main points, however, in my speech would be to express the advantage of Britain showing that there is another alternative besides a Communist revolution to National Socialism. I should stress the character of the opposition which is based on the Churches, and the bureaucracy and certain quarters in the army etc.

Let me have your candid opinion. If you care to amend my Question, or suggest an alternative, all the better.

With all best-wishes to you and your wife
and children for Christmas,
Yours very sincerely,
George Cicestr

The circumstances were now such that they would not permit direct correspondence between Bell and Bonhoeffer. Yet on one occasion Bell could not hold back. Bonhoeffer's birthday was on 4th February. So was Bell's and that of Bonhoeffer's twin sister, Sabine. What a "happy link", Bell wrote to Mrs. Leibholz on 2nd February 1943, "that you and Dietrich and I should have our birthday on the same day," offering her and Dietrich "my affectionate greetings, and best wishes". [Letter to Mrs Leibholz, 2nd February 1943, see Annex 4.]

Bell had an opportunity to manifest his views publicly in the House of Lords when on 11th February 1943 Lord Vansittart moved to resolve, "That, in view of the systematic atrocities committed both by the Gestapo and the German Army, remedies should be proposed before systematic extermination has gone beyond repair". The noble Lord contended that the Germans, the Herrenvolk "are minded to win this war, even if they lose it, and they intend to do so on a basis of population.

They count on achieving that deadly purpose by the wholesale stripping of all territory once occupied by processes of enfeeblement and starvation which prevent the victims from breeding, and by the massacre of the inhabitants, particularly those capable of intellectual leadership". Quoting the German writer, Thomas Mann, Vansittart maintained that German militarism was the manifestation of German morality. That is why Germans did not "protest against anything, however bloody", nor for that matter did even the German Churches ever protest against the atrocities of the German Army. Thus the whole problem lay "in making the Germans protest against their own instincts".[154] The Germans had not "taken seriously our threats of retribution and have gone on their way, murdering and committing atrocities, banking on ultimate impunity and fortified by the remembrance of our weakness towards the war criminals at the end of the last war".[155] That could not be the policy now. Those found guilty must be hanged. Vansittart suggested that "we should not only name fresh culprits but include fresh categories. For instance, I should like to see included among those proclaimed as liable to the penalty of death all those engaged in the German policy of starving whole peoples to death, as in the case of Belgium and Greece".[156] He also ventured to urge that "we should, anyhow for the time being, dispense with the soft sawder and strike out boldly with a new policy and new voices". And what would be the new policy? Vansittart asked for two things: "I ask that henceforth the consideration of the interests of the victims should be the main, though of course not the only, criterion of our broadcasting in German; and secondly, I ask that we should drop conciliation until the Germans drop atrocities".[157]

Viscount Maugham, [158] who followed, "thoroughly" agreed with the idea that those guilty of crimes earn punishment. But he wished to make it quite clear that in his view "this country cannot, in accordance with its ancient traditions, accept the view that we punish people unless we are satisfied that they are guilty of these terrible atrocities".[159]

The Lord Bishop of Chichester, George Bell, said that he was "in whole-hearted agreement" with Lord Vansittart, "as to the grossness of the brutalities which have been committed by the Gestapo and the German Army", but he was not "wholly in agreement with the noble Lord's diagnosis of the sources of the crime". This lead him, he feared, "to a difference of judgement as to the remedies which he has recommended".

And as it was "the remedies which are of supreme importance, and as the nature of a remedy is intimately associated with the question of on whom lies the principal responsibility, I venture to make a few observations on this all-important point".[160] It was not true, argued Bell, that the Germans had not protested against the Nazi rule. Why should there have been so many concentration camps full of so many Germans even before the war began? He had, he said, in his "possession reports of the inside of concentration camps in and since 1934. The tale they tell of unspeakable atrocities against Germans is fully consistent with what the Nazis have perpetrated, and are perpetrating on the largest scale, against the Poles, Yugoslavs, Czechs, and other nationals in occupied territories. It is Hitler and Himmler, the head of the Gestapo, it is Goebbels and Goering, Bormann and Ribbentrop and their partners in Nazi leadership who have carried on and extended during the war atrocities systematically perpetrated long before it. Their reign then was, their reign now is, the reign of the assassin".[161] Many Germans knew of these atrocities, and they [Bell told the House that he knew this at first hand] felt ashamed and humiliated. "Many have protested in spite of the machine guns. Many are in concentration camps, many have been killed, many have committed suicide, as the only form of protest possible to them".

He was not, said Bell, "attempting to deny a dark streak in the character of many Germans, but I do claim that the most powerful, the most significant portion of Germany and the German character, is not all black. I am not attempting to deny the over-docility of the Germans, but I recall that when they had no friends outside to help them in their struggle against Fascism and tyranny for six and a half years before the war, and when during the war they find themselves involved in as heavy a condemnation as the tyrant whom they loathe, their lot is not easy. Whatever our feelings about silence, we must remember that the control exercised by the Party and by the Gestapo is extremely severe and extremely clever, and that it is very difficult for the opposition to get out into the daylight, so that when one ray does appear it becomes almost a miracle".[162]

What then was the remedy? Of one thing Bell was sure. Lord Vansittart had not threatened all Germany with destruction. "To do anything of that kind [reasoned Bell] is to hound on the bestial Germans to more bestialities, and to play the very game that Goebbels wants the

Allies to play, by uniting the anti-Nazis and the non-Nazis with the Nazis, under the lash of despair. The war has never been popular in Germany. It is hated now. But to line up the Nazi assassins in the same row with the people of Germany whom they have outraged, is to make for more barbarism, possibly to postpone peace, and to make quite certain an incredible worsening of the conditions of all Europe when at last peace comes"[163] The true remedy for the atrocities was "to fix the guilt of the atrocities on the real criminals, Adolf Hitler and his co-assassins, the heads of the Nazi Party, the Gestapo and their satellites, and, having boldly and plainly fixed the guilt on them, to declare as plainly that we take a very different view of other Germans who loathe the Nazi régime and repudiate the lust for world dominion, and that we appeal to them to join us from within Germany in overthrowing Hitler and his gang. The remedy is to tell those inside Germany who are anti-Fascist that we want their help, that we will help them in getting rid of the common enemy, and that we intend that a Germany, delivered from Hitlerism, shall have fair play and a proper place in the family of Europe".[164]

Viscount Elibank[165] rose to tell their Lordships that "the only way at the present time in which we can induce Germany to surrender is to let the Germans know that we intend to defeat them, and that we shall go on until we do".

Lord Sempill[166] suggested that "careful consideration" should be given to the suggestions made by Lord Vansittart with regard to broadcasting, namely that vigorous words should be directly spoken.[167]

The Earl of Selborne,[168] the Minister of Economic Warfare, spoke for the Government. He understood that Lord Vansittart had "no desire to exterminate the German people". What was needed was to draw "the difference between acts carried out in the heat of battle and the cold-blooded, inhuman cruelties which the German Government have systematically and deliberately inflicted on the helpless civilian populations at their mercy".[169] He thought that the House was "unanimous on the point that these individuals who can be proved to have been guilty of these atrocities must be brought to justice".

At the end of the debate Lord Vansittart begged to withdraw the Motion.

Bell could not immediately inform Bonhoeffer on the recent debate in the House of Lords. Later it was even more difficult to do so.

Bonhoeffer was arrested on 5th March 1943. Bell, unhappy about the situation, felt more disposed to question the British Government on its policy towards Nazi Germany. When on 10th March 1943 the House of Lords met, The Lord Bishop of Chichester "had the following Notice on the Paper: To call attention to the passage in M. Stalin's speech of 6th November, 1942, in which he said that it was not Russia's aim 'to destroy Germany for it is impossible to destroy Germany'... but that 'the Hitlerite State can and should be destroyed', and to ask whether His Majesty's Government in their war aims make the same distinction between Germany and the Hitlerite State; and to move for Papers".

The Government was not happy with Bell's action. Anthony Eden had tried through Lord Cranborne[170] to persuade Bell not to put the question. But Bell was not convinced.

The question he was to ask, Bell said [opening the debate], had "much to do with the hastening of victory". He was "as clear as any man about the necessity of the complete and final defeat of the present German military machine". But his question also had "much to do with the pattern of European order after the war". It raised "the issue of war aims and the character of the cause for which we and our Allies are contending". It was not "a matter of good or bad Germans; it is a matter of creeds, creeds which pass the frontiers of nations, and of the faith by which the Allies are to overcome the Hitlerite State and the Hitlerite system, wherever found, and build for the future".

Bell put his question very simply: "Do His Majesty's Government make the same distinction as does Premier Stalin between the Hitlerite State and the German people in their prosecution of the war and their view of our war aims"?

The Lord Bishop suggested that "a public announcement by the Government, in emphatic, unhesitating terms, would be particularly valuable now". Bell then set forth to say why.

A mere anti-German slogan would not do. "We must show a positive conception of the future of Europe and of the principles on which a future order will be built". Bell reminded their Lordships that vast number of Germans had been persecuted by the Nazis before and during the war. "It is no mere myth that hundreds of thousands of Aryans were sent to concentration camps, that thousands were executed, that the prisons were overcrowded; it is no mere myth that many hundreds, many thousands, of so-called Aryan families had the ashes of their nearest relatives cynically sent to them from prisons and concentration camps; it is no mere myth that hundreds of thousands, nay probably millions, of Aryans are now living in Nazi Germany as permanent suspects, untouchable from the Nazi point of view, trembling in face of the direct and indirect persecution of the Gestapo. When we are tempted to blame the German people for their docility, we must remember the multitude of assassins and spies".[171]

Bell went on to remind their Lordships that "the opposition that was most effective and world resounding was that of the Christian Church, Catholic and Protestant. The Catholic Church stood up, the Confessional Church stood up". The whole world was "convinced that in the Nazis they faced the destroyers of Christianity and the enemies of God. They were not afraid to denounce the Nazi Government, not simply for interference with religious exercises, but for their denial of freedom, for their rejection of the rights of man, of the individual and of the family, for their idolatry of race and for their contempt of law".[172] And this opposition was still there. It "is an opposition continuous, very subtle, and determined. Much of the opposition has been by implication rather than direct". But let "us never forget they have no arms while the Nazi régime is ruthless. Spies and assassins are everywhere with their machine guns and their revolvers. But no wise statesman will ignore this opposition. They have no weapons, but they have a great faith in the possibility, once given help from outside, of most vigorous action".[173]

Bell, therefore, believed the British Government should "declare in unequivocal terms that a Germany that has overthrown Hitler and all he stands for, a Germany that repudiates all desire for military domination and renounces Hitler's crimes and anti-Jewish laws and Hitler's gains – that such a Germany can be saved and will be welcomed to a proper place in the family of nations".[174]

The Lord Bishop proceeded then to emphasise another important point. That was "the distinction between the Hitlerite State and the German people from the point of view of the future of Europe." The present war, he said, was not a war of nation against nation. "It is a revolutionary war, it is a war of faiths in which the nations themselves are divided. It is necessary to leave no doubt which creed and which leaders in any nation we, the Allies, are ready to support. Our banner is the banner of liberty, democracy and Christian civilisation against slavery, tyranny and barbarism. We must choose, and let the whole world know we choose, between the Hitlerite State for all Europe and the rule of freedom for all Europe. ... We must make the choice as clear as crystal. There is no time to lose".[175]

Bell ended his speech with an apology, for demanding the attention of their Lordships for so long.

Lord Faringdon,[176] who rose next to address the House said that he was sure that "your Lordships who have listened to the brilliant moving speech of the right reverend Prelate will agree with me that no apology was called for".[177] He thought that it was "very difficult to follow that speech", that "there is very little to be added, and that what one can add cannot be added so eloquently as the right reverend Prelate put it". Supporting the motion Lord Faringdon believed "the time has come – indeed it is probably past – when His Majesty's Government would be well advised to make a statement supporting and in line with that of Mr Stalin".[178]

Lord Vansittart commended Bell for his "eloquent and persuasive speech", giving the impression that he agreed with what the right reverend Prelate had said. But in fact he repeated his old arguments that Germany as a whole was to be blamed for Hitler's crimes: "in order to civilise the Germans you have to beat them; and a very handsome job the Russians are making of it".[179] Vansittart did not miss the opportunity to make cynical remarks on Bell's arguments. This invited a critical comment from Lord Lang of Lambeth.[180] Lord Vansittart had begun, Lord Lang said, "by appearing to be ready to agree with the Bishop, but before long I fear, if I may say so, he went back into his old ways. He said he was astonished at his own moderation. He must be alone in that astonishment".[181] The truth was, argued Lord Lang, that though Lord Vansittart brought to bear upon his indictment of the German nation "all his immense knowledge and experience and all his brilliance, he is very apt to do what advocates sometimes are apt to do – namely, to overstate the case and to deprive it of a sense of proportion which is always a mark of wisdom".[182] The Bishop, said Lord Lang, "also showed traces of that similar tendency to overstatement". In principle, however, Lord Lang supported Bell. He thought that Stalin's distinction did "give some encouragement to those who at great risk and often with great difficulty have kept themselves free from the Nazi taint". And for that reason Lord Lang suggested "that one of the most important things we can do at this present juncture is not to exaggerate but not to overlook the distinction which Marshal Stalin has drawn, and I hope that in view of all that depends upon it His Majesty's Government may be disposed to give it, with whatever explanation they think fit, some measure of real endorsement".[183]

Viscount Cecil of Chelwood[184] intervened to express his "gratitude and appreciation of the Motion of the right reverend Prelate because it raises a point of vast importance not only with a view to what we are going to do after the war, but even with a view to what we shall do in order to hasten victory in that war". Hence these questions could not "be disposed of by casual sneers or sarcasm or anything of that kind".[185] Viscount Cecil agreed that there was "a considerable body of non-Nazi opinion in Germany". But he was "extremely doubtful whether you will see anything in the nature of a rebellion in Germany until much later in the war than the stage which we have at present reached".[186] But what could be done might be to do our utmost to assist" those Germans who were opposed to the Nazi Government.[187]

The Earl of Onslow[188] said that he did not trust the Germans: "they will still have the desire for domination and expansion"[189] ... "But I do not see why Germany should not take part in all the peaceful activities of the world and be on equal footing with other nations, provided it is made impossible for Germany to upset the whole world again in an aggressive war".[190]

The Earl of Perth[191] rose to say how much he sympathised "generally" with Bell's Motion. He believed that "there must be in a considerable number of German minds a feeling in favour of peace and opposed to war, and we ought to work on that as far as we can".[192]

The Lord Chancellor, Viscount Simon ,[193] closed the debate. He spoke at length. He declared that he would like now to say "in plain terms on behalf of His Majesty's Government, that we agree with Premier Stalin, first, that the Hitlerite State should be destroyed, and, secondly, that the whole German people is not (as Dr Goebbels has been trying to persuade them) thereby doomed to destruction. I put the two propositions with equal prominence and equal clearness and equal firmness. I want the right reverend Prelate to feel that if those are the questions he wants answered, answered they are, and on behalf of His Majesty's Government I am glad to have this opportunity of making both assertions with equal emphasis afresh".[194] The Lord Chancellor wished further to add that "we British will never seek to take vengeance by wholesale mass reprisals against the general body of the German people. Our methods will be the methods of justice".[195] He also wanted to make it clear that "we are not seeking to deny to Germany a place in the Europe of the future. But the longer the German people tolerate the Nazi régime, the greater becomes their responsibility for the crimes which that régime is committing in their name. If there are men in Germany who realise that they have allowed themselves to be the tools of this wicked system, if there are men in Germany who are ready to wage war against the monstrous tyranny of the Nazis from within, then we seek in every way to encourage them".[196] The Lord Chancellor went even further: "We desire to encourage, in every way we can, the opposition inside Germany which has been described by the right reverend Prelate".[197]

Bell was greatly satisfied with what he called the "deliberate and important answer by the noble and learned Viscount who sits on the Woolsack".[198] The Lord Chancellor had, he said, answered the questions contained in his Motion, which he now begged leave to withdraw.

Bell had now succeeded in achieving his chief aim: that the distinction between the Hitlerite State and the German people should recognised, and that every help possible should given to the opposition inside Germany.

Annex 4

1. George Bell to A. Koechlin, 9 May 1940.
2. George Bell to Prof. Leibholz, 26 December 1941.
3. George Bell to Mrs. Leibholz, 2 February 1943.

9 May 40

THE PALACE,
CHICHESTER.

My dear Kontki

I am very grateful for
your letter. It was a great help
in the final drafting of Message,
as you will see — esp. at the conclusion.
It is to be published in England and
abroad on Saturday.

Thank you also very much for all the
other points in your letter.

272

On Monday Goering's sister in law
(. Sunday) Countess Wilamowitz-
Mollendorf can ?? ?? li
See me. She knows Goering (whom)
will — and knows Hitler. My
folk was. I think, by ?? and I
made. ?? points which she took away
with her. She was a friend of Söderblom.

Yours ever

George ??

THE BISHOP'S LODGING,
22, THE DROVEWAY,
HOVE, SUSSEX.

PRESTON 2518.

My dear Leibholz

I was much touched by your Christmas letter, your kind words and all the friendship they breathe. Believe me your & your wife's friendship has been a great encouragement to me. and a precious possession which must not perish. I append our friendship as threefold, embracing you & your wife (& children) & Dietrich — all together. And just the means to each other, when actually in touch with one.

I don't suppose you listen to the English broadcast in German often. But you may like to know that a broadcast message from me (spoken in German by Hildebrandt) was sent

over the air on Christmas Eve at 9 p.m.
to the oppressed Christians in Germany.
I hope some of our friends there are
listening, and may have been encouraged.
I will have a copy made and sent to you.
I hope your Christmas went peacefully
and with gladness for the children. And
I hope that 1943 may be happier than
1942. You may could have the
enclosed photo.

will hopes also that the ... for many
a family in the immediate future may be
clear soon, and warmest greetings

Yours ...
George ...

THE PALACE,
CHICHESTER.

My dear Mrs Leibholz

This is just a line which
will I hope reach you on your
and Dietrich's birthday to offer

you and him my affectionate
greetings, and best wishes.

I have chanced a telegram of
greeting to Pastor Luß, hoping he

may understand. It is such a happy

link that you - Dietrich and I

should have our birthday on the

same day.   How I hope that

a this year gives. we may not

steadily means peace and order

and a revision of ... and

friends.

Please tell your husband my
debate will now be first.

business on March 10.

It seems a long way off. But
there ~~may have many~~ obstacles.
there will be many

I shall be in Oxford on Feb 9,
and trust I may somehow have

the choice of a word within

My love to the children

Yours most sincerely

George Lucki

6

"The Fundamental menace to our civilisation is Nihilism"

There were anxious moments in other fields. On 28th July 1943 Bell intervened in the debate in the House of Lords on the problem of the temporary asylum of refugees. He pleaded with the Government "not to fall short of that generous and active spirit in dealing especially with the racial victims of the Nazis in these four years of war".[199] More help was needed, and urgently. The question of temporary asylum was "an enormous shelter" in itself and a "safety valve".[200]

The fact that Bonhoeffer was still in prison bothered Bell. He wished Bonhoeffer were free, and wrote to Leibholz how anxious he was. [Bishop Bell to Prof. Leibholz, 21st November 1943. See Annex 5.]

Presently, what concerned Bell still more was the indiscriminate bombing of German cities. He wrote once that "since the time of Grotius,[201] an attempt has been made to draw a distinction between the combatant and the civilian, and that, although one hears people argue that it is better for the whole community to be in the war, the blurring of the distinction in the present war by air bombing, and particularly night bombing, is, from a moral and humanitarian point of view, a retrograde step".[202]

Bell set forth this argument in the September (1943) issue of his Diocesan Gazette. "When [he wrote] a Minister of the Government speaks in exulting terms of a ruthless and destructive bombing of the German people", then "we have a real cause to grieve for a lowering of moral tone, and also to fear greatly for the future ... To bomb cities as cities, deliberately to attack civilians, quite irrespective of whether or not they are actively contributing to the war effort is a wrong deed, whether done by the Nazis or by ourselves".[203]

The undaunted Bishop raised this matter in the House of Lords on 9th February 1944 to the displeasure of the Government and many more. Bell said that it was immoral to obliterate civilian and non-military objects. It was fatal to the future relationships of the peoples of Europe. Why was the British Government blind to the psychological side of their policy? "Why is there this inability to reckon with the moral and spiritual facts? Why is there this forgetfulness of the ideals by which our cause is inspired?"[204]

Bell's speech was welcomed and highly praised by some, and cursed and rejected by others. "May God bless you [wrote one] for your words in the House of Lords yesterday, fearless and forceful: I have been longing and praying for some authoritative voice to be raised in protest against this obliteration bombing, and now the prayer has been completely answered". "It is indeed strange [wrote another] that you should see fit to concern yourself with the sufferings of the people of Berlin, when there are so many cases of tragic suffering around you in this country, caused by his war, which seems to have escaped your notice".[205]

The mass media were equally divided. Bell inferred [in a letter to a friend on 25th February] that "this very fact is an indication of the uneasiness of conscience which great numbers have". One thing certainly cheered him "very much; and that is that of the large flow of letters addressed to me at Chichester, the proportion of supporters to condemners is three to one".[206]

With the invasion of the Allied forces in Normandy in June 1944 the war had entered a new phase. Then came the sensational news from Germany that an assassination attempt on Hitler on 20th July had failed. It seemed clear now that the opposition movement in Germany had not after all been docile. The men involved in this attempt were those whom Bonhoeffer had mentioned to Bell in Stockholm in 1942. Since the attempt had failed the consequences were equally tragic. The conspirators were either hanged, or shot dead. Bell's immediate concern was what would happen to Bonhoeffer, who was in prison at the time of the attempt on Hitler was made. There was no mistaking his association with the opposition. For the moment Bonhoeffer was still in prison in Berlin. Bell now wanted to help those members of the opposition, who had presently escaped Hitler's vengeance. Bell wrote to the Foreign Secretary, Anthony Eden, on July 27th and again on 3rd August (1944), to see if those opposition leaders who were still at large could be helped to leave Germany. Eden's response on 8th and 17th August was negative.[207] How little the Government cared for the future! And yet it was Bell who had prescience of new Europe after the war.

On 14th December 1944 Bell intervened to appealed to His

Majesty's Government that in the liberation of Europe, "freedom, order and food must be linked together as closely as possible. The military administration and the relief administration must work on the common task with the smallest possible interval between them", for let us not forget "how political bitterness is fostered by hunger and enforced idleness".[208]

But it was on the construction of post-war Europe that Bell's vision was deeply profound. In a debate on "Unifying Forces of Europe" in the House of Lords on 19th December Bell set forth in detail his views. In order to rebuild the underlying European unity [he said], "and to secure for every European citizen certain fundamental rights ... we have to go beyond politics". Something deeper than "a political impulse" was "required to secure lasting unity now". The goal of European unity was more likely to be achieved "if we build on the culture which all European peoples have in common". The peoples of Europe all possessed a "common form of culture, based on four common spiritual traditions. There is the humanist tradition, which lies behind the literary and intellectual culture of the educated classes and is largely responsible for the liberal and humanitarian element in our civilisation. There is the scientific tradition, perhaps the clearest example of the part played by intellectual collaboration in European culture. There is the tradition of law and government which, while naturally more affected by national political divisions, possesses important common elements which distinguishes European from Asiatic society. Lastly, there is the Christian religion, which provided the original bond of unity between European peoples and has influenced every part of Europe and every section of European society".[209]

All these traditions were important, but it was the last which seemed to Bell was "the most important and potentially unifying of them all". Few would deny, he said, "and the fact has constantly been affirmed today – that of all the crises in which we are involved the spiritual crisis is the gravest. There is a profound sense of frustration and despair; there is not only a material but a moral disintegration. Without a recovery of purpose, without a restoration of hope, the dissolution of European culture is inevitable". The fundamental menace to "our civilisations" was "Nihilism – the attitude of destruction and negation which calls evil good and good evil".[210]

Bell emphasised the significance of Christianity "as a great unifying force for Europe". The permanent fact was that in spite of "the deep differences in the dogmatic field, there is still such a thing as a common Christian faith".[211] The Church, be it Catholic, Protestant or Orthodox, had a "unifying function to fulfil in the days which follow the liberation".[212]

Bell himself had been for years working towards Christian co-operation. The World Council of the Churches, chiefly initiated by Bell, was in process of formation. The principal purpose of this Council was to promote "the growth of an ecumenical consciousness in the members of all the Churches" and to help in the development of spiritual European identity. It would begin its work the moment hostilities ceased.

In April 1945 that moment had come. There was now occasion to be joyous and optimistic. Not so for Bell. He suffered the most painful moment in his life when news reached him that Bonhoeffer had been executed, together with other members of the opposition movement accused of conspiring against Hitler. Bonhoeffer had been transferred from prison to the concentration camp Buchenwald on 7th February and then executed on 9th April at Flossenbürg. Before Bonhoeffer was taken to the scaffold, he left a message for Bell with a British fellow-prisoner, Captain Payne Best:

"Tell him that for me this is the end but also the beginning – with him I believe in the principle of our Universal Christian brotherhood which rises above all national interests, and that our victory is certain – tell him too that I have never forgotten his words at our last meeting" [in Stockholm on 1 June 1942].[213]

These were powerful words, which moved Bell to tears when he heard them. Bell now resolved, as never before, to carry with passion and dedication the standard of Bonhoeffer: "Our Universal Christian Brotherhood which rises above all National Interests". April 9th was indeed the physical end for Bonhoeffer. But really his spirit never ended with his execution. It survived and has survived. And when Bonhoeffer talked of "the beginning", it also meant the continuity of all that he had stood for.

The "beginning" now meant the spiritual reconstruction of the post-war Europe. Bell laid particular emphasis on the rights of the individual, the "common man". In a speech on 17th April 1945 in the

House of Lords Bell vigorously stressed that the promotion of respect for human rights and fundamental freedom, however interpreted and conditioned, were "not the rights of nations", but "the rights of individuals". They were "part of the indestructible sovereignty of man, the common man".[214] Only when these rights were guaranteed and with them economic and social justice for all nations could world order and peace be permanently secured.

Bell's immediate attention was given up to the post-war situation in Germany. His chief concern was to unite the divided German Evangelical Church. He proceeded to achieve what would have been Bonhoeffer's job, had he been alive. So when the German Evangelical Church Council met at Stuttgart on 19th October 1945 Bell was present together with delegates from France, Holland, Norway and the USA (A. Koechlin and Visser't Hooft among them) representing the World Council of Churches. Bell helped Niemöller and Dibelius in drafting what came to be known as the Stuttgart Declaration of the German Evangelical Church. Dr A. Koechlin wrote later that he was "convinced that it was very much easier for the Germans to give the Declaration to a personality like the Bishop of Chester whom they trusted and loved, than to any other man".[215] With "great pain [the Declaration read] do we say: through us has endless suffering been brought to many peoples and countries", and "we accuse ourselves for not being more courageous, for not praying more faithfully, for not believing more joyously and for not loving more ardently. Now a new beginning is to be made in our churches; founded on the Holy Scriptures, directed with all earnestness on the only Lord of the Church, they now proceed to cleanse themselves from the influences alien to the faith and to set themselves in order ...that in this beginning we may become wholeheartedly united with other Churches in Ecumenical Movement, fills us with deep joy".[216]

The Stuttgart Declaration had indeed echoed Bonhoeffer's last words: "this is the beginning". Bell could not have been more gratified.

With the approval of the British Commander in Germany, Field Marshal Montgomery, Bell travelled in Germany to see conditions there himself. The sight of the devastated cities and the misery of the refugees disturbed him. The evils now afflicting the occupied Germany had to be removed. Food and shelter were urgently needed. Bell contacted the officials of the Allied Control Commission to seek permission for voluntary Christian organisations to begin relief work. Bell's interventions received positive response.

Then the question of punishment of the guilty came up. The process of de-Nazification was causing anxiety in Germany. Bell pleaded for impartial justice, warning the Victorious Powers against its misuse. Bell put the British Government in mind of their responsibility. On 30th January 1946 he told the House of Lords that "We in Great Britain ... are still the champions of human freedom. We must not fail to give a lead to the world in the same great cause today".[217] And in *A Letter to my Friends in the Evangelical Church in Germany* in February 1946, Bell reminded the Victorious Powers of what Pope Pius XII had said in his broadcast of Christmas Eve 1945: "Those who exact today the expiation of crimes and the just punishment of criminals for their misdeeds should take good care not to do themselves what they denounce in others as misdeeds or crimes".[218]

Feelings of apprehension seized Bell when the "war-crimes" trials opened at Nürnberg. Their justification did not convince him. That is what he told their Lordships in the House of Lords on 23rd June 1948. Bell "never wavered", wrote H. A. Smith, sometime Professor of International Law in the University of London, "and was quite prepared to withstand popular disapproval and reproach". Bell was "one of the few whose sense of right and justice" was "absolute, never influenced by popular clamour". At the time of the "war crimes trials [writes Smith], in which the great majority of the British people allowed themselves to work up our national abhorrence of all atrocities into a wild demand for vengeance, irrespective of the law", and "the government of the day bowed to the storm and enacted an entirely new law, ex post facto, to justify them in hanging those who could not have been condemned under the law as it stood at the time", Bell "kept his head, knowing that divine justice is beyond human passion. We may be sure that the judgement of history will uphold him".[219] The judgement of history has indeed upheld Bell.

Hitlerism destroyed, there appeared now the spectre of Marxist Communism in Eastern Europe, threatening the existence of Christian religion and Christian way of life. Bell earnestly felt this threat, and believed that it should be dealt with not by force, since "violence breeds violence." Bell proposed vigorous encouragement of the spirit of the

Christian peoples in these countries. This was possible through the World Council of Churches, which formally took shape in Amsterdam on 22nd August 1948. Its chief aim was to strengthen the Ecumenical Movement, but the Movement would have had more chance of success if peace reigned over the world. One of the greatest needs of the time, Bell argued, was the realisation that violence "is quite incapable of producing a settlement of the unresolved issues which confront the world".[220] The continual teaching of the truth of Christianity alone would defeat the Communist ideology. The employment of the instruments of cold war would be a disaster for the unity of Europe. So much the more the contest for the possession of nuclear arms. This inspired disgust in Bell. The "very notion [he wrote] that forces so overwhelmingly destructive could be employed by civilised men shows the depths to which the standards of international morality have sunk".[221] What really we must "seek is a Christendom of souls – that is to say living human beings, spiritually united and working in a spiritual way upon the people and things of this world".[222]

This rule of conduct in mind Bell lost no time in criticising firmly the Soviet armed intervention in Hungary in 1956, and the British Government's aggressive policy over Suez at the same time.

With so much of Bell's concentration on the Ecumenical Movement, one might entertain the thought that diocesan matters were being left uncared for. Such thoughts would be mistaken. The war damage in Britain was not to be overlooked. The housing problem had become very acute. The Bishop of Chichester paid much attention to it. Much of the credit goes to him in creating Crawley New Town. On Bell's initiative, new schools, theological colleges and a new University were erected in the diocese. Also Chichester Cathedral and its worshippers received constant attention.

Bell retired from the House of Lords at the beginning of 1958. He had sat in the House for twenty-one years. On the last day of his appearance in the House on 30th January, tributes were showered on him by their Lordships. Especially moving and apt were the words addressed to Bell by Lord Pakenham.[223] The right reverend Prelate, he said, had been "a disturbing force, particularly to members of Governments, through his insistence on seeing that the requirements of State were brought before the bar of moral conscience, before the test of higher morality".[224]

On 18th August the World Council of Churches met at Nyborg, Denmark to mark the tenth anniversary of its formation. In spite of his weak health Bell attended the meeting, and on his appearance was very warmly greeted by the assembled members. Bell naturally participated fully in the sessions of the World Council. At the end of the conference Bell delivered a powerful sermon on peace and Church unity in Odense Cathedral on 24th August. In his sermon Bell also quoted the words of his, now dead, close friend, Archbishop of Upsala, Nathan Söderblom: "When God's rule has penetrated man's heart and life so that the divine love and righteousness becomes the main factor, we speak of a saint. A saint is one who reveals God's might. Saints are such as show clearly and plainly in their lives and deeds and in their very being, that God lives".[225]

These words precisely portray the life and actions of the Bishop of Chichester. In his deeds God lived. He showed this "clearly and plainly" right through his life. Bell was a saint, while alive. He died on 3rd October 1958. But saints never die. They are always with us. So George Bell will remain, an eternal saint. And it was no exaggeration when, at the memorial service held for him in Chichester Cathedral on 10th October, the Archbishop of Canterbury stated that Bell "will go down in history as one of the special glories of the Church of England".

Annex 5

Bishop Bell to Professor Leibholz, 21 November 1943.

21 Nov. 1943 TO

THE PALACE,

CHICHESTER.

CHICHESTER 2161.

My dear Leibholz

I send a copy of a letter just received for me at Edinburgh House from Visser t'Hooft. It gives news of Dietrich — though I wish indeed he were free we can take comfort that there is no reason for "special anxiety".

y, I I know will like them write on what fully y care for you an your wife, and for all whom we

dear to you in Germany.

I should be much interested to know

your views of the Moscow Conference.

There are grandes silences

though a beginning to cooperate

is something.

I have written a letter to the Times

2

about Italy (I was asked to

work the point too much by

certain persons right in the midst

of Italian affairs, who are

troubled by the inaction of

government and the possibility of

the republic). But I do not

know if they will print it.

In the enclosed letter Martin is

Micawber. Henry is Leiper.

3

Dear is Boigner

All affectionate remembrances

Yours alway

George West

Appendix

Letters from and to Bishop George Bell on:

Conscientious Objectors, negotiated peace, separating the Nazis from the rest of Germany, international reconstruction, a reasonable place for Germany in Europe, the bombing of enemy, post-war Germany, the Atlantic Charter, death sentence, Vansittart policy, the American Liturgy, the conscription of married women, war prisoners.

[Facsimile]

1) Bishop Bell to Archbishop of Canterbury , 5 September 1942.
2) The Duke of Bedford to Bishop Bell, 17 December 1942.
3) Bishop Bell to the Duke of Bedford, 4 January 1943.
4) The Duke of Bedford to Bishop Bell, 6 January 1943.
5) Bishop Bell to Lord Noel Buxton, 12 January 1943.
6) Lord Noel Buxton to Bishop Bell, 11 March 1943.
7) Bishop Bell to Lord Noel Buxton, 24 March 1943.
8) Lord Noel Buxton to Bishop Bell, 3 May 1943.
9) Lord Noel Buxton: Draft Letter to the Prime Minister (no date).
10) Bishop Bell to the Archbishop of Canterbury, William Temple, 21 May 1943.
11) Bishop Bell to Lord Noel Buxton, 24 May 1943.
12) Bishop Bell to Lord Noel Buxton, 10 June 1943.
13) Bishop Bell to Lord Noel Buxton, 14 July 1943.
14) The Duke of Bedford to George Bell, 30 November 1943.
15) Bishop Bell to the Duke of Bedford, 17 December 1943.
16) Bishop Bell to Stephen Hobhouse, 18 December 1943.
17) Letter to Bishop Bell, 10 February 1944.
18) Letter to Bishop Bell, 14 February 1944.
19) Bishop Bell to Lord Mansfield, 25 February 1944.
20) Bishop Bell to Lord Noel Buxton, 11 April 1944.
21) Bishop Bell to General Eisenhower, 20 May 1944.
22) Bishop Bell to Reinhold Niebuhr,[228] 25 May 1944.
23) Reinhold Niebuhr to Bishop Bell, 7 July 1944.

24)   Denis Hayes to Bishop Bell, 10 July 1944.
25)   Bishop Bell to Lord Halifax,[229] 18 July 1944.
26)   Lord Halifax to Bishop Bell, 31 July 1944.
27)   Bishop Bell to Lord Halifax, 11 August 1944.
28)   Bishop Bell to Lord Noel Buxton, 30 September 1944.
29)   Reinhold Niebuhr to Bishop Bell, 6 October 1944.
30)   Bishop Bell to J.H. Oldham, 24 December 1944.
31)   Central Board for Conscientious Objectors to Bishop Bell,
      6 April 1945.
32)   Lord Halifax to Bishop Bell, 30 May 1945.
33)   Bishop Bell to Lord Halifax, 11 June 1945.
34)   Lord Halifax to Bishop Bell, 4 July 1945.
35)   Mr A. Cassuto to Bishop Bell, 22 August 1946.
36)   Bishop Bell to A. Cassuto, 26 August 1946.
37)   Bishop Bell to Archbishop of Canterbury, Geoffrey Fisher,
      28 May 1951.
38)   Bishop Bell to Lady Milner,[230] 15 September (?).
39)   Bishop Bell to Alfons Koechlin, 25 September 1954.
40)   Typescript: Night Bombing: The Bishop of Chichester
      Replies to his Critics" (no date).

5th September, 1942.

My dear William,

    Fenner Brockway has sent me a copy of his letter of August 31st to you about Conscientious Objectors. I wonder what you feel about it, or rather the method of dealing with the problem ? Archbishop Davidson was constantly worried by the problem of the C.O. and the clumsiness, sometimes worse, of the administration and I think I gave some reference to this in my life, but I had hoped and believed that the experience of the last war had determined the Government to have nothing to do with any cat and mouse method in this war.

                Yours ever,

His Grace the Lord
     Archbishop of Canterbury.

TELEGRAMS & TELEPHONE.
NEWTON STEWART 72.

CAIRNSMORE,
NEWTON STEWART,
WIGTOWNSHIRE.

Dec. 17th. 1942.

Dear Bishop,

The enclosed is very like the pamphlet I sent
you recently, but is written with the special purpose
of giving no offence to people with a pro-war outlook
and inclining them to view more favourably the idea
of a negotiated peace. It contains, therefore, no
direct criticism of the war or of the Government
and no specifically pacifist proposals and, to avoid
arousing needless prejudice, the author's name is
not given.

The objection that Axis statesmen would not
at present consider negotiation on the basis suggested
is not, I think, a very weighty one. Even if this
should be the case - which is by no means certain -
the need would still remain to hamstring their war
propaganda and undermine their popularity with their
own peoples. We could in effect say to the latter:
"As far as we are concerned, provided you are willing
to treat other nations as you yourselves would like
to be treated, you can have peace with honour;
adequate safeguards; and, what you have never yet had,
a share in the world's economic resources proportionate to your needs and numbers. If therefore your
leaders keep you at war, you will not be fighting
for justice or independence, but simply because they
insist on having for their side advantages which
they would consider unjust if claimed by others."

Yours sincerely,

Bedford

298

4th January, 1943.

My dear Duke,

Many thanks for your two letters, together
with the pamphlet and other literature which you
sent me.

I have read the proposals with great interest;
nobody couldcharge you with not having frankly
stated how you, as a pacifist, would face the problem
if a pacifist Prime Minister came into power. But
we have a long way to travel before such an event
became likely.

I myself feel that the most useful line of
approach, which wants pressing harder and harder, is
to draw a distinction between the Nazis and the
anti-Nazis and non-Nazis in Germany; and to show the
anti-Nazis that it is not the aim of the Allies to
destroy Germany, though it is our aim to overthrow
Hitler and all his fellow Nazis who are the perpetrators
of the crimes, and bear practically the whole
responsibility, so far as Germany is concerned, for the
war. I do not forget, of course, the share which
Allied diplomacy and ommissions and commissions
during the past twenty years have also to take.

                          Yours sincerely,

His Grace
    The Duke of Bedford.

TELEGRAMS & TELEPHONE 72.
NEWTON STEWART.

CAIRNSMORE,
NEWTON STEWART,
WIGTOWNSHIRE.

Jan. 6th. 1943.

Dear Bishop,

Many thanks for your letter. As you say, it may
be extremely unlikely that a pacifist Prime Minister
would ever hold office in war time, so that part of
the pamphlet may be of no great practical importance.
I wrote it mainly as an indication of how a difficult
and delicate diplomatic situation could be handled
with imagination; but people destitute of imagination -
and I fear most English people are, especially in
war time! - would not understand it a bit and would
in many cases be irritated by it.

It is, therefore, the suggestions in Wise Diplomacy,
suggestions which could be put into operation by a non-
pacifist Prime Minister, which possess, I think, real
practical value. I am of opinion that it is only by
an approach along these lines that there is the
slightest chance of achieving your object - that of
separating the unreasonable Nazis from the rest of
Germany. After Versailles, we cannot possibly expect
any of the Germans to believe that it is not our aim
to destroy Germany, or at any rate subject her to such
punishments and indignities as we ourselves would never
for a moment tolerate. The Vansittart crowd are
allowed to breathe out threats without any rebuke from
the Government and I myself would trust the word of
the present Government as little as that of any totalitarian statesman and, knowing what I do of them, I
have all too good a reason for my lack of trust! It
is perfectly useless to expect the Germans to believe
that if they lay down arms, they will receive good

treatment from us once Hitler has been got rid of.
The only approach that would make the slightest
appeal to them would be one which left them no more
unprotected against armed attack than we should
consent to allow ourselves to be and, moreover, one
which offered them as drastic safeguards as we ourselves would feel compelled to ask. Also, it would
be no use suggesting peace on terms which did not
assure the Axis Powers of that fundamental justice
which they have never yet enjoyed, i.e. a share of
the world's economic resources proportionate to their
needs and numbers and secured to them in such a way
that it could not easily be snatched away from them
at a moment's notice by the caprice of some jealous
or hostile neighbour. It is also unreasonable, as
we would not allow the Axis to dictate to us about
the personnel of our Government, to attempt to dictate
to them in the same way. That means we have got to
take the risk, if risk it can be called, of the Axis
leaders accepting reasonable terms. It is certainly
not worth wasting good men's lives merely in order to
turn them out, if by wise diplomacy and by full
utilisation of their peoples' aversion to further war,
we can prevent them from causing any more trouble.
It is results and actions that matter, not personalities, and we continually forget that the statesmen of
all countries are apt to be unscrupulous where their
nation's interests are concerned and that peace, therefore, depends, not on the personal reliability of
individuals, but on the absence of conditions which
make it possible for war to be represented as
preferable to peace.

                    Yours sincerely,

                        Bedford

12th January, 1943.

Dear Lord Noel Buxton,

It was most kind of you to write as you
did, and to say that you would be ready to take
part in the debate on January 27th in the House of
Lords. I am very sorry to hear that your eyes are
troubling you so much; but I appreciate all the more
the trouble you are taking.

Emboldened by your good advice I have written
to Lords Addison and Hankey, and also to Lord Keynes.
You will be glad to know that the Archbishop of
Canterbury has told me that he intends to come and
speak. I have also had a letter from Lord Cecil saying
that he is in sympathy and will speak.

In writing to Lord Hankey to-day I have
mentioned your name as emboldening me to write to him.
I do not know whether you would care to send him a line
yourself, for he may wonder why I of all people should
be taking up the matter. I have explained that raising
the matter in this form is the result of my much more
limited question on the R.A.F. leaflets to which the
Government objected; but that this question is asked with
the approval of the Government. It is not my desire at
all to make the question an attack on Lord Vansittart.
As I see it, it is not a question of nationality but
of resistance. It is a European question, viz. the battle
between the Facists everywhere - in the occupied
countries as well as in Germany - and the anti-facists
who stand for democracy and of course include the
Russians.

Yours very sincerely,

Crosslee Hotel,

W O K I N G.

11th March, 1943.

My Dear Bishop,

I hoped to see you after the Debate
yesterday, and to congratulate you on the
success of the Debate, but I was obliged to
leave before seeing you.

It was a great disappointment to me not
to be able to support you, but you could hardly
have a better group of supporters than you had.
I was sorry that the Archbishop did not keep to
his intention to support you, and I felt the
same about Addison, but it was a great score to
get an unexpected supporter like Onslow, and
probably the Chancellor was influenced by the
speeches, to make his statement fairly definite.   I feel that the cause is immensely
benefited by what you have done.

If I could have spoken, I
should have tried to add to
your evidences of anti-Hitler
movements, by adducing the German
Socialists & other minorities.
who were caught unawares
by sudden overwhelming force
in 1933.
Please excuse mistakes as
I do not see what
I have written.
Yours truly
[signature]

24th March, 1943.

Dear Lord Noel-Buxton,

I was very glad that you wrote as you
did to the Times, and I am in agreement with
you. I have not written on the question of
alternative Government. I think this is a very
difficult question. But I am assured by those
who know Germany and the opposition forces within
it that there are outsanding men who would be able
to take charge of things once the opportunity arose.
These men are to be found are to be found in the
old Trade Union movement, in the Highest branches
of the Civil Service, and in certain anti-Nazi circles
connected with the Army, but not militerists.

Yours very sincerely,

18 COWLEY STREET
WESTMINSTER
S·W·1

Crosslee,
Heathside Crescent,
3rd May, 1943.   Woking.

My dear Bishop,

May I make a suggestion? Your debate
of March 10 has attracted much attention and
i think it might be well to try to follow it
up by a joint utterance of peers who wish to su⌐
support you. Few (apart from pacifists) would
come out openly as yet,

So I am enclosing a draft of a possi⌐
ble letter to the Prime Minister, which would b
be strictly private. If you approve the idea,
we might jointly invite others to sign. I woul
undertake the correspondence if it would save
you trouble.

The Prime Minister is said to be
inclined to reason, and he might be glad to
know of support in that direction.

Yours sincerely

Noel Buxton

Draft Letter to the Prime Minister.

Dear Prime Minister,

We beg to write to you in regard to your broadcast on March 21st in which, speaking as "a good European", you outlined the revival of the genius of Europe through a European Council, in which all the main members of the European family must some day be partners.

Your words met with enthusiastic approval, but we, the undersigned, desire to urge that they are entitled to still more attention than they have received. We trust that your allusion to the European Council will recall the public to the fact that the establishment of a durable peace is the true aim of the war. We hope that it will dispel the fantastic vision, which inspires a section of the public, of a post-war settlement in which Germany will be held in subjugation, and German youth will have its aggressive inclinations exorcised by British and other foreign teachers. We are glad, in this connection, of your reminder to the public that the Council must rest on the partnership of all the main branches of the European family. As this obviously includes the German nation, it appears to us to imply the desirability of the formation, as early as possible, following upon the military incapacitation of Hitler and Nazi Germany, of a democratic anti-Nazi Government, with whom negotiation would be possible.

The Foreign Office has from the first days of the war directed to Germany a propaganda which, if it means anything, aims at this end. If our propaganda successfully supplements the military

measures, by political action and thus creates an anti-Hitler
revolt, it will not only produce the greatest assurance of peace
in the future, but it will also minimise the destruction of human
lives and material treasure which must inevitably accompany a war
pursued by military measures alone. Among our reasons for hoping
that you will vigorously pursue the policy of encouraging the
formation of a democratic, anti-Hitler government, with which
negotiations could be carried on, are the following:-

I. The lack of fundamental unity between the United Nations on
anything beyond the aim of defeating Germany; and the danger of
a conflict of rival ambitions once this has been achieved:

II. The imminent danger of widespread anarchy as the result of
chaos and despair:

III. The loss in lives and treasure:

IV. The fact that a peace based on consent would be its own
guarantee while a peace of subjugation would involve the burden
of an Allied occupation, which would become intolerable to the
British and other troops involved in it.

It is not irrelevant to recall this history of the last war,
because in a great measure a comparison can fairly be made.   In
the spring of 1916, President Wilson attempted to bring about a
settlement, but met with insufficient response from Sir Edward Grey.
Writing ten years afterwards, Grey reflected on the results which

might have accrued if he had followed up the President's offer.

He wrote:

"Two years of war, in which expenditure of life and national strength and treasure were at their maximum, would have been avoided. European markets and trade might have recovered quickly, for the impoverishment and exhaustion would have been much less. The future peace of Europe, with the unsevered co-operation of the United States, might have been safer than it is to-day. Prosperity and security might be to-day more fair in prospect for us all than the victory of 1918 and the Treaties of 1919 have made them; and there would have been a peace with no noxious secret ideas of revanche."
                    (Grey: "Twenty-Five Years", Vol. II)

In view of these considerations, we desire to urge the importance of furthering, by a more definite statement, the opposition in Germany, which is already causing great difficulties to the Nazi regime.   We are convinced that in such a policy you would receive strenuous support.

<u>Private.</u>   21st May, 1943.

My dear William,

        It is extremely difficult to know about
Miss Ellis. There is usually a grain of goodness
in what she proposes; but she is ceaseless in
her operations !

        After making my short speech in the House
of Lords on the spiritual aspect of international
reconstruction, I wrote to Baron Palmstierna, who
is Chairman of the World Congress of Faiths, in succession
to Younghusband, and asked him what he thought about
it; and at his suggestion I have written directly to
him (being myself a member of the Council) and asked
him if he would bring it before his Executive Committee
to see whether it can be given a practical shape.
I do think that in the end the big difference is
between those who believe in a spiritual order and
those who reject it. I would be ready to agree that
though their conceptions of a spiritual order are so
different, Moslems and Jews agree with Christians in
this as against Marxists and other materialists.
Perhaps the time is not yet ripe for a public meeting
in which you as Archbishop should take a prominent
part. Miss Ellis knows about my reference to the
World Congress of Faiths (though I realise that one
must walk warily in that circuit).

        There might be something to be said for a
little delay till one sees what they think about it,
if anything. If I get a chance of some further
light on the subject from the Roman Catholic angle,
I will let you know.

                Yours affectionately,

24th May, 1943.

Dear Lord Noel Buxton,

Many thanks for your letter of the 14th May.
Forgive my delay in replying. I think your revision
is a great improvement. I have only one further
suggestion to make in the text, bearing in mind
the critical eyes with which it will be scanned.
I suggest the insertion of the word "democratic"
before "anti-Nazi Government" at the end of the
second paragraph; and the insertion of the same
word, "democratic" before "anti-Hitler Government"
in the revised paragraph at the end of the first
page.

I still should rather like to know what
Cecil thought about it before the others are
approached. His association with such a letter
would be of great importance. And ought we
not to try to get Davies ?   Some of those who
are in your list are, I suppose, persons who were
not anti-Nazi or anti-German before the war. I
have never been anti-German myself, but I have
always been anti-Nazi; and one has got to be a
little careful, I think. But I say this for your
own private eye (and perhaps Cecil's) alone. I do
not really know most of the other members of the
party personally, except Astor, Buccleugh, Holden
and Sempill.

                                    Yours sincerely,

10th June, 1943.

Dear Lord Noel Buxton,

Many thanks for sending me Cecil's letter.
The crux of his objection lies in his remarks
about unconditional surrender; I think that
the language used in the proposed letter to
Churchill is thoroughly defensible. What we are
out for is that the Prime Minister should let the
Axis powers see that while surrender must be
without conditions, and complete defeat must be
acknowledged, the United Nations envisage a
settlement which should appeal to them as just, and
giving them a reasonable place in Europe and the
world.

But I confess that if Cecil takes so decidedly
critical a view of our letter, I am extremely
doubtful as to whether such a letter, sparsely signed,
would carry any weight at all with Churchill, and
whether it might not do more harm than good. What do
you think ? I feel that if only four or five people
sign it, and they are all people whose views Churchill
in any case does not like, he might dismiss it all as
quite unimportant. Cecil's adhesion would make a
difference. I return the letter.

Yours very sincerely,

14th July, 1943.

Dear Lord Noel Buxton,

Many thanks for your letter. I am glad you feel that in the circumstances it is better not to proceed further at present with the proposed letter. I think it is possible that a more favourable situation may arise when there are signs of a German collapse.

I have had some talk with the Bishop of Lichfield on these and similar matters. But I did not feel that an episcopal appeal to the Prime Minister would cut much ice. So till you were able to report about the temporal Peers' willingness to sign such a letter, I have not taken steps with regard to the Bishops.

I had a talk with Captain Liddell Hart last week. He tells me that he has had some correspondence with you, but not a great deal of contact otherwise. I told him in confidence about our letter to the P.M. but he thought that the P.M. was very stiff, and was not likely to be affected for the better by a letter thus signed.

When I am next at the Club I shall hope to get hold of the Contemporary and study your article. I did write an article myself for the International Round Table Conference of Christian leaders which has just been meeting at Princeton, U.S.A. Unfortunately I have no spare copy. I sent it off by air some little time ago, and I know that it reached its destination, for I was rung up on Saturday by the Sunday Express to know whether what I was reported to have said in it was true. They had something about it last Sunday. In it I tried to distinguish between three alternative policies towards a defeated Germany, (1) the policy of appeasement, which I dismissed, (2) the policy of repression, which I also dismissed, and (3) the policy of discrimination, for which I gave various arguments. I drew out what seemed to me the implications of the third policy, both with regard to the military situation after the armistice and permanently, as well as with regard to the economic and political. But I am waiting to hear repercussions

from the U.S.A., and I think it likely that I shall some
time publish it.

You are quite right in saying that when I
first put down my motion I asked the Government whether
it agreed with Stalin's distinction between Hitler's army
and all organised military force in Germany, and Stalin's
statement that while it was necessary to destroy the former,
it was not desirable to destroy the latter.

With regard to the last part of your letter,
which you have written in your own hand, I am afraid I do
not think it would be a good plan for the letter to go to
the P.M. signed just by our two selves.

Yours sincerely,

CAIRNSMORE.
NEWTON STEWART,
WIGTOWNSHIRE.

30th November, 1943.

Dear Bishop,

I have read with interest your letter in the Times.

I do not know how you feel about the situation, but to me it is becoming increasingly obvious that if an Allied victory were secured, under our present political leaders and financial masters we should completely fail to secure practically all our original idealistic war aims.

It is now virtually admitted that we shall have to allow Russia to keep as much as she wants of Poland, Finland, Latvia, Esthonia, Lithuania and Bessarabia, and to dominate Scandinavia and the Balkans as well; so there is the end of our defence of small nations against interference and aggression.

In any areas controlled by Britain and the U.S.A., the tyranny of Big Finance, with its characteristic evil of poverty in the midst of potential abundance, will be re-established, mainly under Wall Street dictatorship. (One good thing the Axis did do was to get rid of the moneylenders' control!) The Morganthau Plan, with the importance it attaches to gold; the defects and omissions of the Keynes Plan; the policy and personnel of AMGOT to which you refer; the unsatisfactory answers given by Chancellors of the Exchequer when questioned by the few M.Ps. who understand the money racket; and the important position occupied by Mr. Churchill's and President Roosevelt's friend, the financier Baruch, all point in the same direction.

As for getting rid of Fascism, its essential features are already firmly established over here and political leaders from time to time make it plain that many of the worst are not to end with the war. We have military conscription; industrial conscription; conscription of money by heavy taxation and of property by requisition orders; + we have more than 9,000 Government regulations, including of course the notorious Regulation 18B.

In a new way, all this seems to give point to what has been my contention all along, viz. that only by a negotiated peace in which all nations agree to give up political interference in the affairs of their neighbours, and in which Britain and America agree to give up the anti-social practices of Big Finance and combine with other countries in developing the world's resources to full capacity, can a reasonable hope of a lasting peace be secured.

Yours sincerely,

Bedford

17th December, 1943.

My dear Duke,

Many thanks for your letter of the
30th November. I am down with 'flu, and
my correspondence has got rather in arrear.

I am very glad you were interested in
my letter in The Times. The situation does
certainly fill me with a great deal of concern.
I am troubled by the drift from an ideological
war to something much more akin to a war based
on power. I feel that I ought to know much
more about the financial side of the international
situation; but I am afraid I know very little,
so that my opinion of what you actually say
about the money lenders and big finance is worth
nothing.   The thing that I am chiefly concerned
for is a re-insistence upon the spirit of the
Atlantic Charter, and the great importance of
viewing Europe as a whole. I don't see much chance
of a negotiated peace at the moment; but I am
all opposed myself to the cry of 'unconditional
surrender'.

Yours sincerely,

18th December, 1943.

Dear Stephen Hobhouse,

I am dreadfully sorry to have kept you
waiting such a long time. I have had 'flu,
but that is not really a very good excuse.
The real truth is that I have been terribly
rushed and all over the place, which is a
bad thing to be and do. I can't help thinking
that if you have got money to spend on one or
other of the two pamphlets, it would be better
spent on <u>Christ and Our Enemies</u>. The fact that
it has been so warmly approved by non-pacifists is
all to the good - so I vote for that.

Thank you for letting me see the Archbishop's
reply to Peace Planners, which I return.
By the way, I took up with Dingle Foot the
quotation which you mentioned about the immense
housing shortage in Germany. I did not tell him
where I got the quotation from. He traced the
words he used, which were not broadcast direct
by him, but extracted from a speech which he had
given somewhere else, broadcast on the Overseas
Service. The words he used, however, did
not differ very much in effect from those you
quoted, but they were much more moderately
couched.

I am asking a question in the House of Lords
early in February about the bombing of enemy
towns, and the government's policy. It was

16/2/44.

The Rt.Rev. the Lord Bishop
of Chichester,
House of Lords,
Westminster, S.W.1.

12, Oakley Road,
Warlingham,
Surrey.

10th February,1944.

Dear Bishop,

   May God bless you for your words
in the House of Lords yesterday, fearless and forceful!
I have been longing and praying for some authoritative
voice to be raised in protest against this obliteration
bombing, and now the prayer has been completely answered.
It may be that you have done far more than you realise
by this stand you have taken. In my knowledge a
considerable number of people will be strengthened in
their own hesitation in supporting the Government's
action and policy.

   Unfortunately, even the religious press
seems to be muzzled. I have tried recently to get a
protest printed in the Methodist Recorder, but the effort
has been fruitless. The Spectator did print a few
letters a few months ago before things got to be as bad
as they are now, but they are refusing them now. All
of which facts make me rejoice the more in your speech
and also in the full account printed in the "Times" this
morning.

   Please do not acknowledge this,

   Heartily yours,

14th. February 1944.

The Right Rev. the Lord Bishop of Chichester,
The House of Lords,
The Houses of Parliament,
LONDON W.1.

My Lord,

THE BOMBING OF BERLIN.

It is indeed strange that you should see fit to concern yourself
with the sufferings of the people of Berlin, when there are so
many cases of tragic suffering around you in this Country, caused
by this war, which seem to have escaped your notice.

What right has my Lord, as a mem'ber of the higher dignitary
of the Church -most members of which have so shamefully failed
in the mission for which they were ordained- I repeat, what
right have you to criticise the actions and purpose of such fine
men as Air Marshal Sir Arthur Harris? Do you have the audacity
to insinuate that such men would be a party to any form of
spiteful revenge, such as to bomb Berlin for any flippant reason?
These men, such as Sir Arthur, have the grave and unenviable
responsibility of sending a high percentage of the crews of some
thirty or forty bombers to a frightful death, each time they
order a heavy raid on that city, and you, My Lord, have the
affrontry to query the sincerity of purpose of their actions.

The British people are glad that such bombing is taking
place, but I have yet to meet one of responsible age, who has not
deplored the fact that these methods have had to be resorted to,
and the inevitable destruction of life and property which must
follow. They believe, through bitter experience, that it is
impossible to teach the German Nation the rudiments of civilisation in theory form, and, therefore, it must be taught them
in practice. They believe that the only way of doing this, is
to let the German people suffer in a like manner to the million s
upon whom they have perpetrated their satanic brutality. They
believe that this bombing will shorten the war and reduce the
casualties amongst the gallant young men who are fighting for us
and fighting for civilization and Christianity.

There are far too many people in high and responsible office
-chiefly in the Church- who state that we are lowering ourselves
to the level of the Germans, by using their methods. These people
are suffering from intellectual indigestion, which prevents them

1

193

The Right Rev. the Lord Bishop of Chichester.

-Continued-

them from using any balanced reasoning and they seldom arrive
at any conclusions based of logical facts, in consequence.
They seem to be quite unable to reason that the motive behind,
and the circumstances leading up to and surrounding a deed, can
make that deed either a bestial cruelty or one of noble courage
and of high purpose. To Quote an example:- A surgeon who cuts
a man open, just for the fun of the thing or to cause the man
pain or death, is a criminal, doing a criminal deed. A surgeon
wo cuts a man open to remove a cancer, is showing courage and
high purpose, and he is to be respected.

The British people believe that Germany contains a disease
centre of the cancer of brutality. The loss of good blood and
tissue caused by the operation of removing this from the world
is unavoidable. They also believe that most of the good tissue
in or around that centre, has already been liquidated or destroyed
by the cancer itself.

My Lord, I feel that your time would be better occupied in
praying for courage to be given to the brave crews of our
bomber forces, who are asked to go through such torture, because
of the lazy mindedness of so many people in this Country before
this war.

Your Lordship's time would be better occupied by pressing
the Government to ease the lot of so many of our elderly people
most of whom did their bit in the last war, and whose only crime
is age- who have to eke out a very miserable existance on rations
that are dreary in the extreme. They have few facilities to
augment and brighten these rations by going to restaurants and
they seldom get a share of any of the tit-bits which the shops
may occasionally have, because their custom is not important to
the shops. These elderly folk, many of whom live alone, have
suffered bitterly during this war and they are surely entitled
to some small measure of comfort in the way of extra milk, tea
and sugar, before any of our food is sent to other countries.

My Lord, I could give you a long list of such wrongs which
ought to be righted, but I am afraid it would be a waste of time,
as you live in a little world of unreality of your own creation
together with your fellow sufferers of intellectual dyspepsia.

I remain, My Lord,

Your Lordship's obedient servant,

Cecil R. Matthews

321

25th February, 1944.

Dear Lord Mansfield,

I see that you are raising a question
about the post-war boundaries of Germany and
other countries, and specially in connection
therewith, the advisability of compulsory transfer
of minorities.   On a former occasion I followed
you in a debate in connection with food conditions
in occupied Europe; but though my remarks were
based on the wording of your motion, they did not
altogether deal with the actual subject with which
your speech dealt.

I was wondering whether on this occasion
you were going to speak about such questions as
East Prussia, or the Polish frontier, and the
advisability of a transfer of population in such
cases; and there are other matters connected with
the post-war boundaries of Germany which would
seem likely to come up if your motion was going to
deal with the problem generally.

If it is not troubling you, I should
be grateful if you could tell me whether I am
correct in thinking that your motion is likely to
deal with questions like East Prussia and Poland
and possibly even the Baltic States.

Yours sincerely,

11th April, 1944.

Dear Lord Noel Buxton,

I was very sorry about the Government's
action on the Atlantic Charter debate. But I do
hope that Roosevelt did not like Churchill's
statement of February 22nd, and that discussion
with the Allies has been hastened.

As to a debate on the crucial point of
annexation soon. Did not Churchill give an
intimation that there would be shortly a debate
on the international situation in the House of
Commons, quite apart from the Atlantic Charter
as such ? I should be very much in favour of a
debate on the international situation in general,
in the course of which the crucial point of
annexation could be raised. But I wonder how you
could get a debate on the specific point of
annexation just now; how would it be for you to
put down a motion calling attention to Stalin's
proclamation, so warmly welcomed by Churchill, on
the moment of entering Roumania ? He made it about
a week or ten days ago. Could you not call attention
to that statement and ask whether His Majesty's
Government was in agreement with it as a statement
of policy generally, in connection with the
impending entry of forces belonging to the United
Nations into enemy countries ?   I think that,
by that means you could say anything you liked on
the subject of annexation, and challenge the

- 2 -

Government specifically about annexation in your
speech.

Yours very sincerely,

20th May, 1944.

Dear Sir,

I am taking the liberty of writing to you, as Commander-in-Chief of the American Army, in connection with the sentence recently passed on two negro soldiers, Private Willie Smith and Private Elijah Bronson who have been condemned to death by military tribunal for rape.

You will not doubt my own abhorrence of rape; but as I believe that the responsibility for the confirmation of the sentence lies with you as Commander-in-Chief, I am venturing to plead that you may see your way to reducing the sentence from sentence of death to a lesser sentence. The crime of rape, whether committed by a negro or a white man, is a very grave crime. But I would plead that the punishment of death, which is ordinarily reserved for those who have committed murder, is a punishment which very large numbers of humane people would find it difficult to justify. I hope I am not doing wrong in making this plea on humane grounds.

With much respect,

I am,

Yours very truly,

General Eisenhower,
Commander-in-Chief,
Allied Headquarters,
S. James' Square,
S.W.1.

26th May, 1944.

My dear Niebuhr,

I was deeply interested, as were many others
in the cable which appeared in the Times of May 4th
speaking of the formation of a Council for a
Democratic Germany, under the chairmanship of
Paul Tillich "with the support of a group of
American liberals, led by Dr Reinhold Niebuhr."
This is obviously a very important move, and I
should greatly like to have any news with regard
to its development.   It would be of particular
interest to us in connection with the starting
of a German Confessional Institute at 14 Lord
North Street, Westminster, which we are hoping to
make not only a place in which students are
trained for the ministry of the German Confessional
Church, under the auspices of Dr Emmerich (there
are now six students, doing part-time work); but
also a centre of discussions between German
churchmen and British friends.   It is not a
political organisation.   We are wanting to make
it in a manner of speaking a forum for discussions
of a personal kind on questions of social, cultural
and international interest.   We are having our
opening ceremony on June 10th; but we are also
having a conference on June 30th between representatives of the different interests I have mentioned,
with a view to mutual understanding.

In this connection, an important developmen
has taken place regarding the Free German League
of Culture and the Communist element amongst the

refugees. There is reason to fear that this
Free German League has been getting more and
more political, and inclined in the Communist
direction. I took an interest in it in the
dark days of 1940, when it was simply a refugee
organisation - non-political. I am told now
that the Communists have got such a sway over it
that the non-Communists are leaving. I have not
verified this; it is however pretty clear that
the German Communists are taking up what is
something like a Vansit artie point of view
with regard to the future. This is most dangerous
and I fear indicates a probable association of
the extreme right with the extreme left in a very
bitter policy.   I wonder whether anything of
this kind is current in U.S.A.

                    Yours ever,

UNION THEOLOGICAL SEMINARY

BROADWAY AT 120TH STREET

NEW YORK 27, N. Y.

July 7, 1944

The Bishop of Chichester
The Palace
Chichester
Sussex, England

Dear Bishop Bell:

It was a pleasure to hear from you again, and in answer to your letter I am asking our office to send you all of the documents relating to our American Association for a Democratic Germany.

I am very much interested in what you say about your Free Germany League. We have excluded communists from our American Committee for obvious reasons, but Tillich's German Committee, because it advocates a solution of the German problem, which also requires accord with Russia, has a few communists on the Committee. But it takes, of course, a completely different line than the organizations that are sponsored by the communists.

I am interested in what you say about the communists taking Vansittart's line. I dont think there is a question about it, that on the whole Russia is supporting the partitioning of Germany, and that wherever communists work on these committees they will give themselves away by an overt, or covert Vansittart policy. If any group in Britain has made a significant statement on this subject we would be very glad to have it for our use.

With kindest personal regards to you, and also to Mrs. Bell,

Sincerely yours,

Reinhold Niebuhr

DH/WLP
July 10th 1944

My Lord Bishop,

Thank you very much for your letter of 7th July; I quite appreciate how crowded with engagements you must be and will take the liberty of writing you again a few days before the hearing on July 25th. I agree that the point of your coming would be as an expression of sympathy with George Elphick, and whilst he is certain to be found guilty, I do think that your attendance might be reflected in the sentence. I was most grateful to learn of your talk with the Mayor of Lewes, though it is difficult to say how far he has taken your advice to heart.

I feel that the position is a most difficult one; there was a good deal of inaccurate talk at the recent Council meeting, but when people feel so strongly on such a subject it is not easy either to correct fact or to counsel moderation effectively.

Yours sincerely,

Denis Hayes

The Rt.Rev.The Lord Bishop of Chichester,
The Palace,
Chichester.

Lord Halifax

18th July, 1944.

My dear Lord,

I venture to write to you about what I
am sure you must feel to be the deplorable
line taken by Vansittart. The kind of
appeal he is now making to the lowest passions
is a menace to all that we stand for; and the
tragedy is that so few people in public resist
what he is saying. I have received a good many
letters since last week's debate in the House
of Lords, and the great majority are written in
strong disapproval of Vansittart. They come
from the most varied types of people, from
Headmasters to R.A.F. Sergeants, and speak in
the strongest terms of the way in which Vansittart
is really setting up a law of the jungle.

I cannot believe that men like Cranborne
can really have any sympathy with such an outburst
as that of Vansittart last Thursday. But the
impression he gives the ordinary man reading the
report of his speech is that the Foreign Office
really does think Vansittart's proposals worth
consideration. He said that His Majesty's
Government "are in the fullest agreement with
the aims of the noble Lord" and "that we welcome
all such proposals and assure him that we will
take full account of them in discussing with our
Allies the large and important issues that they
raise". Of course he did not commit the
Government; but the total effect of his remarks
was taken as encouraging Vansittart.

The purpose of this letter is to beg you
to take any opportunities you can privately
take of discouraging such an anti-Christian
line as Vansittart would have this country
follow.

                    Yours very sincerely,

31st July, 1944.

My dear Lord,

Thank you very much for your letter of 18th July.
I have been away in Yorkshire or I would have answered before.

I am afraid I must confess that I did not read the
report of the debate in the House of Lords to which you refer
quite as carefully as I should have done, and I certainly did
not take so black a view of Vansittart's speech as you do!
In the whole question of the treatment of Germany I feel the
Archbishop is indubitably right in drawing the distinction
between revenge and just retribution. I know the line is
not always very easy to distinguish, but I am sure we must
try to keep to it. Surely what really matters is the spirit
in which we approach the problem, and I should certainly
suppose that in that you and I would find ourselves in
agreement.

Yours sincerely,

Halifax

The Right Reverend,
   The Bishop of Chichester,
      The Palace,
         Chichester.

11th Aug., 1944.

My dear Lord,

Many thanks for your kind letter.
I wish you could take the opportunity of
reading Vansittart's speech of July 13. I
think you really would feel a shrinking from the
more fundamental parts of it. The attempt on
Hitler's life came as a rather ironical
comment on Vansittart's refusal to see any
difference between the Gestapo and the General
Staff.

But as you mention the Archbishop
of Canterbury, I am writing to send you a copy of
his latest public utterance on the treatment of
the enemy. It is an Introduction to a pamphlet
by Stephen Hobouse; and consists of only 3 pages --
but they are extremely important.

Yours sincerely,

Earl of Halifax.

30th September, 1944.

Dear Lord Noel Buxton,

Ever so many thanks for your letter. I
also thought that Vansittart seemed to
be losing ground, and I am very glad you
thought that I had gained.

Cranborne, I think, was reading from
a typed manuscript, and did not really deal
with my speech at all. He came up to me
afterwards and said that he had not meant
to misrepresent me as saying that the German
people were not responsible; but I told him that
I really thought he had missed that point.
I was so glad about what you said in the
debate too.

Yours very sincerely,

UNION THEOLOGICAL SEMINARY
BROADWAY AT 120TH STREET
NEW YORK

Oct. 6th, 1944

Dear Bishop Bell:

   I am very grateful to you for your letter and for the material which you have sent me, which is most informative. Your information about the disinclination of the great powers to dismember Germany, accords with what I know here. At least it seems true that the State Department is opposed to it, though there are other forces in the administration and in influential circles who are of a different mind.

   It seems to me that public hysteria in all the nations has been growing considerably, and that it will not be easy to establish a really workable peace. On the other hand, public sentiment in this country was so strongly against the plan for the complete de-industrialization of Germany, that it had to be quickly disavowed.

   With kindest personal regards to you and to Mrs. Bell,

                    Very sincerely yours,

                    Reinhold Niebuhr

The Lord Bishop of Chichester
The Palace,
Chichester
Sussex, England

24th December, 1944.

My dear Oldham,

I wonder whether you would be willing
to publish as a Supplement to the Christian
News-Letter a speech I made in the House of
Lords on December 19th, in the debate on Lord
Templewood's motion.   The subject of the
speech is the Churches and European Reconstruction.
I enclose a copy of Hansard.   The debate
continued on Wednesday, and I was glad to see
that Lord Cecil noted (in a single sentence) with
appreciation the evidence I gave about the
co-operation of the Christian Churches in the
rebuilding of Europe.

I took a good deal of trouble about
preparing the speech, and made a special point
of an appeal to the Church in Russia. I have
been told that it would be of considerable
value if the speech could be reprinted separately,
for distribution in the right quarters. I am
sending a copy to the Soviet Ambassador, calling
his attention to what I say about Russia.But
it is not only what I say about Russia, but also
what I say about the co-operation of the Churches,
in what was a political context,that might be
useful.   If the Christian News-Letter were
able to pring it this January it would of course
do exactly what was wanted; and I should be
ready to pay for the printing. But if you do
not feel able to print it as a Supplement, could

you let me know in the course of a few days;
for if you cannot, I ought to arrange some
other way without loss of time.

I saw Templewood after the debate, and he
went out of his way to express his gratitude
for what I had said.

Yours ever,

No. 9/4/45.   Und.   26

CENTRAL BOARD FOR CONSCIENTIOUS OBJECTORS

6 ENDSLEIGH STREET, LONDON. W.C.1

Telephone: EUSton 5501

Chairman: FENNER BROCKWAY
Vice-Chairmen: STEPHEN J. THORNE
AND DR. ALEX WOOD
Hon. Treasurer: E. C. REDHEAD
Secretary: NANCY BROWNE

Public Relations Officer:
A. JOSEPH BRAYSHAW
Publications Editor:
DENIS HAYES
Employment Secretary:
JACK CARRUTHERS

AJB/BS
April 6th, 1945

Dear Bishop of Chichester,

        I enclose a draft of a letter for
sending to the New Zealand press and New Zealand
Members of Parliament. We can vouch for the accuracy
of the facts and figures. Already we have signatures
from Bertrand Russell, Vera Brittain, C.E.M. Joad,
Laurence Housman, Sybil Thorndike and Ethel Mannin,
and I am writing to ask whether you feel able to add
your name. If so we shall be most grateful if you
will sign and return the letter as soon as possible.

        Over 700 men unrecognised by the Tribunals
have been kept in indefinite detention, many for more
than three years. A large number of them would probably
be recognised as genuine conscientious objectors if there
were an Appellate Tribunal. Over the last year or two
the New Zealand authorities have given repeated assurances
that they were about to introduce an Appellate Tribunal
and review the whole question of indefinite detention,
but nothing has been done and in the last few months
numbers of men in protest have refused to work and some
have refused food in the detention camps.

        A serious position has arisen and we feel
that this letter to the New Zealand press is an urgent
matter. I should much appreciate an early reply.

        Yours sincerely,

        A.J. Brayshaw

The Rt. Rev the
Bishop of Chichester,
The Palace, CHICHESTER.   Public Relations Officer.

338

UNITED KINGDOM DELEGATION
SAN FRANCISCO CONFERENCE

30th May 1945.

My dear Bishop,

Since our talk a day or two ago a thought
has occurred to me on the Liturgical question
which I would like to pass to you for what it
may be worth.

Like you, I have been greatly impressed by
the American Liturgy, which seems to me in many
respects more satisfactory than ours in the
Church of England. Do you think that, instead
of trying to alter or revise our English Liturgy,
on which there would no doubt be much prejudice
to be encountered, it might be possible to adopt
the American form, with obvious and necessary
alterations, such as the inclusion of a prayer
for The King in the Prayer for the Whole Estate
of Christ's Church? If it were also possible to
authorise the optional use of the nine-fold Kyrie
and of the Gloria following them, I should have
thought/

The Right Reverend
The Bishop of Chichester.

thought it would go far to satisfy those who
criticise our present form. And it would, I
think, have the advantage that in place of
substituting something new and untried for
something old and tried, we should be adopting
a Liturgy which has already been found satisfactory
in a large part of the Anglican communion.

If I am right in believing that the American
Liturgy closely follows that of the Episcopal
Church of Scotland and also that of the Church
in South Africa, we would have behind us the
experience of three provinces of the Communion.
Against such a setting permissive action by the
Bishops could hardly appear revolutionary.

Naturally the proposal would not please
everybody; but no proposal would, and this might
disarm some of the more conservative and suspicious
critics of Prayer Book Revision. At least they

could/

could hardly claim, as they did in 1928 and
1929, that the proposed Liturgy was a dangerous
experiment, or that it would prejudice the Church
of England, vis-a-vis the other branches of
the Catholic Church.

    I hope your journey goes well and that
you will not let this most hospitable people
overwork you! It was a great pleasure to see
you.

        Yours sincerely,

        Halifax

June 11th, 1945.

The Right Honourable Viscount Halifax, K.G.,
United Kingdom Delegation,
San Francisco Conference,
San Francisco,
U. S. A.

My dear Halifax:

Your letter of the 30th of May reached me in Toronto
after travelling from New York. I was delighted to get it
and am much struck with the suggestion you make. I can't help
thinking there is a great deal to be said for the proposal and
will take it up with the Archbishop of Canterbury when I get
home. If you were to write yourself to the Archbishop saying
the same thing as you said to me it would carry great weight
and I would follow it up with a talk with him. I will let
you know if anything develops.

I am ending up a most enjoyable journey and fly
back to England on Tuesday, June 19th. Do hope all will come
out reasonably well in San Francisco.

Sincerely yours,

Bishop of Chichester

BRITISH EMBASSY
WASHINGTON, D. C.
[ZONE 8]

4th July 1945.

My dear Bishop,

Thank you so much for your letter of
June 11th, which reached me while I was still
in San Francisco.

I have written, as you suggest, to
the Archbishop of Canterbury and have told him
that if he thinks there is anything in the idea
I put to you, I believed you would be ready to
have a talk with him about it.

Yours sincerely,

Halifax

he Right Reverend,
The Bishop of Chichester,
The Palace,
Chichester.

29 Rosslyn Crescent,
Wembley. Middlesex.

August 22nd, 1946.

Right Reverend Lord Bishop of Chichester,
The Palace, Chichester.

Dear Dr. Bell,

I have seen your letter in "The Times" of yesterday about the German prisoners of war.

The practical suggestion you make about retaining a large number of German prisoners as civilians by free option to be extende to other civilians in the British zone of Germany might perhaps find some interest among former Italian prisoners of war who have worked in this country. They were not very happy as you know and their home-sickness was even more justified than the Germans', as in many cases they had been as long as five years away from their families while Italy had been a co-belligerent for more than two years without a single prisoner being sent home.

Yet, when these unfortunate young men have been at home for a while they might have found conditions in Italy so difficult as to wish to come back to work in England at least temporarily, this bein perhaps the most practical way of helping their families. Therefore if the invitation you discuss in your letter could be extended to Italian prisoners and other qualified farm labourers, I think this appeal would have a favourable response especially if the conditions offered to the newcomers are not different from those ex-prisoners who have remained here as civilians. There are not more than a few hundred of these who have answered the last minute call of the Briti Government and they are now billeted by farmers and they enjoy full freedom. There has been no complaint about their behaviour and I venture to suggest that there are many more young labourers in Italy who could do useful work in this country. Temporary permits would of course eliminate the dangers of a permanent overcrowding of this country.

I hope to see you sometime in London. Perhaps your views on the general situation are not so gloomy as mine. I am especially interested in and concerned with the fate of Trieste which is in a sense the fate of Europe.

P.T.O.

- 2 -

Besides, I am working hard trying to contribute to the
improvement of British-Italian economic relations and from this
particular angle the outlook is a little brighter, although
political feeling against Great Britain is rising in Italy.
However, I am not particularly impressed by this and knowing my
Italians I venture to forecast that as soon as all the friends of
Britain there are driven underground, there is going to be a tremendous demand for British News and views. The Italians, not unlike
the Irish, like very much to do what they are told not to.

                              Yours sincerely,

                              Aldo Cassuto.

26th August, 1946.

Dear Professor Cassuto,

I am very grateful for your letter about the German prisoners of war; and much interested in what you say about the Italian prisoners who have worked in this country.   I should greatly like to see you when in London: but I am glued to Chichester at the moment, busy writing some lectures for delivery in Sweden next month.

I am afraid my view of the general situation is rather gloomy.   I appreciate what you say about the fate of Trieste.

With all best wishes,
Yours sincerely,

28th May, 1951

My dear Geoffrey,

Conscientious Objectors

I think it would be true to say that the
Convocations, or other official bodies representing
the Church of England, have not made pronouncements
on this matter, for the reasons you mention. The
attitude of the Church of England to conscientious
objectors was I think settled in principle during the
first World War, as a result of Archbishop Davidson's
negotiations with the government. I have not myself
got the House of Lords Hansard for the years 1916-18.
But it might be worth while looking at Archbishop
Davidson's speeches in the House of Lords when the
Military Service Act was passed in 1916. Archbishop
Davidson's actions generally are set out in my Life
(Vol.II,pp.817-821). There is a further letter to
the Chancellor of the Exchequer about the position of
the Civil Service (pp. 952-3). You will I expect have
looked up the reference in the Chronicle of Convocation,
July 4th, 1916 where, under the general heading of
'The Church and the War' the Archbishop spoke about
conscientious objectors, referring to debates that had
taken place in the House of Lords earlier that year.

The position thus secured was not challenged
in the second World War, to the best of my belief. I
do not remember that Archbishop Lang said anything in
the House of Lords on the subject; but I should be
surprised if he did not express his opinion somewhere,
on the lines of the policy settled in the first world
war: and certainly Archbishop Temple took occasion
from time to time in public utterances to defend the
rights of the conscientious objector. I think it
would be perfectly right to say that the legislation in
Great Britain which recognised the position of the
conscientious objector was certainly influenced by the

- 2 -

attitude of the Archbishop of Canterbury and leaders
of the Church of England at the time - and of course
also by the attitude of Free Churchmen, who have no
doubt made their views known quite clearly. It would
be worth while also saying that, as the references to
Archbishop Davidson's Life show, in the administration
of the legislative provision the Church authorities have
from time to time exercised their influence in such a way
as to help in the protection of the rights of the conscientious
objector. I remember vividly the many dealings which
Archbishop Davidson had with individual cases, particularly
in connection with the "cat and mouse" method, and the
difficulties he had with some government authorities.

I believe that in the second world war special
care of the conscientious objector position was taken by
the Right Hon. Ernest Brown, M.P., and I have little doubt
that he was in touch with Archbishop Lang and Archbishop
Temple from time to time.

Yours ever,

The Most Reverend
The Lord Archbishop of Canterbury

15th September, 19

My dear Lady Milner,

It is a real pleasure to hear from you, for it is indeed much too long since I had the pleasure of seeing you.

I also very much appreciate your writing to me about the effects of the conscription of married women. Mrs. Bell and I see a good deal of the breaking up of homes in just the way that you describe. But I had not come across cases in which very young women just married have been actually torn from their husbands under threats. I agree strongly with you that after a forcible sundering there is a big chance of homes never being really started at all.

I agree with you that there has been very little public discussion on the subject. I have had a talk to some sensible people about it, as well as in addition to the knowledge that Mrs. Bell and I have in the ordinary way. One of the elements which cannot be disregarded is, I am afraid, the easy-going way in which many young women marry Service men just for the sake of the allowance. It happened in the last war and it is happening I think even more in the present war. But it is a sorry harvest that men and women should marry in haste, especially when with women it is a question of the allowance, when the war comes to an end, there will be broken homes or homes never made at all and there will also be a crash of a financial kind. At present many of these women are getting a separation allowance and earning good money for war work so are better to do than they have ever been or are ever likely to be. Undoubtedly the Government knows the temptation of the separation allowance well enough.

Then there is this further complication of the lack of houses. Where are these young people, or rather where is the newly married wife to set up the beginning of a home ? This adds to the seriousness of the crisis. Thus there are three elements at least to be considered. (1) the pressing of the newly married wife back to war work, sometimes under threats, (2) the temptation of the separation allowance making for very easy-going marriages, and (3) the lack of housing accommodation.

I shall be staying with the Archbishop of Canterbury next Sunday night at the Old Palace and will put the matter to him.

If you have any further views and care to write further before I see him it would be a great help.   I will also certainly see what I can do myself in my own Diocese by way of either preaching sermons or otherwise calling attention to the gravity of the subject.

Mrs. Bell sends you her love.

Yours very sincerely,

25th September, 1954

y dear Koechlin,

I was greatly touched by your letter,
hich I found on my return to Chichester last
eek-end.   I too was very sorry at not being
ble to say a personal goodbye. I had to leave
he Steering Committee rather quickly for an
ppointment, and somehow I did not realise
though it was foolish of me) that I should not
ee you later that day. It must have seemed
ather abrupt and odd that I left without saying
arewell. But I was very glad that Cooke made
n opportunity of saying something about you at
he luncheon meeting, and gave me also the opportunity
f saying something, very inadequately, by way of
upplement.   I thought your impromptu response was
dmirable, and the warmth of feeling amongst the
embers present must have been felt by you.

Our relationship ever since 1925, and
ur growing friendship, which has become such a
ery strong bond, particularly since our co-operation
n helping the Confessional Church in Germany, has
een one of the happiest and most treasured possessions
n my life in the ecumenical movement. I do very
uch hope that the coming years will give other
pportunities for meeting from time to time. I should
alue this very greatly.   If you are in England, do let
e know - and I will certainly let you know if there
s any chance of my coming to Basel.

You will have had plenty of work in helping
'Espine and your other colleagues to interpret the
essage of Evanston to the Swiss Churches. I was very

glad to meet D'Espine, and was much struck by his
personality and ability. I do greatly hope that he
may play a vigorous part on the Central Committee
and in the ecumenical councils generally.

Mrs Bell joins me in sending warmest
regards and remembrances to you and Mrs Koechlin.

Yours ever sincerely,

George Cicestr:

WAR-TIME ADDRESS:
ST. MARTIN'S VICARAGE
(22 FRANKLIN ROAD).
BRIGHTON.
TEL.: BRIGHTON 198.

THE BISHOP'S LODGING,
22 THE DROVEWAY,
HOVE, SUSSEX

Night Bombing
The Bishop of Chichester Replies To his Critics -

14th June 1941

It is with the greatest interest that I have read the
contributions in the June issue, commenting on my recent
proposal regarding Night Bombing. ~~With your permission,~~ I
should like to offer a few remarks in reply. There are,
first of all, one or two general matters that are worth
bearing in mind. I have no illusions as to the dastardly
character of the Nazi use of bombers against almost, or
quite, defenceless towns. ~~Warsaw, Rotterdam and Belgrade
are among the more hideous examples of the Nazi
annihilating tactics.~~ But the conflict with which we are
concerned is that raging now between Great Britain and
Germany. We have had just over one year of mutual bombing
between these two Powers, commencing May 1940, with
August and September 1940, and April and May 1941, as, up
to now, the peak periods. During that time an immense
amount of damage has been done. In the United Kingdom,
in the ~~eight~~ nine months from September to ~~April~~ May, there were
some ~~30~~ 90,000 classified casualties, including ~~over 34,000~~ 40,000
deaths, ~~i.e.~~ that is, an average of 10,000 casualties per month.
The figures for Germany are not known, but are certainly

high.   The record of British buildings, not being military
or industrial objectives, injured or destroyed, is well-known;
and the number of German buildings, similarly not military or
industrial objectives, injured or destroyed (though not
published), cannot be small, ~~and includes the State Opera~~
~~House, the Library and the Cathedral in Berlin, and the famous~~
~~Bethel Infirmary at Bielefield. (April 5, 1941, the German~~ *on*
~~communiqué reported that the Bethel Infirmary was bombed for~~
~~the second time within a few weeks, and a direct hit destroyed~~
~~a hospital there, killing some people).~~

It is rightly claimed that the British airmen, man for
man, are both braver and aim better than the Germans.   But,
especially in bombing by night, often from great heights, and
with the best intentions, it is impossible for airmen to
succeed completely in discriminating between objectives which
are military or industrial and objectives which are not.   And
I have been told that the effect of an anti-aircraft shell,
within reasonable distance of the bomber, deflects *enormously* the bomb
~~which is being loosed a very considerable distance indeed~~ from
its target.

It is sometimes said that the bombing of objectives of all
kinds from the air is justified, as a means to winning the war
in the shortest possible time.   I agree that this is a
military question.   But anyone can look at a map and use
common sense.   We are now in the position of light weight

354

3

boxers matched with heavy weight boxers, in the matter of air
force equipment.   Any advantages we might have if, and when,
equally matched in the number of aeroplanes, are proportionately
lessened by our *present* inequality.   But, assuming the achievement of
equality, the distance of the British airmen's base from ~~which~~ *German targets*
~~they can attack Germany~~ is three times as great as that between
the base of ~~the~~ German airmen in the Occupied Territories. and
their targets in this country.   We have, besides, an immense
concentration of population in our island*.* They have *almost* ~~also~~ the
entire Continent under their control, with immense possibilities *for*
~~of~~ the withdrawal of population and factories far into the
interior.

Mr. Attlee, replying to a question in the House of Commons
on May 21, said that the suggestion of a mutual cessation of
night bombing, by agreement, was not acceptable to the Government.
On being asked why, he replied that it was impossible to trust
Hitler to keep his word.   In other words, he based his
negative attitude, not on military considerations, but on the
lack
~~latter~~ of international trust.   An agreement, however, could be
put to the test.   After all, we could maintain all anti-aircraft
defences, weakening nothing, but at the same time refraining from
the bombing of Germany by night, having announced that we should
refrain.   If Germany suddenly broke the agreement, we should not
be taken by surprise.   The arrangement could, in any event, do
us no harm, ~~on the assumption that~~ we were always prepared.   But

4

the fact that our Government had taken the initiative, and
had made the attempt to secure the cessation of night bombing,
and failed, would be a great asset to our moral cause.   The
practical abstention from bombing of any kind, in the form of
a tacit mutual bombing truce, was achieved when Athens and
Cairo were believed to be in danger of bombing.   The British
Government then announced that Rome would be bombed, if Athens and
Cairo were bombed.   The New Statesman of May 24, commenting
on this, said   "That is to say, it used our growing strength
in the air, not in ways which were bound to lead to general
and inconclusive destruction, but in a way which was likely to
impress the enemy and incidentally to save important centres of
civilization.   It was a welcome attempt to use brain as well
as bombing power.   In addition to this, there is the precedent
of an actual agreement between England and Germany, announced
by the G.P.O. as recently as June 7 with regard to air services
for correspondence with prisoners of war.   The text of the
announcement is as follows:-

The Postmaster General announces that agreement has now
been reached with the German authorities, through the good
offices of the United States Government, for the reciprocal
use of the air services between Lisbon and Germany and between
Lisbon and the United Kingdom for the conveyance of correspondence
to and from prisoners of war and interned civilians.

Under the new arrangements letters and postcards posted in

the United Kingdom for British prisoners of war and interned

civilians in German hands ~~and prepaid for transmission by~~

~~air (5d. for letters and 2½d. for postcards)~~ will be conveyed

from Lisbon to Germany by air as well as from this country to

Lisbon, ~~letters and postcards which are not prepaid for air~~

transmission will also normally be conveyed from Lisbon to

Germany by air.   In the reverse direction, all letters and

postcards from British prisoners in German hands will be

conveyed from Germany to the United Kingdom throughout by

air without charge.

It is hoped that further improvement of the prisoner of

war service beyond that recently achieved will soon result

from the new arrangements.   The possibility of establishing

similar arrangements for British prisoners of war in Italian

hands is being considered: meanwhile letters to and from

these prisoners are conveyed by air between Lisbon and the

United Kingdom, subject in the outward direction to payment

of the air mail fee.

General Post Office   7th June, 1941"

If agreement is possible between the British and the German

Governments for air services of this kind, it should not be ruled

out as impossible in the case of the cessation of night

bombing.

I shall be told that it is impossible to make a
distinction between military and industrial objectives on
the one hand, and non-military and non-industrial objectives
on the other hand. My reply is that since the time of
Grotius, an attempt has been made to draw a distinction between
the combatant and the civilian, and that, although one hears
people argue that it is better for the whole community to be in
the war, the blurring of the distinction in the present war by
air bombing, and particularly night bombing, is, from a moral
and humanitarian point of view, a retrograde step. In any
case, if the agreement were an agreement to cease altogether
from night bombing, that particular difficulty would, in that
field, not arise.

Lord Cyrene argues that we ought to concentrate on the
prevention of war rather than to attempt to render it more
humane. I agree, but in view of the terrible destructiveness
of night bombing, surely there could be no harm in attempting
this limitation. The declaration or the agreement could clearly define
definitely state what was meant by night bombing. And if
all night bombing were to cease, there would be no need to define
the areas to be regarded as immune.

Lord Sankey says that the time and advisability of any
solemn declaration are better entrusted to the Prime Minister.
Naturally, the decision must rest with the Prime Minister. But,

judging from his own expressed opinions, he ~~they not~~ *is not likely to* reject ~~any kind of~~ suggestion~~s~~ from the public, and this is a matter which raises important moral as well as political considerations.

Lord Esher ~~suggests~~ *remarks* that there are no non-combatants in totalitarian war, and ~~says~~ that an agreement ~~such as mine~~ would impose a grave military handicap upon ourselves. I have spoken about non-combatants, and I have suggested at least questions to be raised from the purely military point of view.

I agree with Miss Storm Jameson's fear of the unspeakable difficulty of recovery if the destruction and devastation in Europe go much further, and I am very glad of the reasons she gives for her support.

To Miss Sayers I would say, as I have said above, "Is there any harm in trying the agreement, though Hitler's ideology and ours are, indeed, poles apart?"

Mr. St. John Ervine reminds me of the outcry in the last war by devout men against our use of poison gas. So far poison gas has not been used on either side, nor have wells been poisoned. There is something to be said for making a halt now, lest worse befall.

I would add one final argument which should be weighed at least as fully as that which warns us against the mutual devastation and destruction which will be caused to all Europe if bombing goes on. Little has been said of the effect on the airmen themselves: they know well what spiritual degradation it must be to them to have to fly over territory, dropping bombs, with

8

the certain knowledge that in innumerable cases the bombs
must kill the women and children.   At the beginning of the
war, on September 14, ~~the Government~~ announced that "Whatever
be the lengths to which others may go, His Majesty's Government
will never resort to the deliberate attack of women and children
and other civilians for purposes of mere terrorism."   Granted
that there never is deliberate attack by British airmen on
German civilians, it is inevitable that civilians should suffer,
and suffer far more than can be excused by military necessity,
when there is bombing by night. *Let us spur our airmen ...*

... Spaunton, by noting ... the declaration that we do Slotin ... no night bombing ovurlay. the grunung will also cease.

Yours etc. *[signature]*

The Editor,
The Fortnightly Review.

Notes

1 Rt Rev. Peter Knight Walker, Canon of Christ Church, Oxford, 1972-77; Bishop of Ely, 1977-89; entered The House of Lords, 1984; President, British Section of International Bonhoeffer Society, 1987-96.

2 Peter Walker, "Commemorating George Bell," *Oxford Magazine* (Oxford), Michaelmas Term, 2000, p.5.

3 George Bell, *Christianity and World Order*, Penguin Books (New York, 1940), pp.140-1.

4 *Ibid.*, p. 128.

5 *Ibid.*, p. 154.

6 Oliver O'Donovan, "The Act of Judgement" (Bampton Lectures I, 2003, Oxford). Typescript, pp. 3-4.

7 For details see Ronald C.D. Jasper's *George Bell. Bishop of Chichester* (Oxford University Press, London,1967) I acknowledge my obvious debt to this book.

8 Rt. Rev. William Boyd Carpenter (1841-1918), Bishop of Ripon, 1884-1911; Canon of Westminstrer,1911.

9 Rt Rev. Thomas Banks Strong (1861-1944), Dean of Christ Church, Oxford, 1901-20; Vice Chancellor, 1913-17; Bishop of Ripon, 1920-25; Bishop of Oxford, 1921-37.

10 Henry Scott Holland (1847-1918), Regius Professor of Divinity, Cannon of Christ Church, Oxford, 1911.

11 Rt Rev. Ronald Arbuthnot Knox (1888-1957), received into the Church of Rome, 1917; Catholic Chaplain at the University of Oxford, 1926-39; Domestic Prelate to His Holiness,1936.

12 Jasper, *op. cit.*, p. 16-17.

13 *Ibid.*, p. 17.

14 Randall Davidson (1848-1930), Archbishop of Canterbury, 1903-1928.

15 Jasper, *op. cit.*, p.19.

16 *Ibid.*, p.19.

17 Bell's entry in his journal, dated 10 December 1914.Jasper, *op. cit.*, p.21.

18 Jasper, *op. cit.*, p. 22.

19 *Ibid.*

20 Ven. Francis Norman Thicknesse (1858-1946), Rural Dean of Westminster, 1912-27; Rector of St George's Hanover Square, 1912-27.

21 William Temple (1881-1944), later Archbishop of York, 1929, Archbishop of Canterbury , 1942.

22 Jasper, *op.cit.*, p.30.

23 *Ibid.*, p.30.

24 *Ibid.*

[25] Very Rev. Henry Wace (1836-1924), Dean of Canterbury, since 1903.

[26] Jasper, *op.cit.*, p.32-3.

[27] *Ibid.*, p.33.

[28] *Ibid.*

[29] Rt Hon James Ramsay Macdonald (1866-1937); Prime Minister, First Lord of Treasury, Jan.-Nov. 1924; 1929-35.

[30] Rev. Arthur James Mason (1851-1928); Canon of Canterbury, 1895; Lady Margaret Professor of Divinity, Cambridge University, 1895-1903; Master of Pembroke College, Cambridge, 1903-12.

[31] Charles Patrick Duff (1889-1972); Private Secretary to successive Prime Ministers (Stanley Baldwin, Ramsay Macdonald), 1923-33.

[32] Dean of Christ Church since 1920.

[33] Jasper, *op. cit.*, p. 37.

[34] John Masefield (1878-1967), Poet Laureate, 1930.

[35] Gustaw Holst (1874-1934), Composer, and Teacher of Music at St Paul's Girls' School, Brook Green.

[36] Jasper, *op. cit.*, p. 42.

[37] *Ibid.* p. 43.

[38] Thomas Stearns Eliot (1818-1965; Nobel Prize for Literature, 1948.

[39] Christopher Fry, poet, publ. *The Boy with a Cart*, 1939; *The Firstborn*, 1946; *The Lady's Not For Burning*, 1949.

[40] Dorothy Leigh Sayers (1893-1957); wrote verse, fiction, plays.

[41] Jasper, *op. cit.*, p. 44.

[42] Rev. William Lewis Robertson (1860-1947); Secretary of the Federal Council of the Evangelical Free Church of England, 1918-35.

[43] Rt Hon. Stanley Baldwin (1867-1947); Prime Minister, 1923-24, 1924-29, 1935-37.

[44] Rt Rev. Winfrid Burrows (1858-1929); Bishop of Chichester, 1919.

[45] Nathan Söderblom (1866-1931), Archbishop of Upsala, 1914-1931.

[46] Jasper, *op. cit.*, p. 56.

[47] Jasper, *op. cit.*, p. 60. Also George Bell, *The Stockholm Conference on Life and Work 1925* (1926), p. 1.

[48] Jasper, *op. cit.*, p. 62.

[49] *Ibid.*

[50] *Ibid.*, p. 65.

[51] *Ibid.*, p. 67.

[52] *Ibid.*, p. 95-6.

[53] *Ibid.*, p. 68.

[54] A. D. Lindsay (1879-1952); Master of Balliol College, Oxford, 1924-49.

[55] Jasper, *op. cit.*, pp. 71-2.

[56] *Ibid.*, p. 74.

[57] M. K. Gandhi (1869-1948), started Satyagraha movement in 1918.

[58] Alphons Koechlin (1885-1965), Swiss Pastor, president of the Church Council Basel, Swiss member of the Council for Life and Work.

[59] Bell and Koechlin wrote to each other on German situation for many years. A German translation of this correspondence was published in 1969. See *George Bell - Alphons Koechlin. Biriefwechsel 1933-1954.* Herausgegeben von Andreas Lindt (EVZ-Verlag, Zürich, 1969.

[60] Letters to the Editor: "The German Church – Political Conflict", *The Times*, 14 June 1933.

[61] Friedrich von Bodelschwingh (1877-1946), pastor, State Bishop.

[62] Ludwig Müller (1883-1945), a former army chaplain, State Bishop, 1933.

[63] President of the German Church Federation, 1933.

[64] Friedrich Siegmund-Schultze (1885-1969), Professor of Sociology at the University of Berlin.

[65] Karl Barth (1886-1968), pastor, Professor of Theology at the University of Bonn.

[66] "Church and State in Europe: The Jewish Question", *The Times*, 4 October 1933, p.8.

[67] *Ibid.*

[68] Jasper, *op. cit.*, pp. 107-8.

[69] Dietrich Bonhoeffer (1906-1945), pastor, took charge of the German Church in Forest Hill, London in September 1933; a prominent leader of the Confessional Church. On his life and times see two most valuable studies: Eberhard Bethge, *Dietrich Bonhoeffer. Eine Biographie* (Chr. Kaiser Verlag, München,1983); Edwin Robertson, *The Shame and the Sacrifice. Dietrich Bonhoeffer's Life and Preaching* (Hodder & Stoughton, London,1987).

[70] See Bonhoeffer's letters to Bell also in: Dietrich Bonhoeffer, *Gesammte Schriften.* Herausgegeben von Eberhard Bethge (Chr. Kaiser Verlag, München, 1958), volumes 1 & 2.

[71] Hans Schönfeld (1900-1954), German Theologian, Director of the Research Department, Life and Work, Geneva.

[72] Karl Fezer (1891-1960), Professor of Theology in Tübingen.

[73] Gerhard Jacobi, pastor, an active member of the Confessional Church.

[74] "The German Church: Meeting with the Chancellor", *The Times*, 17 January 1934.

[75] Konstantin Freiherr von Neurath (1873-1953), Reichs Foreign Minister, 1932-38.

[76] Wilhelm Frick (1877-1946), Reichs Interior Minister, 1933.

[77] Reference is here to the German edition of Bell's *A brief sketch of the Church of England,* soon to appear in Germany.

[78] Martin Niemöller (1892-1984), a prominent leader of the Confessional

Church.

79 Theodor Heckel (1894-1967), Reich bishop and 'Ecumenical Bishop' (1934).

80 Jasper, *op. cit.*, p.109.

81 Erling Eidem, Archbishop of Upsala, 1931-1950.

82 Jasper, *op. cit.*, p.109.

83 *Ibid.*, p.110.

84 August Jäger (1887-1945), legal adviser to the State Bishop, 1934.

85 Jörgen Wilhelm Winterhager, Director of Studies, International Committee for Friendship of Churches.

86 Friedrich Coch (1887-1945).

87 Karl Koch (1876-1951), a leader of the Confessional Church; president of the Synod in Barmen, 1934.

88 Valdemar Ammundsen (1875-1936), Danish Theologian, Bishop of Haderslev (1923), an active member of the ecumenical movement.

89 Jasper, *op. cit.*, p.119.

90 *Ibid.*

91 *Ibid.*, p.117.

92 Joachim von Ribbentrop (1893-1946), Ambassador to London, 1936, Foreign Minister, 1938.

93 Franz von Papen (1879-1969), German Chancellor, 1932, Vice Chancellor, 1934.

94 Paul von Hindenburg (1847-1934), Reichs-President, 1925-1934.

95 Sir Wyndham Henry Deedes, Brigadier General.

96 Rev. R. S. Cragg , chaplain to the British Embassy in Berlin.

97 Hans Lilje edited *Junge Kirche*, journal of the Confessional Church.

98 Joseph Goebbels (1897-1945), Reichs Minister for Propaganda, 1933.

99 Jasper, *op. cit.*, p. 204.

100 Joseph Houldsworth Oldham (1874-1969), Theologian, a prominent member of The Life and Work movement.

101 Jasper, *op. cit.*, p. 204.

102 Hans Kerrl (1887-1941), Minister for Church Affairs, July 1935.

103 Jasper, *op. cit.*, p. 207.

104 *Ibid.* p. 210.

105 *Ibid.*

106 Wilhelm Zoellner (1860-1937).

107 Alfred Rosenberg (1893-1946), leading Nazi thinker, author of *The Myth of the 20ᵗʰ Century*.

108 Jasper, *op. cit.*, pp. 210-1.

109 Otto Dibelius (1880-1967), Bishop of Berlin-Brandenburg, 1945-66.

110 Jasper, *op. cit.*, p. 227.

[111] *Ibid.*, p. 233.

[112] Eberhard Bethge, German pastor, Bonhoeffer's biographer.

[113] Gerhard Leibholz, Professor of Public and International Law at the University of Göttingen was married to Bonhoeffer's twin sister Sabine.

[114] Willem Adolf Visser't Hooft, Dutch Theologian, Joint General Secretary, Provisional Committee of World Council of Churches, 1938.

[115] Jasper, *op. cit.*, p.241.

[116] *Ibid.*

[117] *Ibid.*

[118] Franz Hildebrandt, German Pastor, Bonhoeffer's friend, worked closely with B. in the German Church in London, 1933-34.

[119] Henry Smith Leiper, secretary of the American Section of Life and Work.

[120] Jasper, *op. cit.*, p. 146.

[121] Rev. William Paton (1886-1943), secretary, International Missionary Council; Joint General Secretary, Provisional Committee of World Council of Churches, 1938.

[122] *Ibid.* p. 257.

[123] George Bell, *Christianity and World Order*, Penguin Books (New York), 1940, p. 100-1.

[124] Cardinal Arthur Hinsley (1865-1943), Archbishop of Westminster, 1935-43.

[125] Barbara Ward (1914-1981), author; Assistant Editor of the *Economist*; Member of Council of Royal Institute of International Affairs, 1943-44; Governor of BBC, 1946.

[126] Christopher Dawson (1889-1970), Editor of *Dublin Review*, 1940.

[127] Arthur Charles Frederick Beals (1905-1974); Talks Producer, Religious Broadcasting Dept. BBC, 1941-45; Hon. Sec. Sword of the Spirit Movement, 1941-47.

[128] Jasper, *op. cit.*, p. 250.

[129] Cosmo Gordon Lang (1864-1944), Archbishop of York, 1908-1928; Archbishop of Canterbury, 1928- 1942.

[130] Jasper, *op. cit.*, p. 250.

[131] *Ibid.*

[132] Edward Noel-Buxton (1869-1948), M.P. (Labour), 1910-18, 1922-30; Minister of Agriculture , 1924, 1929-30; publ. include: *Oppressed Peoples and the League of Nations*.

[133] R.W. Chambers (1874-1942); Quain Professor of English Language and Literature, University College, London, 1922-41.

[134] George Leonard Prestige (1889-1955); Fellow of New College, Oxford, 1913-20; Editor, *The Church Times*, 1941-47; Acting Gen. Sec., Church of England Council on Foreign Relations, 1949-50; Canon of St Paul's, 1950.

[135] Very Rev. Norman Sykes (1897-1961); Lecturer in Ecclesiastical History, Trinity College, Cambridge, 1931-33; Dixie Professor of Ecclesiastical History, Cambridge University, 1944-48; Dean of Winchester, 1958.

[136] Geoffrey Francis Fisher (187-1972), Bishop of London, 1939-45.

[137] Bell and Leibholz corresponded with each other extensively. A German translation of these letters appeared later. See *An der Schwelle zum gespaltenen Europa. Der Briefwechsel zwischen George Bell und Gerhard Leibholz.* Herausgegeben von Eberhard Bethge und Ronald C. D. Jasper (Kreuz Verlag, Stuttgart, 1974).

[138] Alfred Duff Cooper (1890-1954), Secretary of State for War, 1935-37; First Lord of Admiralty, 1937-38; Minister of Information, 1940-41; Chancellor of Duchy of Lancaster, 1941-43.

[139] Sir Robert Vansittart (1818-1957), Chief Diplomatic Adviser to Foreign Secretary, 1938-41.

[140] George Bell, *The Church and Humanity* (1946), p. 50; Jasper, *op. cit.*, 261.

[141] Bell, *Christianity and World Order*, p. 105-6.

[142] *Ibid.*, p. 92.

[143] Jasper, *op. cit.*, p. 262.

[144] George Bernard Shaw (1856-1950); Nobel Prize for Literature, 1925.

[145] Gilbert Murray (1866-1957); Regius Professor of Greek, Oxford University, 1908-36; Chairman League of Nations Union, 1923-38.

[146] George Bell, "The Church and the Resistance Movement". Speech delivered in Göttingen on 15 May 1957. Published in: Dietrich Bonhoeffer, *Gesammtte Schriften*. Herausgegeben von Eberhard Bethge (Chr. Kaiser Verlag, München, 1958), Band I, pp. 401-8.

[147] Victor Alexander Louis Mallet (1893-1969); Minister at Stockholm, 1940-45.

[148] Heinrich Himmler (1900-1945), Head of Gestapo.

[149] Hjalmar Schacht, president of the Reichsbank, 1933-39.

[150] Sir Stafford Cripps (1889-1952); British Ambassador to Russia, 1940-42; Minister of Aircraft Production, 1942-45.

[151] Helmuth James Graf von Moltke (1907-45), advocated a new Christian Socialist morality during the War; helped victims of Nazism, maintained secret contacts with the West; interned in Jan.1944; after the July plot of 1944 was charged with treason, hanged in Plötzensee prison in Berlin on 23 Jan. 1945.

[152] Anthony Eden (1897-1977); Secretary of State for Foreign Affairs, 1940-45; Leader of the House of Commons, 1942-45.

[153] Bell, "The Church and the Resistance Movement", *op. cit.*, p. 409.

[154] *The Parliamentary Debates.* Fifth Series, vol.. 125, House of Lords, 11 February 1943, c. 1058.

[155] *Ibid.*, c.1067.

[156] *Ibid.*, c.1067.

[157] *Ibid.*, c.1066.

[158] Frederic Herbert Maugham (1866-1958), Lord Chancellor, 1938-39.

[159] *The Parliamentary Debates*. Fifth Series, vol.. 125, House of Lords, 11 February 1943, c.1070.

[160] *Ibid.*, c.1076.

[161] *Ibid.*, c.1077.

[162] *Ibid.*, c.1080.

[163] *Ibid.*

[164] *Ibid.*, c.1080-1.

[165] Gideon Murray Elibank (1877-1951), Member of Speaker's Parliamentary Devolution Conference, 1919-20; President West India Committee, 1930-36.

[166] William Francis Sempill (1893-1965), a Representative Peer for Scotland, 1935-63.

[167] *The Parliamentary Debates*. Fifth Series, vol.. 125, House of Lords, 11 February 1943, c.1084.

[168] Roundell Cecil Palmer Selborne (1887-1971), Minister of Economic Welfare, 1942-45.

[169] *The Parliamentary Debates*. Fifth Series, vol.. 125, House of Lords, 11 February 1943, c.1086.

[170] Secretary of State for the Colonies and Leader of the House of Lords, since 1942.

[171] *The Parliamentary Debates*. Fifth Series, vol. 126, House of Lords, c. 538.

[172] *Ibid.*, c. 538-9.

[173] *Ibid.*, c. 541.

[174] *Ibid.* c. 543.

[175] *Ibid.* c. 544.

[176] Alexander Gavin Henderson Faringdon (1902-1977), Treasurer, Nat. Council for Civil Liberties, 1940-45.

[177] *The Parliamentary Debates*. Fifth Series, vol. 126, House of Lords, c. 545.

[178] *Ibid.*, c. 548.

[179] *Ibid.*, c. 553.

[180] Archbishop of Canterbury, 1928-42.

[181] *The Parliamentary Debates*. Fifth Series, vol. 126, House of Lords, c. 556.

[182] *Ibid.*

[183] *Ibid.*, c. 561.

[184] E. A. R. Cecil (1864-1958), President League of Nations Union, 1923-45; Nobel Peace Prize, 1937.

[185] *The Parliamentary Debates*. Fifth Series, vol. 126, House of Lords, c. 561.

[186] *Ibid.*, c. 563.

[187] *Ibid.*, c. 566.

[188] Richard William Alan Onslow (1876-1945), Chairman of Committees and Deputy Speaker House of Lords, 1931-44.

[189] *The Parliamentary Debates.* Fifth Series, vol. 126, House of Lords, c. 571.

[190] *Ibid.*

[191] J. E. D. Perth (1876-1951), Secretary General to League of Nations, 1919-33; Chief Adviser on Foreign Publicity, Minister of Information, 1939-40; Representative Peer of Scotland since 1941.

[192] *The Parliamentary Debates.* Fifth Series, vol. 126, House of Lords, c. 572.

[193] John Allsebrook Simon (1873-1954), Secretary of State for Foreign Affairs, 1931-35; Chancellor of the Exchequer, 1937-40; Lord Chancellor, 1940-45.

[194] *The Parliamentary Debates.* Fifth Series, vol. 126, House of Lords, c. 575.

[195] *Ibid.*, c. 577.

[196] *Ibid.*, c. 579.

[197] *Ibid.* c. 580.

[198] *Ibid.* c. 581.

[199] *The Parliamentary Debates*, Fifth Series, vol. 128, House of Lords, Vol. c.346-7.

[200] *Ibid.*, c. 850.

[201] Hugo Grotius (1583-1645), famous for his work on the laws of War and Peace.

[202] See Appendix: *Night Bombing. The Bishop of Chichester Replies to his Critics* (no date).

[203] Jasper, *op. cit.*, p. 276.

[204] Bell, *The Church and Humanity*, pp,129-41; Also Jasper, *op. cit.*, p. 277.

[205] See Appendix: Letters to Bell dated 10 February and 14 February 1944.

[206] Jasper, *op. cit.*, p. 278.

[207] *Ibid.*, p. 281.

[208] *The Parliamentary Debates*, Fifth Series, vol. 134. House of Lords, c. 341.

[209] *Ibid.*, c.402-3.

[210] *Ibid.*, c.403.

[211] *Ibid.*, c.404.

[212] *Ibid.*, c.406.

[213] George Bell, "The Church and the Resistance Movement" in : Dietrich Bonhoeffer, *Gesammte Schriften, op. cit.*, Band I, p. 412.

[214] *The Parliamentary Debates*, vol. 135, House of Lords, c.1137.

[215] Jasper, *op. cit.*, p. 295.

[216] *Ibid.*, p.294.

[217] *The Parliamentary Debates*, vol. 139, House of Lords, c. 68-77.

[218] Jasper, *op. cit.*, p. 307.

[219] *Ibid.*, p. 309-10.

[220] *Ibid.*, p. 341.

[221] *Ibid.*, p. 340.

[222] *Ibid.*, p. 347.

[223] Francis Aungier Pakenham (1905-2001), a Lord in Waiting to the King, 1945-46; Parl. Under-Sec. of State, War Office, 1946-47; Chancellor of the Duchy of Lancaster, 1947-48; First Lord of the Admiralty, 1951.

[224] *The Parliamentary Debates*, vol. 207, House of Lords, c. 342-3; Also Jasper, *op. cit.*, p. 344.

[225] Jasper, *op. cit.*, p. 385.

[226] H.W.S.R. Bedford (1888-1953), publ.: *The Road to Real Success*; *Poverty and Over-Taxation – the Way Out*.

[227] The Earl of Mansfield (1900-1971), Hon. Sec., British Group, Inter-parliamentary Union, 1932-35; Past President, British Empire Union.

[228] Rev. Reinhold Niebuhr (1892-1971), Professor of Christian Ethics and Philosophy of Religion, Union Theological Seminary, New York City, since 1928.

[229] The Earl of Halifax (1881-1959), British Ambassador at Washington, 1941-46.

[230] Violet Georgina Milner, Viscountess, died 1958, Editor, National Review, 1932-1948.

Index

Printed in the United Kingdom
by Lightning Source UK Ltd.
107885UKS00001B/1-39